Literature Connections Day-by-Day

Books and Activitites that Celebrate More Than 100 Special Days of the Year

by Kathy Everts Danielson and
Sheri Everts Rogers

SCHOLASTIC PROFESSIONAL BOOKS

New York • Toronto • London • Auckland • Sydney

In memory of our dad

Cover design by Vincent Ceci
Interior design by Sydney Wright
Cover and interior illustrations by Claude Martinot
ISBN 0-590-49471-6

C·O·N·T·E·N·T·S

INTRODUCTION

Special days throughout the year warrant special attention. This book was created to capitalize on students' interests about different topics. Specific days throughout the year have been selected with a list of picture books, novels, poems, and activities relating to the days. Teachers may want to spend more than one day on each of the dates. Students and teachers could complete many of the activities before the actual date, or teachers could tie the dates into units they already teach. Older students may want to divide the books up and read one from the list, making a text set for a literature discussion group. Teachers may want to read aloud some of the books from the list for younger children.

It is our goal to provide teachers with a variety of resources about different topics. Although most of the books included are picture books, it is our belief that picture books are for every age level (not just primary grades). Poetry has been included because it is important to share poetry throughout the curriculum with students. Reading a poem a day is not an unreachable goal, especially with the list of poems in this book.

On a personal level, we would like to thank our families for their support through this project and for pretending not to notice that we spent a lot of time at the library and with our computers.

Resources

Chase's Annual Events: Special Days, Weeks and Months. Chicago: Comtemporary Books, Inc. (published yearly)

Dahlstrom, L. M. (1990). *Writing Down the Days: 365 Journaling Ideas for Young People.* Minneapolis: Free Spirit Publishing.

Hopkins, L. B. & Arenstein, M. (1990). *Do You Know What Day Tomorrow Is? A Teacher's Almanac.* New York: Scholastic.

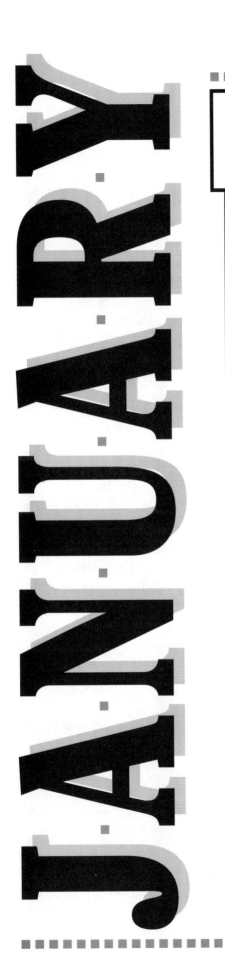

■ **Date:** Any day in January

■ **This month is special because:** It is National Hobby Month.

Books that relate to this month

■ Picture Books:

Bulla, C. (1979). *Daniel's Duck*. Ill. by Joan Sandin. New York: HarperCollins. (wood carving)

Carlson, N. (1984). *Bunnies and Their Hobbies*. Minneapolis: Carolrhoda. (many hobbies)

Carlson, N. (1993). *Take Time to Relax!* New York: Puffin.

Coyle, R. (1988). *My First Baking Book*. Ill. by Tedd Arnold. New York: Workman. (cooking)

Ernst, L. C. (1991). *Miss Penny and Mr. Grubbs*. New York: Bradbury. (gardening and raising rabbits)

Kimmel, E. A. (1992). *Anasi Goes Fishing*. Ill. by Janet Stevens. New York: Holiday House.

Long, E. (1984). *Gone Fishing*. Ill. by Richard Brown. Boston: Houghton Mifflin. (fishing)

Owen, C. (1993). *My Nature Craft Book*. Boston: Little, Brown. (crafts)

Ripley, C. (1988). *Kitchen Fun*. Boston: Little, Brown. (cooking and crafts)

Temko, F. (1993). *Origami Magic*. New York: Scholastic.

Williams, K. L. (1990). *Galimoto*. Ill. by Katherine Stock. New York: Lothrop, Lee & Shepard. (African—making toys)

■ Poetry:

"I'm Thankful" in:
Prelutsky, J. (1984). *The New Kid on the Block*. Ill. by James Stevenson. (pages 28–29)

"I am Sitting Here and Fishing" in:
Prelutsky, J. (1990). *Something BIG Has Been Here*. Ill. by James Stevenson. New York: Greenwillow. (pages 112–113)

"My Hobby" in:
Silverstein, S. (1974). *Where the Sidewalk Ends*. New York: Harper & Row. (page 129)

1. Brainstorm a list of possible hobbies.

2. Invite students to share their hobbies with the class. Students might want to present it in a report.

3. Invite other students, teachers, the principal, the secretary, etc., to come to talk about their hobbies.

4. Interview other students, teachers, and parents about their hobbies. Organize the information into a graph. Talk about the most unusual hobbies and the most common hobbies.

5. Start a class collection of stamps, buttons, rocks, or some other area of interest.

6. Match the following hobbies to the corresponding words in a pocket chart activity:

Hobby	Objects used for this hobby
Coin Collecting	1920 penny
Stamp Collecting	Olympic stamps
Painting	Paintbrush
Gardening	Hoe
Ballet Dancing	Ballet Slippers
Bowling	Bowling Ball
Fishing	Lure
Reading	Books
Knitting	Needles

J·A·N·U·A·R·Y 1

■ Date: January 1

■ This date is special because:
It is New Year's Day.

Books that relate to this date

■ Picture Books:

Baylor, B. (1986). *I'm in Charge of Celebrations*. Ill. by Peter Parnall. New York: Scribner.

Behrens, J. (1981). *Gung Hay Fat Choy: Happy New Year*. Photos by Terry Behrens & Ronnie Ramos. Chicago: Childrens Press. (Chinese)

Chin, S. (1993). *A Dragon Parade*. Ill. by Mou-Sien Tseng. New York: Steck-Vaughn.

Grifalconi, A. (1992). *Flyaway Girl*. Boston: Little, Brown. (African folktale)

Pittman, H. C. (1986). *A Grain of Rice*. New York: Hastings House. (Chinese folktale)

Stevenson, J. (1989). *Un-Happy New Year, Emma!* New York: Greenwillow.

Waters, K. and Slovenz-Low, M. (1990). *Lion Dancer: Ernie Wan's Chinese New Year*. Photos by Martha Cooper. New York: Scholastic. (Chinese)

Wood, A. (1988). *The Horrible Holidays*. Ill. by Rosekrans Hoffman. New York: Dial.

■ Novels:

Giff, P. R. (1991). *Emily Arrow Promises to Do Better This Year*. Ill. by Blanche Sims. New York: Dell.

Kelley, E. (1984). *Happy New Year*. Ill. by Priscilla Kiedrowski. Minneapolis: Carolrhoda.

Pinkwater, D. M. (1975). *Wingman*. New York: Dodd. (Chinese)

■ Poetry:

Carlstrom, N. W. (1992). *How Do You Say It Today, Jesse Bear?* Ill. by Bruce Degen. New York: Macmillan. (poem of months of the year)

"New Year's Eve" in:
Livingston, M. C. (1985). *Celebrations*. Ill. by Leonard Everett Fisher. New York: Holiday House. (page 4)

Livingston, M. C. (1987). *New Year's Poems*. Ill. by Margot Tomes. New York: Holiday House.

"Beginning a New Year Means" by Ruth Whitman in:
Low, A. (1991). *The Family Read-Aloud Holiday Treasury*. Ill. by Marc Brown. Boston: Little, Brown. (page 4)

"Bouquet of Roses" in: Low, A. (1991). *The Family Read-Aloud Holiday Treasury*. Ill. by Marc Brown. Boston: Little, Brown. (page 5) (Puerto Rican)

"Chinese New Year" in:
Low, A. (1991). *The Family Read-Aloud Holiday Treasury*. Ill. by Marc Brown. Boston: Little, Brown. (page 5)

"Happy New Year" in:
Merriam, E. (1973). *Out Loud*. Ill. by Harriet Sherman. New York: Atheneum. (page 50)

"January" by John Updike in: Prelutsky, J. (1983). *The Random House Book of Poetry for Children*. Ill. by Arnold Lobel. New York: Random House. (page 36)

■ Resource Books:

Greene, C. (1982). *Holidays Around the World*. Chicago: Childrens Press.

Van Straalen, A. (1986). *The Book of Holidays Around the World*. New York: Dutton.

Activities for Extension:

1. Invite students to write New Year's goals or resolutions.

2. Reflect on the past year by listing the top ten events, accomplishments, and days.

3. Prepare a calendar for the new year. Invite students to draw a picture for each month and attach it to calendar pages.

4. Write down important events that will occur in this new year: birthdays, vacations planned, school trips, and so on.

5. Discuss: What is one new thing you would like to learn this year? What is one thing you would like to teach someone this year?

6. Encourage students to predict events that will occur this year. Put the predictions in a special box and then open the box at the end of the year or the school year and see if any happened.

7. Learn how to say "Happy New Year" in other languages. Use the following words in a pocket chart activity. Put the languages in the chart and have students match the words to the language.

Chinese: Guo nien!
German: Gluckliches neues Jahr!
Spanish: Felíz año nuevo!
French: Bonne Annee!
Norwegian: Godt nyt dr!
Italian: Buon Anno!
Russian: Snovom godom!

8. Invite students to research the New Year's customs of a country or culture of their choice.

J·AN·U·A·R·Y 4

■ **Date:** January 4

■ **This date is special because:**
It is Louis Braille's birthday (1809).

Books that relate to this date

■ Picture Books:

Adler, D. A. (1990). *A Picture Book of Helen Keller*. Ill. by John and Alexandra Wallner. New York: Holiday House.

Alexander, S. H. (1992). *Mom's Best Friend*. Photos by George Ancona. New York: Macmillan.

Alexander, S. (1990). *Mom Can't See Me*. Ill. by George Ancona. New York: Macmillan.

Ancona, G. and Beth, M. (1989). *Handtalk Zoo*. New York: Four Winds.

Arnold, C. (1991). *A Guide Dog Puppy Grows Up*. Photos by Richard Hewett. San Diego: Harcourt Brace Jovanovich.

Charlip, R., Beth, M., and Ancona, G. (1974). *Handtalk*. New York: Macmillan.

Charlip, R., Beth, M. and Ancona, G. (1987). *Handtalk Birthday*. New York: Four Winds.

Cohen, M. (1983). *See You Tomorrow, Charles*. New York: Greenwillow.

Davidson, M. (1974). *Louis Braille: The Boy Who Invented Books for the Blind*. New York: Scholastic.

Fort, P. (1988). *Redbird*. New York: Orchard.

Gross, R. B. (1991). *You Don't Need Words*. Ill. by Susannah Ryan. New York: Scholastic.

Keeler, S. (1986). *Louis Braille*. Ill. by Richard Hook. New York: Bookwright.

MacLachlan, P. (1971). *Through Grandpa's Eyes*. Ill. by Deborah Ray. New York: HarperCollins.

Martin, B. and Archambault, J. (1987). *Knots on a Counting Rope*. Ill. by Ted Rand. New York: Holt.

Miller, M. B. and Ancona, G. (1991). *Handtalk School*. New York: Four Winds.

Parker, S. (1989). *The Eye and Seeing*. New York: Watts.

Pearson, S. (1987). *Happy Birthday, Grampie*. Ill. by Ronald Himler. New York: Dial.

Rankin, L. (1991). *The Handmade Alphabet*. New York: Dial.

Smith, E. S. (1987). *A Guide Dog Goes to School: The Story of a Dog Trained to Lead the Blind*. Ill. by Bert Dodson. New York: Morrow.

Sullivan, M. B., and Bourke, L. (1980). *A Show of Hands*. New York: Scholastic.

Yolen, J. (1975). *The Seeing Stick*. Ill. by Remy Charlip and Demetra Maraslis. New York: HarperCollins.

■ Novels:

Clifford, E. (1987). *The Man Who Sang in the Dark*. Ill. by Mary Beth Owens. Boston: Houghton Mifflin.

■ **Poetry:**

"Smells" by Kathryn Worth in:
Prelutsky, J. (1983). *The Random House Book of Poetry for Children.* Ill. by Arnold Lobel. New York: Scholastic. (page 39)

"Ears Hear" by Lucia and James L. Hymes, Jr. in:
Prelutsky, J. (1986). *Read-Aloud Rhymes for the Very Young.* Ill. by Marc Brown. New York: Knopf. (page 84)

Activities for Extension:

1. Examine a children's book printed in Braille, such as:

Clifton, L. (1986). *The Boy Who Didn't Believe in Spring.* Ill. by Brinton Turkle. Boston: National Braille Press.

2. Make a "feeling box." Put some uniquely shaped objects in a shoe box and have students feel and identify the objects in the box. Items included can be a comb, a piece of sandpaper, an orange, a mitten, a cotton ball, a nail clipper, a bottle cap, etc.

3. Invite students to learn sign language from any of the Handtalk books and practice signing their names and other messages to one another.

4. Take students outside and have them close their eyes. What do they hear, smell, feel, and taste? Discuss the importance of all the senses.

J·A·N·U·A·R·Y 15

■ **Date:** January 15

■ **This date is special because:**
It is Martin Luther King, Jr.'s birthday (1929).

Books that relate to this date

■ **Picture Books:**

Adler, D. A. (1986). *Martin Luther King Jr.: Free at Last.* Ill. by Robert Casilla. New York: Holiday House.

Adler, D. A. (1989). *A Picture Book of Martin Luther King Jr.* Ill. by Robert Casilla. New York: Holiday House.

Behrens, J. (1979). *Martin Luther King Jr.: The Story of a Dream.* Ill. by Anne Siberell. Chicago: Childrens Press.

Davidson, M. (1986). *I Have a Dream: The Story of Martin Luther King Jr.* New York: Scholastic.

De Kay, J. T. (1989). *Meet Martin Luther King Jr.* New York: Random House.

Hakim, R. (1991). *Martin Luther King Jr. and the March Toward Freedom.* Brookfield, CT: Millbrook.

Harris, J. L. (1983). *Martin Luther King Jr.* New York: Watts.

Hunter, N. (1985). *Martin Luther King Jr.* Ill. by Richard Cook. New York: Bookwright.

Levine, E. (1990). *If You Lived at the Time of Martin Luther King Jr.* New York: Scholastic.

Marzollo, J. (1993). *Happy Birthday, Martin Luther King.* Ill. by J. Brian Pinkney. New York: Scholastic.

■ **Novels:**

Haskins, J. (1992). *I Have a Dream: The Life and Words of Martin Luther King Jr.* Brookfield, CT: Millbrook.

Jakoubek, R. E. (1989). *Martin Luther King Jr.* New York: Chelsea House.

Lowery, L. (1987). *Martin Luther King Day.* Ill. by Hetty Mitchell. Minneapolis: Carolrhoda.

Patrick, D. (1991). *Coretta Scott King.* New York: Watts.

Tate, E. (1990). *Thank You, Dr. Martin Luther King, Jr!* New York: Watts.

■ **Poetry:**

"Martin Luther King Day" in: Livingston, M. C. (1985). *Celebrations.* Ill. by Leonard Everett Fisher. New York: Holiday House. (page 6)

Livingston, M. C. (1992). *Let Freedom Ring: A Ballad of Martin Luther King Jr.* Ill. by Samuel Byrd. New York: Holiday House.

"Dreams" by Langston Hughes in: Low, A. (1991). *The Family Read-Aloud Holiday Treasury.* Ill. by Marc Brown. Boston: Little, Brown. (page 7)

"We Shall Overcome" by Zilphia Horton, Frank Hamilton, Guy Carawan, and Pete Seeger in:
Low, A. (1991). *The Family Read-Aloud Holiday Treasury*. Ill. by Marc Brown. Boston: Little, Brown. (page 6)

"Martin Luther King" by Myra Cohn Livingston in:
Prelutsky, J. (1983). *The Random House Book of Poetry for Children*. Ill. by Arnold Lobel. New York: Random House. (page 37)

Activities for Extension:

1. Encourage students to write a clerihew poem (the first two lines rhyme, as do the last two lines) about Martin Luther King, Jr. Use the following example as a model:

> Martin Luther King
> Let freedom ring.
> He was a peaceful man
> Who helped others through his plan.

2. Using the books listed, ask students to make a time line of the important events in Dr. King's life.

3. Ask students to make a mural of the events found in Activity 2 or draw pictures of the most important event in Dr. King's life.

4. Dr. King fought for the equal rights of African Americans. Discuss whether all people have equal rights now.

5. Learn the popular song of the 1960's that was Dr. King's theme song. Music and verses are provided in *If You Lived at the Time of Martin Luther King Jr.* (Levine, 1990).

"We Shall Overcome"

We shall overcome.
We shall overcome.
Black and white together,
We shall overcome some day.
Oh deep in my heart, I do believe
We shall overcome some day.

J·A·N·U·A·R·Y 17

■ **Date:** January 17

■ **This date is special because:**
It is Hat Day.

Books that relate to this date
■ Picture Books:

Barkan, J. (1992). *That Fat Hat*. Ill. by Maggie Swanson. New York: Scholastic.

Blos, J. W. (1984). *Martin's Hats*. Ill. by Marc Simont. New York: Morrow.

Christelow, E. (1987). *Olive and the Magic Hat*. New York: Clarion.

Clark, E. C. (1990). *Catch That Hat*. Boston: Little, Brown.

Cushman, D. (1988). *Uncle Foster's Hat Tree*. New York: Dutton.

Geringer, L. (1985). *A Three Hat Day*. Ill. by Arnold Lobel. New York: Harper.

Howard, E. F. (1991). *Aunt Flossie's Hats (and Crab Cakes Later)*. Ill. by James Ransome. New York: Clarion.

Johnston, T. (1984). *The Witch's Hat*. Ill. by M. Tomes. New York: Putnam.

Kojima, N. (1989). *The Chef's Hat*. San Francisco: Chronicle.

Krisher, T. (1992). *Kathy's Hats: A Story of Hope*. Ill. by Nadine Bernard Westcott. Morton Grove, IL: Whitman.

Lear, E. (1988). *The Quangle Wangle's Hat*. Ill. by Janet Stevens. San Diego: Harcourt Brace Jovanovich.

Leemis, R. (1991). *Mister Momboo's Hat*. Ill. by Jeni Bassett. New York: Dutton.

Mariana, (1987). *Miss Flora McFlimsey's Easter Bonnet*. New York: Lothrop.

Miller, M. (1988). *Whose Hat?* New York: Greenwillow.

Morris, A. (1989). *Hats, Hats, Hats*. Photos by Ken Heyman. New York: Lothrop. (many cultures)

Parr, L. (1991). *A Man and His Hat*. New York: Putnam.

Rohmer, H. (1989). *Uncle Nacho's Hat-El Sombrero Del Tio Nacho*. Ill. by Beg Reisberg. Emeryville, CA: Children's Book Press.

Roy, R. (1990). *Whose Hat Is That?* Ill. by Rosemarie Hausherr. Boston: Houghton Mifflin.

Scheller, M. (1992). *My Grandfather's Hat*. Ill. by Keiko Narahashi. New York: McElderry.

Slobodkina, E. (1947). *Caps for Sale*. New York: Harper.

Wild, J. (1987). *Florence and Eric Take the Cake*. New York: Dial.

■ Poetry:

"Tight Hat" in:
Silverstein, S. (1974). *Where the Sidewalk Ends*. New York: Harper & Row. (page 83)

Smith, W. J. (1989). *Ho for a Hat!* Ill. by Lynn Munsinger. Boston: Little, Brown.

"Hats" in:
Smith, W. J. (1990). *Laughing Time*. Ill. by Fernando Krahn. New York: Farrar, Straus & Giroux. (page 10)

Activities for Extension:

1. Invite students to wear their favorite hats to school.

2. Categorize the hats worn to school according to color, size, soft, hard, etc. Play "20 Questions" with all the hats brought to school. Pick one out (in your mind) and then have students ask yes and no questions about it. Play continues until the hat is discovered. Students can play the game with a partner.

3. Invite students to role play situations by selecting hats of different occupations, such as a baker's hat, a firefighter's hat, etc.

4. Using the book *Hats, Hats, Hats* (Morris, 1989), categorize the hat next to the culture represented in a pocket chart:

Japan: straw hats

Israel: yarmulke

Egypt: kaffiyeh

Ask students to add other hats and cultures to this activity.

5. Invite students to match the hat to the activity in a pocket chart.

chef: chef's hat
cowboy: cowboy hat
sleeper: nightcap
baseball: baseball cap
construction worker: hard hat
navy service person: sailor hat
race car driver: crash helmet
football player: helmet

J·A·N·U·A·R·Y 22

■ Date: January 22

■ This date is special because:
It is National Popcorn Day.

Books that relate to this date

■ Picture Books:

de Paola, T. (1978). *The Popcorn Book.* New York: Holiday House.

Hall, C. V. (1976). *I Love Popcorn.* New York: Doubleday.

Low, A. (1993). *The Popcorn Shop.* Ill. by Patti Hammel. New York: Scholastic.

Selsam, M. (1976). *Popcorn.* Photos by Jerome Wexler. New York: Morrow.

Thayer, J. (1989). *The Popcorn Dragon.* Ill. by Lisa McGue. New York: Morrow.

Williams, B. (1976). *Cornzapoppin'.* New York: Holt.

Wyler, R. (1986). *Science Fun with Peanuts and Popcorn.* Ill. by Pat Stewart. New York: Messner.

■ Poems:

"A Popcorn Song" by Nancy Byrd Turner in:
de Regniers, B. S., and others. (1988). *Sing a Song of Popcorn: Every Child's Book of Poems.* Ill. by Marcia Brown, Leo and Diane Dillon, Richard Egielski, Trina Schart Hyman, Arnold Lobel, Maurice Sendak, Marc Simont, and Margot Zemach. New York: Scholastic. (page 23)

"Pigeons and Popcorn" in:
Livingston, M. C. (1989). *Remembering and Other Poems.* New York: McElderry. (page 24)

"The Turkey Shot Out of the Oven" in:
Prelutsky, J. (1990). *Something BIG Has Been Here.* Ill. by James Stevenson. New York: Greenwillow. (pages 18–19)

1. Help students make popcorn. After it is done, invite students to fill in the following sensory chart about the popcorn.

Looks like:	
Feels like:	
Smells like:	
Tastes like:	
Sounds like:	

Use the words in the chart to write poems about popcorn.

2. Encourage students to discuss and write about their favorite ways to prepare or eat popcorn.

3. Introduce the following tongue twister to your class: "How many pecks of popcorn does a popcorn popper pop when it pops a pound of popcorn kernels?" from *Science Fun with Peanuts and Popcorn* (Wylie, 1986). Encourage students to write more popcorn tongue twisters.

4. Store popcorn in different locations (refrigerator, freezer, in a warm place, in a dark place, and so on). Ask students to predict which will pop better. Then, pop the popcorn and see which did pop better. Discuss why this might have happened.

5. Encourage students to write away for a Jolly Time Pop Corn Ball Maker. Send $1.00 to: Jolly Time Pop Corn, American Pop Corn Company, P.O. Box 178, Department H, Sioux City, IA 51102. Ask for a Jolly Time Pop Corn Ball Maker. (from *Free Stuff for Kids*, Meadowbrook Press, 1993, page 86)

J·A·N·U·A·R·Y 23

■ Date: January 23

■ This date is special because:
It is National Handwriting Day.

Books that relate to this date
■ Picture Books:

Arnosky, J. (1983). *Mouse Writing*. San Diego: Harcourt Brace Jovanovich.

Cobb, V. (1989). *Writing It Down*. Ill. by Marylin Hafner. New York: HarperCollins.

Fisher, L. E. (1985). *Symbol Art*. New York: Four Winds.

Goldstein, P. (1993). *Long is a Dragon: Chinese Writing for Children*. New York: Scholastic.

Heide, F. P. and Gilliland, J. H. (1990). *The Day of Ahmed's Secret*. Ill. by Ted Levin. New York: Lothrop.

Lee, H. V. (1994). *At the Beach*. New York: Holt. (Mandarin Chinese)

Mitgutsch, A. Reidel, M., Fuschshuber, A., and Hogner, F. (1985). *From Graphite to Pencil*. Minneapolis: Carolrhoda.

Morris, N. (1984). *The Lettering Book*. New York: Scholastic.

Pulver, R. (1991). *Holiday Handwriting School*. Ill. by G. Brian Karas. New York: Four Winds.

Roehrig, C. (1990). *Fun with Hieroglyphs*. New York: The Metropolitan Museum of Art.

■ Novels:

Burch, J. J. (1991). *Fine Print: A Story about Johann Gutenberg*. Ill. by Kent Alan Aldrich. Minneapolis: Carolrhoda.

Cleary, B. (1990). *Muggy Maggie*. New York: Morrow.

Ransom, C. F. (1991). *Ladies and Jellybeans*. New York: Bradbury.

■ Poetry:

"Beginning on Paper" by Ruth Krauss in:
de Regniers, B. S., and others. (1988). *Sing a Song of Popcorn: Every Child's Book of Poems*. Ill. by Marcia Brown, Leo and Diane Dillon, Richard Egielski, Trina Schart Hyman, Arnold Lobel, Maurice Sendak, Marc Simont, and Margot Zemach. New York: Scholastic. (page 95)

"Pencils" and "Homework" in:
Esbensen, B. (1992). *Who Shrank My Grandmother's House? Poems of Discovery*. Ill. by Eric Beddows. New York: HarperCollins. (pages 9, 36)

"A New Pencil" in:
Merriam, E. (1986). *Fresh Paint*. Ill. by Eve Merriam. New York: Macmillan.

"My Snake" in:
Prelutsky, J. (1990). *Something BIG Has Been Here*. Ill. by James Stevenson. New York: Greenwillow. (page 116-117)

1. Encourage students to learn how letters are made in other languages using *Symbol Art* (Fisher, 1985).

2. Using the book *Long Is a Dragon* (Goldstein, 1993), invite students to practice writing the words for the characters in Chinese. Then make pocket chart cards out of the words and match the character in Chinese with the English word or numeral.

3. Invite students to copy their favorite poems in their best handwriting.

4. Encourage students to ask their parents or primary caregivers to copy their favorite quote in their best handwriting. Discuss: What do you notice about the handwriting? How many print? How many write in cursive? Make a graph of the results.

5. Using *The Lettering Book* (Morris, 1984), invite students to try different styles of lettering.

6. Invite students to survey their family and friends. Here are some questions they might ask.

> What is your favorite writing tool?
> (pen, pencil, crayon, marker, other)

> What is your favorite type of paper?
> (Lined paper, notebook paper, yellow paper, other)

> Where do you feel most comfortable writing?

> What is your favorite thing to write about?

7. Encourage students to write for a Wrist Writer (flexible pen bracelet). Enclose a long self-addressed, stamped envelope and $1.00. Send the request to: Neetstuff, Department N-3, P.O. Box 207, Glenside, PA 19038 and ask for the pen bracelet. (from *Free Stuff for Kids*, Meadowbrook Press, 1993, page 30)

J·A·N·U·A·R·Y 27

■ Date: January 27

■ This date is special because:

It is Mozart's birthday (1736).

Books that relate to this date

■ Picture Books:

Brett, J. (1992). *Berlioz the Bear*. New York: Scholastic.

Brighton, C. (1990). *Mozart: Scenes from the Childhood of the Great Composer*. New York: Doubleday.

Carlson, N. (1982). *Harriet's Recital*. Minneapolis: Carolrhoda.

Downing, J. (1990). *Mozart Tonight*. New York: Bradbury.

Griffith, H. (1986). *Georgia Music*. Ill. by James Stevenson. New York: Greenwillow.

Haseley, D. (1990). *The Old Banjo*. Ill. by Stephen Gammell. New York: Macmillan.

Johnston, T. (1988). *Pages of Music*. Ill. by Tomie de Paola. New York: Putnam.

Kraus, R. (1990). *Musica Max*. Ill. by Jose Aruego and Ariane Dewey. New York: Simon & Schuster.

Micucci, C. (1989). *A Little Night Music*. New York: Morrow.

Ober, H. (1994). *How Music Came to the World*. Ill. by Carol Ober. Boston: Houghton Mifflin. (Mexican myth)

Pettigrew, M. (1987). *Music and Sound*. New York: Gloucester.

Storms, L. (1983). *Careers with an Orchestra*. Photos by Milton J. Blumenfield. Minneapolis: Lerner.Tomes, R. (1991). *Mozart*. New York: Watts.

Walter, M. P. (1984). *Ty's One-Man Band*. Ill. by Margot Tomes. New York: Scholastic.

Weil, L. (1989). *The Magic of Music*. New York: Holiday House.

Zolotow, C. (1987). *Everything Glistens and Everything Sings*. Ill. by Margot Tomes. New York: Harcourt Brace Jovanovich.

■ Novels:

Monjo, F. N. (1975). *Letters to Horseface*. Ill. by Don Bolognese & Elaine Raphael. New York: Viking.

■ Poetry:

Fleischman, P. (1988). *Rondo in C*. Ill. by Janet Wentworth. New York: Harper.

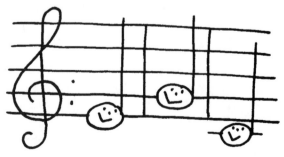

1. Invite students to make a birthday card for Mozart.

2. Introduce your class to some of Mozart's music. Then ask students to draw a picture of how this music makes them feel. You might want to read the book *Rondo in C* (Fleischman, 1988) to your class before playing Mozart's music.

3. Ask students to interview their parents about their favorite musicians. Graph the information.

4. Students can figure out how old Mozart would be today.

5. Ask students to write an acrostic poem using the letters in Mozart's name. Some students might want to use his full name, Wolfgang Amadeus Mozart.

6. Encourage a class discussion: How different is Mozart's music from that of today's?

7. Invite students to learn about other classical composers. Ask them to share their research with the class.

J·A·N·U·A·R·Y 29

■ **Date:** January 29

■ **This date is special because:**

It is Tony Johnston's birthday (1942).

Tony Johnston is a children's writer who is often mistaken for a man because of her name.

Books that relate to this date

■ Picture Books about Names:

Engel, D. (1989). *Josephina Hates Her Names*. Ill. by Diana Engel. New York: Morrow.

Goodman, B., and Krulik, N. E. (1991). *What's Your Name? A Guide to First Names and What They Mean*. New York: Scholastic.

Henkes, K. (1991). *Chrysanthemum*. New York: Greenwillow.

Kimmel, E. A. (1989). *Charlie Drives the Stage*. Ill. by Glen Rounds. New York: Holiday House.

Kline, R. (1990). *Watch Out for These Weirdos!* Ill. by Nancy Carlson. New York: Viking.

Lester, H. (1986). *A Porcupine Named Fluffy*. Ill. by Lynn Munsinger. Boston: Houghton Mifflin.

Waber, B. (1976). *But Names Will Never Hurt Me*. Boston: Houghton Mifflin.

■ Novels:

Miller, M. J. (1990). *Me and My Name*. New York: Viking.

■ Poetry:

"Beginning On Paper" by Ruth Krauss in:
de Regniers, B. S., and others. (1988). *Sing a Song of Popcorn*. New York: Scholastic. (page 95)

"My Name Is ..." by Pauline Clarke in: Prelutsky, J. (1983). *The Random House Book of Poetry for Children*. Ill. by Arnold Lobel. New York: Random House. (page 118)

■ Picture Books by Tony Johnston:

Johnston, T. (1990). *The Badger and the Magician*. Ill. by Tomie de Paola. New York: Putnam.

Johnston, T.(1986). *Farmer Mack Measures His Pig*. Ill. by Megan Lloyd. New York: Harper.

Johnston, T. (1979). *Little Mouse Nibbling*. Ill. by Diane Stanley. New York: Putnam.

Johnston, T. (1977). *Night Noises and Other Mole and Troll Stories*. Ill. by Cyndy Szekeres. New York: Putnam.

Johnston, T. (1994). *The Old Lady and the Birds*. Ill. by Stephanie Garcia. San Diego: Harcourt Brace Jovanovich.

Johnston, T. (1988). *Pages of Music*. Ill. by Tomie de Paola. New York: Putnam.

Johnston, T. (1985). *The Quilt Story*. Ill. by Tomie de Paola. New York: Putnam.

Johnston, T. (1990). *The Soup Bone*. Ill. by Margot Tomes. New York: Putnam.

Johnston, T. (1983). *The Vanishing Pumpkin*. Ill. by Tomie de Paola. New York: Putnam.

Johnston, T. (1987). *Whale Song*. Ill. by Ed Young. New York: Putnam.

Johnston, T. (1988). *Yonder*. Ill. by Lloyd Bloom. New York: Dial.

■ **Resource Book:**

Kovacs, D. and Preller J. (1993). *Meet the Authors and Illustrators: Volume Two*. New York: Scholastic. (pages 38-39)

Activities for Extension:

1. Brainstorm names that are sometimes hard to distinguish between male and female.

2. Ask students to list three reasons why they like their name.

3. Discuss: If you could have any name, what would it be and why?

4. After reading *Watch Out for These Weirdos!* (Kline, 1990) invite students to make up their own names and characteristics. (Example: Erin "Starin" McCarron who likes to peek at people.)

5. Ask students to read Tony Johnston's books. Which is their favorite and why? What do the books have in common? How are they different? Chart or graph the results.

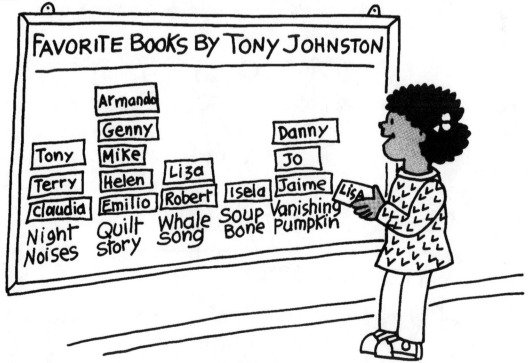

J·A·N·U·A·R·Y 31

■ **Date:** January 31

■ **This date is special because:**
It is Jackie Robinson's birthday (1919).

Books that relate to this date
■ **Picture Books:**

Adler, D. A. (1989). *Jackie Robinson: He Was the First.* Ill. by Robert Casilla. New York: Holiday House.

Blackstone, M. (1993). *This Is Baseball.* Ill. by John O'Brien. New York: Holt.

Christopher, M. (1988). *The Dog That Pitched a No-Hitter.* Ill. by Daniels Vasconcellos. Boston: Little, Brown.

Christopher, M. (1993). *The Dog That Stole Home.* Ill. by Daniel Vasconcellos. Boston: Little, Brown.

Cohen, B. (1989). *Thank You, Jackie Robinson.* Ill. by Richard Cuffari. New York: Scholastic.

Davidson, M. (1988). *The Story of Jackie Robinson: Bravest Man in Baseball.* New York: Dell.

Egan, T., Friedmann, S., and Levine, M. (1992). *The Macmillan Book of Baseball Stories.* New York: Macmillan.

Golenbock, P. (1990). *Teammates.* San Diego: Harcourt Brace Jovanovich.

Horenstein, H. (1988). *Spring Training.* New York: Macmillan.

Jaspersohn, W. (1989). *Bat, Ball, Glove: The Making of Major League Baseball Gear.* Boston: Little, Brown.

Kovalski, M. (1993). *Take Me Out to the Ballgame.* New York: Scholastic.

Latimar, J. (1991). *Fox under First Base*. Ill. by Lisa McCue. New York: Scribners.

O'Connor, J. (1989). *Jackie Robinson and the Story of All-Black Baseball*. Ill. by Jim Butcher. New York: Random House.

Robbins, K. (1988). *At the Ballpark*. New York: Viking.

Spohn, D. (1993). *Home Field*. New York: Lothrop.

Stadler, J. (1984). *Hooray for Snail*. New York: Crowell.

Teague, M (1993). *The Field Beyond Outfield*. New York: Scholastic.

■ Novels:

Lord, B. B. (1984). *In the Year of the Boar and Jackie Robinson*. New York: Harper.

■ Poetry:

Hopkins, L. B. (1993). *Extra Innings: Baseball Poems*. Ill. by Scott Medlock. San Diego: Harcourt Brace Jovanovich.

Morrison, L. (1992). *At the Crack of the Bat*. Ill. by Steve Cieslawski. New York: Hyperion.

Norworth, J. (1993). *Take Me Out to the Ballgame*. Ill. by Alec Gillman. New York: Four Winds.

"The Base Stealer" by Robert Francis in:
Prelutsky, J. (1983). *The Random House Book of Poetry for Children*. Ill. by Arnold Lobel. New York: Random House. (page 219)

Thayer, E. L. (1993). *Casey at the Bat*. Ill. by Patricia Polacco. New York: Scholastic.

■ Resource Books:

McKissack, P.C. and McKissack, F. (1994). *Black Diamond: The Story of the Negro Baseball Leagues*. New York: Scholastic.

Palmer, P. (1993). *Total Baseball: The Ultimate Encyclopedia of Baseball*. 3rd Edition. New York: HarperCollins.

Activities for Extension:

1. Jackie Robinson was the first black American to play in the Major Leagues. Ask students to write or discuss what they would like to be firsts at?

2. Discuss with your class: Who is your favorite baseball player? Graph or chart the results.

3. Invite students to make a time line of important events in Jackie Robinson's life.

4. Invite students to write a journal entry that Jackie Robinson might have written when he began to play in the Major Leagues.

5. Ask students to read *Teammates* (Golenbock, 1990), then discuss what the country was like back then. Have things changed? Why or why not?

FEBRUARY

■ **Date:** Any day in February

■ **This month is special because:** It is Black History Month.

Books that relate to this month
■ **Picture Books:**

Adler, D. A. (1993). *A Picture Book of Frederick Douglass*. Ill. by Samuel Byrd. New York: Holiday House.

Adler, D. A. (1992). *A Picture Book of Martin Luther King, Jr.* Ill. by Robert Casilla. New York: Holiday.

Campbell, T. L. (1990). *Honey Brown in Search of her Identity*. New York: TL Campbell.

Cavan, S. (1993). *Thurgood Marshall and Equal Rights*. Brookfield, CT: Millbrook.

Celsi, T. (1991). *Jesse Jackson and Political Power*. Brookfield, CT: Millbrook.

Crews, D. (1991). *Big Mama's*. New York: Greenwillow.

Crews, D. (1992). *Shortcut*. New York: Greenwillow.

Cwiklik, R. (1993). *Stokeley Carmichael and Black Power*. Brookfield, CT: Millbrook.

Dragonwagon, C. (1990). *Home Place*. Ill. by Jerry Pinkey. New York: Macmillan.

Everett, G. (1992). *Li'l Sis and Uncle Willie*. New York: Rizzoli.

Grifalconi, A. (1992). *Flyaway Firl*. Boston: Little, Brown.

Grifalconi, A. (1990). *Osa's Pride*. Boston: Little, Brown.

Hamilton, V. (1991). *The All Jahdu Storybook*. Ill. by Barry Moser. San Diego: Harcourt Brace Jovanovich.

Hoffman, M. (1991). *Amazing Grace*. Ill. by Caroline Binch. New York: Dial.

Hudson, C. W., and Ford, B. G. (1990). *Bright Eyes, Brown Skin.*. Ill. by George Ford. New York: Just Us Books.

Johnson, J. W. (1993). *Lift Every Voice and Sing*. Ill. by Elizabeth Catlett. New York: Walker.

Kroll, V. (1992). *Masai and I*. Ill. by Nancy Carpenter. New York: Four Winds.

Marsh, C. (1989). *Black "Jography" the Paths of Our Black Pioneers*. New York: Gallopade.

Marsh, C. (1989). *Black Trivia A-Z*. New York: Gallopade.

McKissack, P. C. (1988). *Mirandy and Brother Wind*. Ill. by Jerry Pinkey. New York: Knopf.

Medearis, A. S. (1993). *Picking Pennies for a Penny*. Ill. by Charles Shaw. New York: Scholastic.

Myers, W. D. (1993). *Malcolm X: By Any Means Necessary*. New York: Scholastic.

Polacco, P. (1992). *Chicken Sunday*. New York: Philomel.

Polacco, P. (1992). *Mrs. Katz and Tush*. New York: Putnam.

Sealy, A. V. (1980). *The Color Your Way into Black History Book*. New York: Assn Family Living.

Steptoe, J. (1987). *Mufaro's Beautiful Daughters*. New York: Lothrop.

Strickland, D. S. (1986). *Listen Children: An Anthology of Black Literature*. New York: Bantam.

Vigna, J. (1992). *Black Like Kyra, White Like Me*. Morton, IL: Whitman.

Williams, S. A. (1992). *Working Cotton*. Ill. by Carole Byard. San Diego: Harcourt Brace Jovanovich.

▪ Novels

Hart, P. S. (1992). *Flying Free: America's First Black Aviators*. Minneapolis: Lerner.

Levine, E. (1993). *Freedom's Children: Young Civil Right Activists Tell Their Own Stories*. New York: Putnam.

Myers, W. D. (1991). *Now Is Your Time! The African-American Struggle for Freedom*. New York: HarperCollins.

Patrick, D. (1991). *Coretta Scott King*. New York: Watts.

Taylor, M. D. (1990). *Mississippi Bridge*. New York: Bantam Doubleday.

Taylor, M. D. (1988). *The Friendship and The Gold Cadillac*. New York: Bantam Doubleday.

▪ Poetry

Adoff, A. (1982). *All the Colors of the Race*. Ill. by John Steptoe. New York: Lothrop.

Adoff, A. (1973). *Black Is Brown Is Tan*. Ill. by Emily Arnold McCully. New York: Harper & Row.

Adoff, A. (1970). *Black Out Loud: An Anthology of Modern Poems by Black Americans*. Ill. by Alvin Hollingsworth. New York: Macmillan.

Adoff, A. (1977). *Celebrations: A New Anthology of Black American Poetry*. Chicago: Follett.

Adoff, A. (1974). *My Black Me: A Beginning Book of Black Poetry*. New York: Dutton.

Adoff, A. (1973). *The Poetry of Black America: Anthology of the 20th Century*. New York: Harper & Row.

Giovanni, N. (1985). *Spin a Soft Black Song*. Ill. by George Martins. New York: Hill and Wang.

Greenfield, E. (1978). *Honey I Love*. Ill. by Diane & Leo Dillon. New York: HarperCollins.

Greenfield, E. (1988). *Nathaniel Talking*. Ill. by Jan Spivey Gilchrist. New York: Black Butterfly.

Greenfield, E. (1988). *Under the Sunday Tree*. Ill. by Amos Ferguson. New York: Harper & Row.

Hudson, W. (1993). *Pass It On: African-American Poetry for Children*. Ill. by Floyd Cooper. New York: Scholastic.

Johnson, J. W. (1993). *Lift Every Voice and Sing*. Ill. by Elizabeth Catlett. New York: Walker.

1. Encourage students to decorate the room for Black History Month. They can include drawings and facts from the listed titles.

2. Ask students to read a poem a day from the recommended poetry books.

3. You might want to invite several prominent role models from the African American community to speak to your class.

4. Ask students to read *Mufaro's Beautiful Daughters* (Steptoe, 1987). Then ask them to compare and discuss the similarities between this title and Cinderella.

5. Ask students to read *Masai and I* (Kroll, 1992). Some students might want to read with another teacher or adult. Afterwards, allow them to discuss the similarities and differences between Linda (who is African American) and Linde (who is African Masai).

F·E·B·R·U·A·R·Y 3

■ Date: February 3

■ This date is special because:

It is Elizabeth Blackwell's birthday.

Elizabeth Blackwell was the first female doctor.

Books that relate to this date

■ Picture Books:

Berger, M. (1985). *Germs Make Me Sick!* Ill. by Marylin Hafner. New York: Crowell.

Chalmers, M. (1981) *Come to the Doctor, Harry.* Ill. by Mary Chalmers. New York: HarperCollins.

Cherry, L. (1988) *Who's Sick Today?* New York: Dutton.

Cole, J.(1981). *Get Well, Clown Arounds!* Ill. by Jerry Smath. New York: Parents.

Klingel, C. (1987). *Women of America: Elizabeth Blackwell.* New York: Creative Ed.

Kuklin, S. (1988) *When I See My Doctor.* New York: Bradbury.

Latham, J. L.(1991). *Elizabeth Blackwell: Pioneer Woman* Doctor. Ill. by Ethel Gold. New York: Chelsea House.

Patent, D. H. (1983). *Germ!* New York: Holiday House.

Robison, D. & P. (1982). *Your Turn, Doctor.* Ill. Deborah Robison. New York: Dial.

Rockwell, A. & Rockwell, H. (1982). *Sick in Bed.* New York: Dial.

■ Poetry:

"Why Can't A Girl Be the Leader of the Boys?" in:
Dakos, Kalli. (1990). *If You're Not Here Please Raise Your Hand.* Ill. by G. Brian Karas. New York: Four Winds. (page 25)

"Louisa's Liberation" in:
Little, J. (1989). *Hey World, Here I Am!.* Ill. by Sue Truesdell. New York: Harper & Row. (page 59)

Activities for Extension:

1. Invite a doctor to come into the classroom and ask her or him questions the students have prepared. Then, ask students to write an article about the doctor's visit for the class or school newspaper.

2. Allow children to spend time with a doctor play kit. Kit should contain items such as stethoscope, prescription pad, tongue depressors, reflex hammer, etc. Challenge students to describe the purpose or use of each item.

3. Challenge students to name famous doctors (e.g., Dr. Doolittle, Dr. Suess).

F·E·B·R·U·A·R·Y 11

- **Date:** February 11

- **This date is special because:**
It is National Inventor's Day.

Books that relate to this date
■ Picture Books:

Bender, L. (1991). *Inventions*. New York: Knopf.

Bendick, J. (1993). *Eureka! It's a Telephone!* Ill. by Sal Murdocca. Brookfield, CT: Millbrook.

Brown, J., and Hott, M. (1990). *Inventing Things*. New York: Bareth Stevens.

Caney, S. (1985). *Steven Caney's Invention Book*. New York: Workman.

Carroll, J. and Wells, C. (1987). *Inventors*. Ill. by Tom Foster. New York: Good Apple.

Cartwright, P. (1990). *Mr. Butterby's Amazing Machines*. New York: Steck-Vaughn.

Davidson, M. (1990). *The Story of Thomas Alva Edison, Inventor*. New York: Scholastic.

Elting, M. (1984). *The Answer Book about Robots and Other Inventions*. Ill. by Rowen Barnes-Murphy. New York: Putnam.

Himmelman, J. (1990). *The Day-Off Machine*. Englewood Cliffs, NJ: Silver.

Jacobs, D. (1990). *What Does It Do? Inventions Then and Now*. New York: Raintree.

Jones, C. F. (1991). *Mistakes That Worked*. Ill. by John O'Brien. New York: Doubleday.

Konigsburg, E. L. (1991). *Samuel Todd's Book of Great Inventions*. New York: Atheneum.

Macaulay, D. (1988). *The Way Things Work*. Boston: Houghton Mifflin.

Quinn, K. (1986). *Inventive Inventions*. New York: Price Stern.

Smith, D., and Cassin, S.(1990). *The Amazing Book of Firsts: Great Ideas*. New York: BDD Promos Bk.

Towle, W. (1993). *The Real McCoy: The Life of an African-American Inventor*. Ill. by Wil Clay. New York: Scholastic.

Weiss, H. (1980). *How to Be an Inventor*. New York: Crowell.

■ Poetry:

"How to Assemble a Toy" in:
Ciardi, J. (1990). *Mummy Took Cooking Lessons*. Ill. by Merle Nacht. Boston: Houghton Mifflin. (page 40)

"Invention" in:
Silverstein, S. (1974). *Where the Sidewalk Ends*. New York: Harper & Row. (page 48)

"The Inventor" in:
Simmie, L. (1984). *Auntie's Knitting a Baby*. Ill. by Anne Simmie. New York: Orchard. (page 26)

1. Ask students to create a new invention using scraps and "junk" items. Then allow them to write about what each invention does.

2. Encourage students to interview their class, other classes, the office staff, teachers, and parents about their choice for most important invention. Make a picture graph of the results.

3. Share with the class an unusual fact about an invention. See Stephen *Caney's Invention Book* (Caney, p. 85). Invite students to do the same.

4. Invite students to draw a picture or write an advertisement for their favorite invention.

5. Encourage students to make a "What We Have Learned About Inventions" book with all the information they have gathered. Share the book with another class, and invite them to add to it.

6. Challenge students to think of life today without a certain invention. Invite each student to record their thoughts in a report or short story form.

F·E·B·R·U·A·R·Y 12

■ **Date:** February 12

■ **This date is special because:**
It is Abraham Lincoln's birthday (1809).

Books that relate to this date
■ Picture Books:

Adler, D. A. (1989). *Picture Book of Abraham Lincoln.* New York: Holiday.

Barkan, J. (1990). *Abraham Lincoln.* Ill. by Lyle Miller. New York: Silver.

Colver, A. (1992). *Abraham Lincoln: For the People.* New York: Chelsea House.

Fradin, D. B. (1990). *Lincoln's Birthday.* New York: Enslow.

Gibbons, T. (1989). *Lincoln and the Lady.* New York: Sonos.

Greene, C. (1989). *Abraham Lincoln: President of a Divided Country.* Ill. by Steven Dobson. New York: Childrens.

Gross, R. B. (1985). *If You Grew Up with Abraham Lincoln.* New York: Scholastic.

Gross, R. B. (1988). *True Stories About Abraham Lincoln.* Ill. by Charles Turzak. New York: Scholastic.

Hanneman, T. (1992). *The Election Book: People Pick a President.* New York: Scholastic.

Kunhardt, E. (1993). *Honest Abe.* Ill. by Malcah Zeldis. New York: Greenwillow.

McGovern, A. (1985). *If You Grew up with Abe Lincoln.* Ill. by Brinton Turkle. New York: Scholastic.

Provensen, A. (1990). *The Buck Stops Here.* New York: HarperCollins.

Shorto, R. (1991). *Abe Lincoln and the End of Slavery.* New York: Millbrook.

■ Poetry:

"To Meet Mr. Lincoln" by Eve Merriam in:
de Regniers, B. S., and others. (1988). *Sing a Song of Popcorn.* Ill. by nine Caldecott Medal artists. New York: Scholastic. (page 92)

Livingston, M. C. (1993). *Abraham Lincoln: A Man for All the People.* Ill. by Samuel Byrd. New York: Scholastic.

"Lincoln" by N. B. Turner in:
Prelutsky, J. (1983). *The Random House Book of Poetry.* Ill. by Arnold Lobel. New York: Random House. (page 37)

1. Ask students to calculate how old Lincoln would be today.

2. Encourage students to pretend they lived during Lincoln's time. Ask them to write Lincoln letters persuading him to ignore the opposition and pass the Emancipation Proclamation.

3. Invite students to draw a picture of Abraham Lincoln. Some students might choose do a report on him.

4. Encourage students to ask an adult: Who is their favorite president? Why? Allow students to share their findings with the class. Chart the results.

5. Ask students to bring in articles about the current president. Students might want to bring in selections from any newspaper or magazine. Challenge students to discuss differences.

6. Using a map of the United States, find cities named after Lincoln.

7. Children might want to dress up like Lincoln as they learn about him.

F·E·B·R·U·A·R·Y 14

■ Date: February 14

■ This date is special because:
It is Valentine's Day.

Books that relate to this date
■ Picture Books:

Bennett, M. and Peltier P. (1985). *My First Valentine's Day Book*. New York: Childrens.

Bond, F. (1986). *Four Valentines in a Rainstorm*. New York: HarperCollins.

Brown, M. (1980). *Arthur's Valentine*. Boston: Little, Brown.

Carlson, N. (1987). *Louanne Pig in the Mysterious Valentine*. New York: Puffin.

Cohen, M. (1978). *Bee My Valentine*. New York: Bantam Doubleday.

Cole, B. (1989). *Cupid*. New York: Putnam.

Davis, N. M., and others. (1986). *February and Valentines*. Ill. by Nancy Davis. New York: DaNa.

Delvin, W., and Devlin, H. (1986). *Cranberry Valentine*. New York: Macmillan.

Dinardo, J. (1992). *Henry's Secret Valentine*. New York: Bantam Doubleday.

Folmer, A. P. (1991). *Valentine Pop-Up Cards to Make*. New York: Scholastic.

Fradin, D. B. (1990). *Valentine's Day*. New York: Enslow.

Gantz, D. (1990). *Biggest Valentine.* New York: Scholastic.

Kessel, J. K. (1988). *Valentine's Day.* Ill. by Karen Ritz. New York: Lerner.

Kraus, R. (1986). *How Spider Saved Valentine's Day.* New York: Scholastic.

Kroll, S. (1993). *Will You Be My Valentine?* Ill. by Lillian Hoban. New York: Holiday House.

Modell, F. (1981). *One Zillion Valentines.* New York: Greenwillow.

Mooser, S. (1990). *Crazy Mixed-Up Valentine's.* New York: Greenwillow.

Pretlusky, J. (1985). *It's Valentine's Day.* Ill. by Yossi Abolafia. New York: Scholastic.

St. Pierre, S. (1990). *Valentine Kittens.* New York: Scholastic.

Stevenson, J. (1987). *Happy Valentine's Day, Emma!* New York: Greenwillow.

Stock, C. (1991). *Secret Valentine Stock.* New York: Macmillan.

Watson, W. (1993). *A Valentine for You.* New York: Clarion.

Wittman, S. (1987). *The Boy Who Hated Valentines Day.* Ill. by Chaya Burstein. New York: HarperCollins.

■ Poetry:

"My Valentine" in:
Livingston, M. C. (1985). *Celebrations.* Ill. by Leonard Everett Fisher. New York: Holiday House. (page 10)

Low, A. (1991). *The Family Read-Aloud Holiday Treasury.* Ill. by Marc Brown. Boston: Little, Brown. (pages 8–11)

"Valentine" in:
Prelutsky, J. (1983). *The Random House Book of Poetry for Children.* Ill. by Arnold Lobel. New York: Random House. (page 38)

Activities for Extension:

1. Allow students to create their own pop-up valentines for a loved one.

2. Challenge students to find out whether Valentine's is celebrated in other countries.

3. You might want to share the history of Valentine's with your class.

4. Invite students to create personal valentines with compliments.

5. You might want to bring candy hearts into the classroom. Sort the hearts according to color or message or other categories that students invent.

6. Ask students to group the candy hearts in a box by color. Others might want to group the candies by message. Then ask them to graph the results.

F·E·B·R·U·A·R·Y 18

Date: February 18

This date is special because:
It is the day the planet Pluto was discovered.

Books that relate to this date

Picture Books:

Anderson, J. (1993). *Richie's Rocket*. Photos by George Ancona. New York: Morrow.

Bailey, D. (1990). *The Far Planets*. New York: Steck-Vaughn.

Bailey, D. (1990). *The Near Planets*. New York: Steck-Vaughn.

Berger, M. (1992). *Discovering Mars: The Amazing Story of the Red Planet*. Ill. by Joan Holub. New York: Scholastic.

Branley, F. M. (1987). *The Planets in Our Solar System*. Ill. by Don Maden. New York: HarperCollins.

Cole, J. (1990). *The Magic School Bus Lost in the Solar System*. Ill. by Bruce Degen. New York: Scholastic.

Fradin, D. B. (1989). *Pluto*. New York: Childrens.

Gibbons, G. (1993). *The Planets*. New York: Holiday House.

Gibbons, G. (1992). *Stargazers*. New York: Holiday House.

Glyman, C. A. (1992). *What's Above the Sky?: A Book about Planets*. Ill. by Dee Biser. New York: Forest.

Greenburg, J. E., and Carey, H. H. (1990). *Space*. Ill. by Rick Karpinski. New York: Raintree.

Hirst, R., and S. (1988). *My Place in Space*. Ill. by Roland Harvey with Joe Levine. New York: Orchard.

Ingves, G. (1992). *To Pluto and Back: A Voyage in the Milky Way*. New York: R & S Books.

Jay, M. (1987). *Planets*. New York: Watts.

Kerrod, R. (1990). *Big Book of Stars and Planets*. New York: Smithmark.

Leedy, L. (1993). *Postcards from Pluto*. New York: Holiday House.

Petty, K. (1984). *The Planets*. Ill. by Mike Saunders. New York: Watts.

Reigot, B. P. (1981). *A Book About Planets*. Ill. by Ted Hanke. New York: Scholastic.

Robson, D. (1991). *The Planets*. New York: Watts.

Rosen, S. (1992). *Can You Find a Planet?* Ill. by Dean Lindberg. Minneapolis: Carolrhoda.

Simon, S. (1992). *Our Solar System*. New York: Morrow.

Wiesner, D. (1992). *June 29, 1999*. New York: Clarion.

■ Poetry:

A Wonderful Trip in a Rocketship" in Lee, D. (1991). *The Ice Cream Store*. Ill. by David McPhail. New York: Scholastic.

Livingston, M. C. (1988). *Space Songs*. Ill. by Leonard Everett Fisher. New York: Holiday House.

Activities for Extension:

1. Allow students to design a solar system using styrofoam balls.

2. Ask students to pretend they've landed on their favorite planet and write about it.

3. Allow students to make a papier mâché model of each of the planets. Remind them to decorate the surface in an appropriate style.

4. Invite students to draw, design, and describe their own planet. Who lives there? What does it look like? What language is spoken? What do people do all day on your planet? What do they eat?

5. Ask students to make a cookbook of pretend foods eaten on Pluto, such as Pluto Pudding, Pluto Pie, Pluto Pretzels, Pluto Popcorn, etc.

F·E·B·R·U·A·R·Y 20

■ **Date:** February 20

■ **This date is special because:**
It is Tana Hoban's birthday.

Tana Hoban is a children's book author and photographer.

Books that relate to this date

■ Picture Books:

Freeman, T. (1983). *Photography.* New York: Childrens.

Hoban, T. (1991). *All About Where.* New York: Greenwillow.

Hoban, T. (1987). *Dots, Spots, Speckles, and Stripes.* New York: Greenwillow.

Hoban, T. (1990). *Exactly the Opposite.* New York: Greenwillow.

Hoban, T. (1983). *I Read Signs.* New York: Greenwillow.

Hoban, T. (1983). *I Read Symbols.* New York: Greenwillow.

Hoban, T. (1988). *Look, Look, Look.* New York: Greenwillow.

Hoban, T. (1992). *Look Up, Look Down.* New York: Greenwillow.

Hoban, T. (1989). *Of Colors and Things.* New York: Greenwillow.

Hoban, T. (1990). *Shadows and Reflections.* New York: Greenwillow.

Hoban, T. (1992) *Spirals, Curves, Fanshapes and Lines.* New York: Greenwillow.

Lasky, K. (1992). *Think Like an Eagle: At Work with a Wildlife Photographer.* Photos by Christopher Knight & Jack Swedberg. Boston: Little, Brown.

Osinki, C. (1986). *I Can Be a Photographer.* New York: Childrens.

Stokes. (1992). *The Photography Book.* New York: Scholastic.

Yates, M. (1987). *It's School Picture Day.* Ill. by Blanche Sims. New York: Abingdon.

Yolen, J. (1993). *The Moon Was the Best.* Photos by Tana Hoban. New York: Greenwillow.

■ Novels:

Mitchell, B. (1986). *Click: A Story about George Eastman.* Ill. by Jan Hosking Smith. Minneapolis: Carolrhoda.

■ Poetry:

"Old Photograph Album: Grandfather" in:
Esbensen, B. (1992). *Who Shrank My Grandmother's House?* Ill. by Eric Beddows. New York: Harper & Row. (page 19)

1. Ask students to bring in their favorite photograph. Create frames out of shoebox lids.

2. Using the book, *Look, Look, Look* (Hoban, 1992), invite students to create their own book versions with magazine pictures.

3. Many of Tana Hoban's books are concept books. Invite students to create their own classroom concept book.

4. Invite a photographer into the classroom to discuss, explain and display their work.

5. Ask each student to take one photo of himself or herself, and describe themselves with facts that are important to them. Display photos and facts on the bulletin board.

F·E·B·R·U·A·R·Y 22

■ Date: February 22

■ This date is special because:
It is George Washington's birthday (1732).

Books that relate to this date

■ Picture Books:

Adler, D. A. (1988). *George Washington: Father of Our Country*. Ill. by Jacqueline Garrick. New York: Holiday.

Adler, D. A. (1989). *A Picture Book of George Washington*. Ill. by John & Alexandra Wallner. New York: Holiday House.

Fritz, J. (1984). *George Washington's Breakfast*. Ill. by Paul Galdone. New York: Putnam.

Fritz, J. (1992). *George Washington's Mother*. Ill. by Dy Anne DiSalvo-Ryan. New York: Grosset.

Giblin, J. C. (1992). *George Washington: A Picture Book Biography*. Ill. by Michael Dooling. New York: Scholastic.

Gross, R. B. (1985). *If You Grew Up with George Washington*. Ill. by Jack Kent. New York: Scholastic.

Marshall, J. (1987). *George and Martha*. Boston: Houghton Mifflin.

McGovern, A. (1985). *If You Grew Up with George Washington*. New York: Scholastic.

Moncure, J. B. (1987). *My First President's Day Book*. Ill. by Lydia Halverson. New York: Childrens.

Provensen, A. (1990). *The Buck Stops Here*. New York: HarperCollins.

Quackenbush, Robert. (1989). *I Did It with My Hatchet: A Story of George Washington*. New York: Pippin.

Roop, P. and Roop, C. (1986). *Buttons for General Washington*. Ill. by Peter E. Hanson. Minneapolis: Carolrhoda.

Tunnel, M. O. (1993). *The Joke's on George*. Ill. by Kathy Osborn. New York: Tamborine.

Waricha, J. (1992). *George Washington Was Not the First President! And Other Crazy Facts about Our Presidents*. New York: Parachute Press.

■ Poetry:

"President's Day" in:
Livingston, M. C. (1985). *Celebrations*. Ill. by Leonard Everett Fisher. New York: Holiday House. (page 9)

Provensen, A. (1990). *The Buck Stops Here*. New York: Harper & Row.

1. Using a map of the United States, ask students to find the cities, towns, and states named after our first president.

2. Ask students to make an acrostic poem using George Washington's name.

3. Make a chart entitled "Facts about George Washington." Each student can contribute a fact from the above titles.

4. Ask students to research who the first governor of the state was, who the first mayor of the city was, or who the first principal of the school was. Students can make a class book using this information. Some might want to illustrate the book.

5. Ask students to pretend George Washington paid a visit to the classroom. What would they ask him?

F·E·B·R·U·A·R·Y 26

■ **Date:** February 26

■ **This date is special because:**
It is "Buffalo Bill" Cody's birthday (1846).

Books that relate to this date

■ Picture Books:

Adler, D. A. (1988). *Wild Bill Hickok and Other Old West Riddles*. Ill. by Glen Rounds. New York: Holiday House.

Baker, O. (1981). *Where the Buffaloes Begin*. Ill. by Stephen Gammell. New York: Warner.

Brusca, M. C. (1991). *On the Pampas*. New York: Henry Holt.

Everett, P. L. (1992). *The One That Got Away*. Ill. by Dirk Zimmer. New York: Clarion.

Freedman, R. (1992). *Children of the Wild West*. New York: Scholastic.

Gorsline, M. & Forsline, D. (1980). *Cowboys*. Ill. by Doug Forsline. New York: Random House.

Guthrie, M. M. (1992). *Woody's 20 Grow Big Songs*. Ill. by Woody Guthrie. New York: HarperCollins.

Hooker, R. (1990). *Matthew the Cowboy*. Ill. by Cat Bowman Smith. Niles, IL: Whitman.

Khalsa, Dayal K. (1990). *Cowboy Dreams*. New York: McKay.

Kimmel, E. A. (1990). *Four Dollars and Fifty Cents*. Ill. by Glen Rounds. New York: Holiday.

Lenski, L. (1980). *Cowboy Small*. New York: McKay.

Levine, E. (1992) *. . . If You Traveled West in a Covered Wagon*. Ill. by Elroy Freem. New York: Scholastic.

Martini, T. (1981). *Cowboys*. New York: Childrens.

Noble, T. H. (1987). *Meanwhile Back at the Ranch*. Ill. by Tony Ross. New York: Dial.

Reed, L. R. (1990). *Rattlesnake Stew*. New York: Farrar, Straus & Giroux.

Rounds, G. (1991). *Cowboys*. New York: Holiday.

Scott, A. H. (1990). *One Good Horse: A Cowpuncher's Counting Book*. Ill. by Lynn Sweat. New York: Greenwillow.

Scott, A. H. (1989). *Someday Rider*. Ill. by Ronald Himler. New York: Clarion.

Sewall, M. (1985). *Riding That Strawberry Roan*. New York: Viking.

Shepard, A. (1993). *The Legend of Lightning Larry*. Ill. by Toni Goffe. New York: Scribner.

Sullivan, C. 1993). *Cowboys*. New York: Rizzoli.

■ Novels:

Scieszka, J. (1993). *The Good, the Bad, and the Goofy.* Ill. by Lane Smith. New York: Puffin.

■ Resource Book:

Greenlaw, M. J. (1993). *Ranch Dressing; The Story of Western Wear.* New York: Lodestar.

■ Poetry:

Medearis, A. S. (1992). *The Zebra-Riding Cowboy.* Ill. by Maria Cristina Brusca. New York: Holt.

Metropolitan Museum of Art. (1991). *Songs of the Wild West.* New York: Simon & Schuster.

Activities for Extension:

1. Discuss how cowboys are portrayed in westerns. Is this accurate or fair?

2. Ask students to locate and trace the path taken by the cattle drives.

3. Ask students to match the cowboy expressions to their meanings in the following pocket chart activity:

grub pile	time to eat
bread sack	stomach
narrow at the equator	feeling hungry
splatter dabs	pancakes
sinkers	biscuits
Texas butter	gravy
side winder	snake
frog sticker	long knife
wipes	handkerchief
hoosegow	jail
leaving Cheyenne	leaving town

4. Plan a pocket chart activity with the book *On the Pampas* (Brusca, 1991). Ask students to match the Spanish words to their meanings.

horneo—bird
mate—bitter, greenish tea
nandu—South American ostrich
asado—meat roasted outdoors over a fire
estancia—South American cattle ranch
las pampas—Grasslands

mulita—armadillo
recado—saddle
facon—gaucho knife
gaucho—cowboy
rastra—gaucho belt

5. Sing some of the songs from *Songs of the Wild West* (Metropolitan Museum of Art, 1991). Ask students to pretend they are gathered around a campfire.

M·A·R·C·H

■ **Date:** Any day in March

■ **This month is special because:** It is National Women's History Month.

Books that relate to this month

■ Picture Books:

Adler, D. A. (1993). *A Picture Book of Anne Frank*. Ill. by Karen Ritz. New York: Holiday House. (World War II)

Adler, D. A. (1993). *A Picture Book of Rosa Parks*. Ill. by Robert Casilla. New York: Holiday House. (civil rights movement)

Accorsi, W. (1993). *Rachel Carson*. New York: Holiday House. (naturalist)

Baker, R. (1987). *The First Woman Doctor*. Ill. by Eveln Copelman. New York: Scholastic.

Blaine, M. (1975). *The Terrible Thing That Happened at Our House*. New York: Scholastic.

Giff, P. R. (1987). *Mother Teresa: Sister to the Poor*. Ill. by Ted Lewin. New York: Puffin.

Johnston, J. (1987). *They Led the Way: 14 American Woman*. New York: Scholastic.

Knight, A. S. (1993). *The Way West: Journal of a Pioneer Woman*. Ill. by Michael McCurdy. New York: Simon & Schuster.

Steelsmith, S. (1987). *Elizabeth Blackwell: The Story of the First Woman Doctor*. Ill. by Judy Kerstetter. New York: Parenting Press.

■ Novels:

Crofford, E. (1989). *Healing Warrior: A Story about Sister Elizabeth Kenny*. Ill. by Steve Michaels. Minneapolis: Carolrhoda. (nurse)

Ferris, J. (1988). *Go Free or Die: A Story about Harriet Tubman*. Ill. by Karen Ritz. Minneapolis: Carolrhoda. (underground railroad)

Ferris, J. (1991). *Native American Doctor: The Story of Susan Flesche Picotte*. Minneapolis: Carolrhoda.

Giblin, J. C. (1993). *Edith Wilson: The Woman Who Ran the United States*. Ill. by Michelle Laporte. New York: Puffin. (Woodrow Wilson's wife)

Macy, S. (1993). *A Whole New Ballgame. New York: Henry Holt.* (All-American Girls Professional Baseball League)

McPherson, S. S. (1992). *I Speak for the Women: A Story about Lucy Stone.* Ill. by Brian Liedahl. Minneapolis: Carolrhoda. (women's rights activist)

McPherson, S. S. (1990). *Rooftop Astronomer: A Story about Maria Mitchell.* Ill. by Henry Mitchell. Minneapolis: Carolrhoda. (astronomer)

McPherson, S. (1992). *The Workers' Detective: A Story about Alice Hamilton.* Ill. by Janet Schulz. Minneapolis: Carolrhoda.

O'Connor, B. (1992). *Mammolina: A Story about Maria Montessori.* Ill. by Sara Campitelli. Minneapolis: Carolrhoda. (Montessori schools)

Ransom, C. F. (1993). *Listening to the Crickets: A Story about Rachel Carson.* Ill. by Shelly O. Haas. Minneapolis: Carolrhoda. (nature lover, writer)

Vare, E. A. (1992). *Adventurous Spirit: A Story About Ellen Swallow Richards.* Minneapolis: Carolrhoda. (first professional woman chemist in the U.S.)

Weidt, M. N. (1991). *Stateswoman to the World: A Story About Eleanor Roosevelt.* Ill. by Lydia M. Anderson. Minneapolis: Carolrhoda.

■ Poetry:

"Herstory-Her Story" in:
Dakos, K. (1993). *Don't Read This Book, Whatever You Do!* Ill. by G. Brian Karas. New York: Four Winds. (page 17)

"No Girls Allowed" by Jack Prelutsky and "Girls Can Too" by Lee Bennett Hopkins in:
Prelutsky, J. (1983). *The Random House Book of Poetry for Children.* Ill. by Arnold Lobel. New York: Random House. (page 111)

Activities for Extension:

1. Invite students to write about the most important woman to them and why that woman is important. Illustrate and make a class book.

2. Students can make a time line of important dates in women's history using the above books.

3. Allow students to illustrate the above time line for a mural effect.

4. Invite students to interview their parents and grandparents about famous women in history. Have them list three women that made a difference. Discuss the results.

5. Using a newspaper, ask students to find women who they predict will make a difference in their time.

M·A·R·C·H 3

■ **Date:** March 3

■ **This date is special because:**
It is Doll Day in Japan.

Books that relate to this date
■ **Picture Books:**

Bonners, S. (1991). *The Wooden Doll*. New York: Lothrop.

Brett, J. (1992). *Trouble with Trolls*. New York: Putnam.

Brown, R. (1990). *I Don't Like It*. New York: Dutton.

Buffet, J., and Buffet, J. (1991). *Trouble Dolls*. Ill. by Lambert Davis. San Diego: Harcourt Brace Jovanovich.

Conrad, P. (1989). *The Tub People*. Ill. by Richard Egielski. New York: Harper.

Freidman, T. (1986). *Henriette: The Story of a Doll*. Ill. by Vera Rosenbery. New York: Scholastic.

Garelick, M. (1990). *Just My Size*. Ill. by William Pene Du Bois. New York: HarperCollins.

Godden, R. (1992). *The Story of Holly and Ivy*. Ill. by Barbara Cooney. New York: Scholastic.

Goffstein, M. B. (1988). *Our Prairie Home: A Picture Album*. New York: Harper & Row.

Haskin, J. (1991). *Count Your Way Through Japan*. Minneapolis: Carolrhoda.

Kroll, S. (1983). *The Hand-Me-Down-Doll*. Ill. by Evaline Ness. New York: Holiday House.

McKissack, P. C. (1989). *Netti Jo's Friends*. Ill. by Scott Cook. New York: Knopf.

Polacco, P. (1990). *Babushka's Doll*. New York: Simon & Schuster.

Pomerantz, C. (1989). *The Chalk Doll*. Ill. by Frane Lesac. New York: HarperCollins.

Rosenberg, L. (1991). *The Scrap Doll*. Ill. by Robin Ballard. New York: HarperCollins.

Rowland, D. (1990). *A World of Toys*. Ill. by J. Fried. Chicago: Contemporary Books.

Taylor, C. (1990). *Yesterday's Dolls*. New York: Scholastic.

Tsutsui, Y. (1990). *Anna's Special Present*. Ill. by Akiko Hayushi. New York: Puffin.

Well, R. (1983). *Peabody*. New York: Dial.

Winthrop, E. (1983). *Katherine's Doll*. Ill. by Marylin Hafner. New York: Dutton.

Winthrop, E. (1985). *Tough Eddie*. Ill. by Lillian Hoban. New York: Dutton.

Zolotow, C. (1972). *William's Doll*. Ill. by William Pene Du Bois. New York: HarperCollins.

■ Novels:

Griffith, H. V. (1990). *Caitlin's Holiday*. Ill. by Susan Condie Lamb. New York: Greenwillow.

Griffith, H. V. (1993). *Doll Trouble*. Ill. by Susan Condie Lamb. New York: Greenwillow.

Hiser, C. (1993). *The Missing Doll*. Ill. by Marcy Ramsey. New York: Holiday House.

■ **Poetry:**

"Doll" and "My Cousin's Dollhouse" in: Livingston, M. C. (1985). *Worlds I Know and Other Poems*. Ill. by Tim Arnold. New York: McElderry. (page 5, 22, 23)

Activities for Extension:

1. Ask students to bring a favorite family doll to class. Categorize the dolls according to size, color of hair, height, and so on.

2. Using the dolls from the activity above, invite students to write a description of one of the dolls and have the others guess which one it is.

3. Introduce paper doll chains to the class. Allow students to make some of their own.

4. Read *William's Doll* (Zolotow, 1972) and *Tough Eddie* (Winthrop, 1985) and discuss toys and gender.

5. Ask students to draw designs for a new doll. Some students might also write advertisements for the dolls they design.

6. Invite a doll collector to come and show his or her doll collection to the class.

MARCH 5

- **Date:** March 5

- **This date is special because:**
It is Mem Fox's birthday (1946).

Books that relate to this date
■ Picture Books:

Fox, M. (1990). *Guess What?* Ill. by Vivienne Goodman. San Diego: Harcourt Brace Jovanovich.

Fox, M. (1987). *Hattie and the Fox*. Ill. by Patricia Mullins. New York: Bradbury.

Fox, M. (1988). *Koala Lou*. Ill. by Pamela Lofts. San Diego: Harcourt Brace Jovanovich.

Fox, M. (1989). *Night Noises*. Ill. by Terry Denton. San Diego: Harcourt Brace Jovanovich.

Fox, M. (1987). *Possum Magic*. Ill. by Julie Vivas. Nashville: Abingdon.

Fox, M. (1990). *Shoes from Grandpa*. Ill. by Patricia Mullins. New York: Orchard.

Fox, M. (1985). *Wilfrid Gordon McDonald Partridge*. Ill. by Julie Vivas. Brooklyn, NY: Kane Miller.

Fox, M. (1988). *With Love, At Christmas*. Ill. by Gary Lippincott. Nashville: Abingdon.

■ Novels:

Fox, M. (1992). *Dear Mem Fox, I Have Read All Your Books, Even the Pathetic Ones*. San Diego: Harcourt Brace Jovanovich.

■ Video:

Trumpet Club Video. *Trumpet Video Visit: Mem Fox*. Holmes, PA: Trumpet Club.

Activities for Extension:

1. Ask students to read some of Mem Fox's books and vote on their favorite. Make a bar graph of the results.

2. Read *Wilfrid Gordon McDonald Partridge* (Fox, 1985). Allow students to create their own memory boxes or write about their favorite memories.

3. Read *Hattie and the Fox* (Fox, 1987). Invite students to make paper sack puppets for each character and act out the story.

4. With the help of your students, you might want to create a tape of sounds that could be used while reading *Night Noises* (Fox, 1989). Or tape record other sounds for students to guess, such as brushing teeth, lawn mower, typewriter, etc.

M·A·R·C·H 6

■ Date: March 6

■ This date is special because:
It is Michelangelo's birthday (1475).

Books that relate to this date

■ Picture Books:

Agee, J. (1988). *The Incredible Paintings of Felix Clousseau*. New York: Farrar, Straus & Giroux.

Alcorn, J. (1991). *Rembrandt's Beret*. Ill. by Stephen Alcorn. New York: Tambourine.

Bonafoux, P. (1992). *A Weekend with Rembrandt*. New York: Rizzoli.

Bulla, C. R. (1987). *The Chalk Box Kid*. Ill. by Thomas B. Allen. New York: Random House.

Carle, E. (1992). *Draw Me a Star*. New York: Philomel.

Carrick, D. (1985). *Morgan and the Artist*. Boston: Houghton Mifflin.

Christiana, D. (1990). *Drawer in a Drawer*. New York: Farrar Straus & Giroux.

Clement, C. (1986). *The Painter and the Wild Swans*. Ill. by Frederic Clement. New York: Dial.

Cohen, M. (1986). *No Good in Art*. New York: Dell.

Collins, P. L. (1992). *I Am an Artist*. Ill. by Robin Brickman. Brookfield, CT: Millbrook.

Cooney, B. (1990). *Hattie and the Wild Waves*. New York: Viking.

Cummings, P. (1992). *Talking with Artists*. New York: Bradbury.

Demi. (1991). *The Artist and the Architect*. New York: Holt.

de Paola, T. (1989). *The Art Lesson*. New York: Putnam.

de Paola, T. (1991). *Bonjour, Mr. Satie*. New York: Putnam.

Dubelaar, T and Bruijn, R. (1992). *Looking for Vincent*. New York: Checkerboard Press.

Edwards, M. (1991). *A Baker's Portrait*. New York: Lothrop.

Ernst, L. C. (1986). *Hamilton's Art Show*. New York: Lothrop.

Everett, G. (1991). *Li'l Sis and Uncle Willie: A Story Based on the Life and Paintings of William H. Johnson*. New York: Rizzoli. (African American)

Fischetto, L. (1993). *Michael the Angel*. New York: Doubleday.

Florian, D. (1993). *A Painter*. New York: Greenwillow.

Goffstein, B. (1987). *Artists' Helpers Enjoy the Evenings*. New York: HarperCollins.

Hendry, D. (1991). *The Rainbow Watchers*. Ill. by Thor Wickstrom. New York: Lothrop.

Heslewood, J. (1993). *Introducing Picasso*. Boston: Little, Brown.

Kesselman, W. (1993). *Emma*. New York: Dell.

Lepskcky, I. (1992). *Pablo Picasso*. Ill. by Paolo Cardoni. New York: Trumpet Club.

Locker, T. (1989). *The Young Artist*. New York: Dial.

Markun, P. M. (1993). *The Little Painter of Sabana Grande*. Ill. by Robert Casilla. New York: Bradbury. (Panama)

McPhail, D. (1988). *Something's Special*. Boston: Little, Brown.

Moss, M. (1990). *Regina's Big Mistake*. Boston: Houghton Mifflin.

Muhlberger, R. (1993). *What Makes a Bruegel a Bruegel?* New York: Viking.

Muhlberger, R. (1993). *What Makes a Degas a Degas?* New York: Viking.

Muhlberger, R. (1993). *What Makes a Monet a Monet?* New York: Viking.

Muhlberger, R. (1993). *What Makes a Raphael a Raphael?* New York: Viking.

Muhlberger, R. (1993). *What Makes a Rembrandt a Rembrandt?* New York: Viking.

Muhlberger, R. (1993). *What Makes a Van Gogh a Van Gogh?* New York: Viking.

Peet, B. (1981). *Encore for Eleanor*. Boston: Houghton Mifflin.

Richmond, R. (1992). *Introducing Michelangelo*. Boston: Little, Brown.

Rodari, F. (1992). *A Weekend with Picasso*. New York: Rizzoli.

Rodari, F. (1992). *A Weekend with Velazquez*. New York: Rizzoli.

Rylant, C. (1988). *All I See*. Ill. by Peter Catalanotto. New York: Orchard.

Schick, E. (1987). *Art Lessons*. New York: Greenwillow.

Skira-Venturi, R. (1992). *A Weekend with Degas*. New York: Rizzoli.

Skira-Venturi, R. (1992). *A Weekend with Leonardo Da Vinci*. New York: Rizzoli.

Skira-Venturi, R. (1992). *A Weekend with Renoir*. New York: Rizzoli.

Turner, R. M. (1993). *Frida Kahlo*. Boston: Little, Brown.

Turner, R. M. (1991). *Georgia O'Keeffe*. Boston: Little, Brown.

Turner, R. M. (1991). *Mary Cassatt*. Boston: Little, Brown.

Waddell, M. (1988). *Alice, the Artist*. Ill. by Jonathan Langley. New York: Dutton.

Wolkstein, D. (1992). *Little Mouse's Paintings*. Ill. by Mary Jane Begin. New York: Morrow.

Yenawine, P. (1991). *Lines*. New York: Delacorte.

▪ Novels:

Bjork, C. (1987). *Linnea in Monet's Garden*. Ill. by Lena Anderson. New York: R & S Books.

Turner, A. (1987). *Time of the Bison*. Ill. by Beth Peck. New York: Macmillan.

▪ Resource Book:

Chertok, B., Hirshfeld, G., and Rosh, M. (1992). *Meet the Masterpieces: Strategies, Activities, & Posters*. New York: Scholastic.

▪ Poetry:

"Art Class" in:
Kennedy, X. J. (1985). *The Forgetful Wishing Well*. Ill. by Monica Incisa. New York: Atheneum. (page 6)

"Crayons" by Marchette Chute in:
Prelutsky, J. (1986). *Read-Aloud Rhymes for the Very Young*. Ill. by Marc Brown. New York: Knopf. (page 86)

"The Paint Box" in E. V. Rieu:
Prelutsky, J. (1983). *The Random House Book of Poetry for Children*. Ill. by Arnold Lobel. New York: Scholastic. (page 226)

1. Visit an art gallery.

2. Create your own classroom art gallery using ideas and styles from the books above.

3. Invite a local artist to display and discuss his or her work.

4. Encourage students to interview their parents and ask who their favorite artists are. Chart the results.

5. After looking at the artwork from the suggested book list, have students vote for their favorite artist. Create a picture graph of the results.

MARCH 17

■ **Date:** March 17

■ **This date is special because:**
It is Saint Patrick's Day.

Books that relate to this date
■ **Picture Books:**

Baker, J. W. (1989). *St. Patrick's Day Magic*. Ill. by George Overlie. Minneapolis: Lerner.

Barth, E. (1982). *Shamrocks, Harps, and Shillelaghs: The Story of the Saint Patrick's Day Symbols*. Ill. by Ursula Arndt. Boston: Houghton Mifflin.

Cooper, S. (1986). *The Selkie Girl*. Ill. by Warwich Hutton. New York: McElderry.

de Paola, T. (1981). *Fin M'Coul: The Giant of Knockmany Hill*. New York: Holiday House.

de Paola, T. (1992). *Jamie O'Rourke and the Big Potato: An Irish Folktale*. New York: Putnam.

Fairclough, C. (1986). *We Live in Ireland*. New York: Bookwright.

Fradin, D. B. (1984). *The Republic of Ireland*. Chicago: Childrens Press.

Geography Department. (1990). *Ireland in Pictures*. Minneapolis: Lerner.

Geography Department. (1991). *Northern Ireland in Pictures*. Minneapolis: Lerner.

Giff, P. R. (1989). *The Great Shamrock Disaster*. New York: Dell.

Jacobsen, P. O. (1985). *A Family in Ireland*. New York: Bookwright.

James, I. (1983). *Take a Trip to Ireland*. New York: Watts.

Kessel, J. K. (1982). *St. Patrick's Day*. Ill. by Cathy Gilchrist. Minneapolis: Carolrhoda.

Kroll, S. (1991). *Mary McLean and the St. Patrick's Day Parade*. Ill. by Michael Doling. New York: Scholastic.

Low, A. (1991). *The Family Read-Aloud Holiday Treasury*. Ill. by Marc Brown. Boston: Little, Brown. (pages 24–29)

McDermott, G. (1986). Daniel O'Rouke: *An Irish Tale*. New York: Viking.

McDermott, G. (1990). *Tim O'Toole and the Weefolk: An Irish Tale*. New York: Viking.

Moran, T. (1986). *A Family in Ireland*. Minneapolis: Lerner.

O'Brien, E. (1986). *Tales for the Telling: Irish Folk and Fairy Stories*. Ill. by Michael Foreman. New York: Atheneum.

O'Shea, P. (1987). *Fin MacCool and the Small Men of Deeds*. Ill. by Stephen Lavis. New York: Holiday House.

Schertle, A. (1987). *Jeremy Bean's St. Patrick's Day*. Ill. by Linda Shute. New York: Lothrop.

Shute, L. (1988). *Clever Tom and the Leprechaun: An Old Irish Story*. New York: Lothrop.

■ **Novels:**

Giff, P. R. (1982). *The Gift of the Pirate Queen*. Ill. by Jenny Rutherford. New York: Delacorte.

Marzollo, J. (1981). *Halfway Down Paddy Lane*. New York: Dial.

Snyder, Z. K. (1991). *Squeak Saves the Day*. New York: Delacorte.

■ Poetry:

"Little People's Express" in:
Kennedy, X. J. (1989). *Ghatlies, Goops & Pincushions*. Ill. by Ron Barrett. New York: McElderry.(pages 29–30)

"Saint Patrick's Day" in:
Livingston, M. C. (1985). *Celebrations*. Ill. by Leonard Everett Fisher. New York: Holiday House. (page 12)

"What Is Green?" in:
O'Neill, M. (1989). *Hailstones and Halibut Bones*. Ill. by John Wallner. New York: Dell.

"Wearing of the Green" by Aileen Fisher in:
Prelutsky, J. (Ed.) (1983). *The Random House Book of Poetry for Children*. Ill. by Arnold Lobel. New York: Random House. (page 41)

Activities for Extension:

1. Ask students to make a list of all the green things they can think of.

2. Allow students to write poems about green things, or collect poems with the color green.

3. Discuss green foods: lettuce, grapes, avocados, peppers, beans, peas, green onions, parsley, broccoli, cabbage, brussel sprouts. Allow students to vote on their favorite green food. Graph or chart the results.

4. After looking at illustrated books of Ireland, ask students to draw a picture of an Irish setting and write a paragraph describing it.

5. Ask students to write about what it would be like to be small like a leprechaun after reading some of the following books about being small.

Picture Books:

Joyce, W. (1985). *George Shrinks*. New York: Harper & Row.

Morimoto, J. (1984). *The Inch Boy*. New York: Viking.

Zolotow, C. (1987). *I Like to Be Little*. Ill. by Erik Blegvad. New York: Crowell.

Novel:

Peterson, P. J. (1990). *The Fire Plug Is First Base*. New York: Dutton.

Poetry:

"One Inch Tall" in:
Silverstein, S. (1974). *Where the Sidewalk Ends*. New York: Harper & Row. (page 55)

M·A·R·C·H 20

▪ Date: March 20

▪ This date is special because:
It is Mitsumasa Anno's birthday (1926).

Books that relate to this date
▪ Picture Books:

Anno, M. (1986). *All in a Day*. New York: Philomel.

Anno, M. (1975). *Anno's Alphabet*. New York: Crowell.

Anno, M. (1984). *Anno's Flea Market*. New York: Philomel.

Anno, M. (1977). *Anno's Journey*. New York: Philomel.

Anno, M. (1990). *Anno's Masks*. New York: Philomel.

Anno, M. (1987). *Anno's Math Games*. New York: Philomel.

Anno, M. (1989). *Anno's Math Games II*. New York: Philomel.

Anno, M. (1991). *Anno's Math Games III*. New York: Philomel.

Anno, M. (1987). *Anno's Sundial*. New York: Philomel.

Anno, M. (1983). *Anno's USA*. New York: Philomel.

Anno, M. (1982). *Britain*. New York: Philomel.

Anno, M. (1977). *Counting Book*. New York: Crowell.

Anno, M. (1982). *Counting House*. New York: Philomel.

Anno, M. (1988). *In Shadowland*. New York: Orchard.

Anno, M. (1978). *Italy*. New York: Collins.

Anno, M. (1976). *The King's Flower*. New York: Collins.

Anno, M. (1981). *Magical ABC: An Anamorphic Alphabet*. New York: Philomel.

Anno, M. (1972). *Magical Midnight Circus*. New York: Weatherhill.

Anno, M. (1980). *Medieval World*. New York: Philomel.

Anno, M. (1983). *The Mysterious Multiplying Jar*. New York: Philomel.

Anno, M. (1987). *Peekaboo*. New York: Philomel.

Anno, M. (1989). *Topsy-Turvies: More Pictures to Stretch the Imagination*. New York: Philomel.

Anno, M. (1988). *Upside-Downers: Pictures to Stretch the Imagination*. New York: Philomel.

Mori, T. (1986). *Socrates and the 3 Little Pigs*. Ill. by Anno. New York: Philomel.

Nozaki, A. (1985). *Anno's Hat Tricks*. Ill. by Anno. New York: Philomel.

▪ Resource Book:

Kovacs, D. and Preller, J. (1991). *Meet the Authors and Illustrators: 60 Creators of Favorite Children's Books Talk about Their Work*. New York: Scholastic. (an interview with Anno) (pages 12-13)

1. Invite students to read some of Anno's books, then discuss their favorites.

2. Read *All in a Day* (Anno, 1986) and ask students to write some of their own daily activities.

3. Using Anno's notes at the end of the books, challenge students to find all of the hidden characters.

4. Anno does mostly wordless books. Encourage students to make their own wordless picture book.

5. Students can make and use their own sun dials using *Anno's Sun Dial* (Anno, 1987) as a guide.

M·A·R·C·H 22

■ **Date:** March 22

■ **This date is special because:**
It is Randolph Caldecott's birthday.

Books that relate to this date

■ Picture Books:

Caldecott, R. (1986). *A First Caldecott Collection.* New York: Warne.

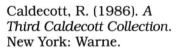

Caldecott, R. (1986). *A Second Caldecott Collection.* New York: Warne.

Caldecott, R. (1986). *A Third Caldecott Collection.* New York: Warne.

Caldecott, R. (1976). *Yours Pictorially: Illustrated Letters of Randolph Caldecott.* Ed. by Michael Hutchins. London: F. Warne.

Cummings, P. (1992). *Talking with Artists.* New York: Bradbury.

Kovacs, D., and Preller, J. (1991). *Meet the Authors and Illustrators.* New York: Scholastic.

■ Recent Caldecott Winners:

Ackerman, K. (1988). *Song and Dance Man.* Ill. by Stephen Gammell. New York: Knopf.

Macaulay, D. (1990). *Black and White.* Boston: Houghton Mifflin.

McCully, E. A. (1992). *Mirette On the High Wire.* New York: Putnam.

Say, A. (1993). *Grandfather's Journey.* Boston: Houghton Mifflin.

Van Allsburg, C. (1985). *Polar Express.* Boston: Houghton Mifflin.

Wiesner, D. (1991). *Tuesday.* New York: Clarion.

Yolen, J. (1987). *Owl Moon.* Ill. by John Schoenherr. New York: Philomel.

Yorinks, A. (1986). *Hey, Al.* Ill. by Richard Egielski. New York: Farrar, Straus & Giroux.

Young, E. (1989). *Lon Po Po: A Red-Riding Hood Story from China.* New York: Philomel.

■ Poetry:

"Art Class" in:
Kennedy, X. J. (1985). *The Forgetful Wishing Well.* Ill. by Monica Incisa. New York: Atheneum. (page 6)

"Crayons" by Marchette Chute in:
Prelutsky, J. (1986). *Read-Aloud Rhymes for the Very Young.* Ill. by Marc Brown. New York: Knopf. (page 86)

"The Paint Box" by E. V. Rieu in: Prelutsky, J. (1983). *The Random House Book of Poetry for Children.* Ill. by Arnold Lobel. New York: Scholastic. (page 226)

1. Ask students to vote on their favorite illustrated picture book. Make a picture graph of the results.

2. Display recent Caldecott Medal books and discuss the different art styles.

3. Challenge students to find out who is depicted on the Caldecott medal.

4. Ask students to predict which picture book will win next year's Caldecott award. Chart the results.

Note: This award is given by the American Library Association and is announced in mid-January. Only books published during the previous year are considered for the award.

5. Students might want to invent another award that could be given to picture books. Ask them to design the medal and the criteria. Give the award to a deserving book voted on by the class.

M·A·R·C·H 24

■ **Date:** March 24

■ **This date is special because:**
It is Harry Houdini's birthday (1874).

Books that relate to this date
■ Picture Books:

Bailey, V. (1990). *Magic Tricks: Games and Projects for Children.* New York: Watts.

Brisson, P. (1991). *Magic Carpet.* Ill. by Amy Schwartz. New York: Bradbury.

Brown, M. (1985). *Arthur's April Fool.* Boston: Little, Brown.

Chew, R. (1982). *Mostly Magic.* New York: Scholastic.

Christelow, E. (1987). *Olive and the Magic Hat.* New York: Clarion.

Cole, J. (1987). *Mixed-Up Magic.* Ill. by True Kelly. New York: Scholastic.

Combs, P. (1984). *The Magician and McTree.* New York: Lothrop.

de Paola, T. (1982). *Strega Nona's Magic Lessons.* San Diego: Harcourt Brace Jovanovich.

Ernst, L. C. and Ernst, L. (1990). *The Tangram Magician.* New York: Abrams.

Evans, C. and Keable-Elliot, I. (1989). *The Usborne Complete Book of Magic.* Ill. by Kim Raymond. London: Usborne.

Howe, J. (1993). *Harold and Chester in Rabbit-Cadabra!* Ill. by Alan Daniel. New York: Morrow.

Karaske, R. (1989). *Harry Houdini: Master of Magic.* New York: Scholastic.

Kroll, S. (1987). *The Big Bunny and the Magic Show.* Ill. by Janet Stevens. New York: Scholastic.

Lester, H. (1990). *The Revenge of the Magic Chicken.* Ill. by Lynn Munsinger. Boston: Houghton Mifflin.

Lester, H. (1988). *The Wizard, the Fairy, and the Magic Chicken.* Ill. by Lynn Munsinger. Boston: Houghton Mifflin.

Levy, E. (1981). *Running Out of Magic with Houdini.* Ill. by Blanche Sims & Jenny Rutherford. New York: Knopf.

Nozaki, A. and Anno, M. (1985). *Anno's Hat Tricks.* New York: Putnam.

Penrose, G. (1989). *Dr. Zed's Science Surprises.* New York: Simon & Schuster.

Selznick, B. (1991). *The Houdini Box.* New York: Knopf.

Van der Meer, R. (1983). *The Pop-Up Book of Magic Tricks.* New York: Viking.

Walter, M. (1989) *Magic Mirror Tricks.* Ill. by Navah Haber-Schaim. New York: Scholastic.

Wyler, R. and Ames, G. (1990). *Magic Secrets.* Ill. by Arthur Dorros. New York: HarperCollins.

■ Poetry:

"Magic Things" in:
Livingston, M. C. (1984). *A Song I Sang to You*. Ill. by Margot Tomes. San Diego: Harcourt Brace Jovanovich. (pages 66–79)

"Miraculous Mortimer" in:
Prelutsky, J. (1984). *The New Kid on the Block*. Ill. by James Stevenson. New York: Greenwillow. (page 139)

"Magic" in:
Silverstein, S. (1974). *Where the Sidewalk Ends*. New York: Harper & Row. (page 11)

Activities for Extension:

  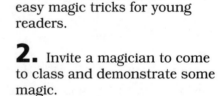

1. Invite students to demonstrate their favorite magic tricks. *Magic Secrets* (Wyler and Ames, 1990) has some easy magic tricks for young readers.

2. Invite a magician to come to class and demonstrate some magic.

3. Ask students to make up new magic tricks.

4. Students might want to put on a class magic show using the tricks from Activities 1 and 3.

5. Encourage students to write a story with a magical character.

M·A·R·C·H 26

■ Date: March 26

■ This date is special because: It is Sandra Day O'Connor's birthday (1930).

Books that relate to this date
■ Picture Books:

Fox, M. V. (1983). *Justice Sandra Day O'Connor*. Hillside, NJ: Enslow.

Greene, C. (1982). *Sandra Day O'Connor: First Woman on the Supreme Court*. Chicago: Childrens Press.

Greene, C. (1985). *The Supreme Court*. New York: Childrens.

Macht, N. L. (1992). *Sandra Day O'Connor*. New York: Chelsea House.

O'Neal, Z. (1990). *A Long Way to Go*. Ill. by Michael Dooling. New York: Viking.

Stein, R. C. (1989). *The Story of the Powers of the Supreme Court*. New York: Childrens.

Woods, H. (1985). *Equal Justice: A Biography of Sandra Day O'Connor*. Minneapolis: Dillon.

Zolotow, C. (1992). I *Know a Lady*. Ill. by James Stevenson. New York: Morrow.

■ Nonfiction:

Gherman, B. (1991). *Sandra Day O'Connor*. New York: Viking.

■ Poetry:

Hopkins, L. B. (1972). *Girls Can Too! A Book of Poems*. Ill. by Emily McCully. New York: Watts.

Activities for Extension:

1. You might want to arrange a visit to a local courtroom, then ask your students to write a story about their experiences.

2. Invite a local judge or attorney into the classroom. Allow students to prepare questions for the visitor.

3. Ask students to design their own classroom bill of rights.

4. Read about Sandra Day O'Connor's life. Ask students to role play selected events from her life.

5. Ask students to find out why judges wear robes. Some may want to design a new one.

■ **Date:** Any day in April

■ **This month is special because:** It is National Humor Month.

Books that relate to this month:
■ Picture Books:

Ahlberg, J. and Ahlberg, A. (1990). *Funnybones*. New York: Morrow.

Allard, H. (1985). *The Stupids Die*. Ill. by James Marshall. Boston: Houghton Mifflin.

Berger, M. (1989). *101 Wacky Science Jokes*. New York: Scholastic.

Berger, M. (1990). *101 President Jokes*. New York: Scholastic.

Berger, M. (1991). *101 Wacky State Jokes*. New York: Scholastic.

Brown, J. (1992). *The Emergency Excuses Kit*. New York: Puffin.

Cole, J. and Calmenson, S. (1986). *The Laugh Book*. Ill. by Marylin Hafner. New York: Doubleday.

Denim, S. (1994). *The Dumb Bunnies*. Ill. by Dav Pilkey. New York: Scholastic.

Hall, K. (1990). *101 Cat and Dog Jokes*. New York: Scholastic.

Kline, R. (1990). *Watch Out for These Weirdos*. New York: Viking.

McNaughton, C. (1991). *Guess Who Just Moved in Next Door?* New York: Random House.

Nixon, J. (1992). *That's the Spirit, Claude*. New York: Viking.

Phillips, L. (1990). *Loose Leaf*. Ill. by Joseph Farri. New York: Atheneum.

Pollack, P. (1988). *The Random House Book of Humor*. Ill. by Paul O. Zelinsky. New York: Random House.

Walker, B. K. (1992). *Laughing Together: Giggles and Grins from Around the Globe*. Ill. by Simms Taback. Minneapolis: Free Spirit.

Wood, A. and Wood, D. (1994). *The Tickle-Octopus*. San Diego: Harcourt.

■ Poetry:

Prelutsky, J. (1991). *For Laughing Out Loud: Poems to Tickle Your Funny Bone*. Ill. by Marjorie Priceman. New York: Knopf.

"Captain Hook" in:
Silverstein, S. (1974). *Where the Sidewalk Ends*. New York: Harper & Row. (page 18)

Smith, W. J. (1990). *Laughing Time: Collected Nonsense*. Ill. by Fernando Krahn. New York: Farrar, Straus & Giroux.

Activities for Extension:

1. Celebrate a classroom joke day. All students can tell their favorite joke.

2. Students might want to write a classroom humor book using the jokes from above.

3. Discuss why we laugh. What makes something funny? Ask students to brainstorm ideas.

4. Allow students to write a poem using the brainstormed ideas from above.

5. Encourage students to keep a diary of things they find humorous. Share with the class.

A·P·R·I·L 1

> ■ **Date:** April 1
>
> ■ **This date is special because:**
> It is National Census Day.

Books that relate to this date

■ Picture Books:

Aker, S. (1990). *What Comes in 2's, 3's, & 4's?* Ill. by Bernie Karlin. New York: Simon & Schuster.

Allen, P. (1983). *Who Sank the Boat?*. New York: Coward.

Anderson, M. K. (1980). *Counting on You: The United States Census*. New York: Vanguard.

Anno, M. (1982). *Anno's Counting House*. New York: Philomel.

Anno, M., and Anno, M. (1983). *Anno's Mysterious Multiplying Jar*. New York: Philomel.

Ashabranner, M. (1989). *Counting America: The Story of the United States*. New York: Putnam.

Bright, R. (1985). *My Red Umbrella*. New York: Morrow.

Ehlert, L. (1990). *Fish Eyes: A Book You Can Count On*. San Diego: Harcourt Brace Jovanovich.

Gray, C. (1988). *1, 2, 3, & 4: No More?* Ill. by Marissa Moss. Boston: Houghton Mifflin.

Katz, M. J. (1990). *Ten Potatoes in a Pot and Other Counting Rhymes*. Ill. by June Otani. New York: Harper & Row.

McMillan, B. (1992). *Eating Fractions*. New York: Scholastic.

Ockenga, S. (1988). *World of Wonders: A Trip Through Numbers*. Photographs by Starr Ockenga. Boston: Houghton Mifflin.

Petty, K. (1986). *What's That Number?* New York: Watts.

Pragnoff, F. (1987). *How Many?* New York: Doubleday.

Riedel, M. G. (1978). *Winning with Numbers: A Kid's Guide to Statistics*. Ill. by Paul Coker, Jr. New York: Prentice-Hall.

Schwartz, D. (1986). *How Much Is a Million?* Ill. by Steven Kellogg. New York: Scholastic.

Schwartz, D. (1989). *If You Made a Million*. Ill. by Steven Kellogg. New York: Lothrop.

■ Poetry:

"How Much Is a Gross?" in: Ciardi, J. (1985) *Doodlesoup*. Ill. by Merle Nacht. Boston: Houghton Mifflin. (page 28)

"There's Nothing to It" in: Ciardi, J. (1985) *Doodlesoup*. Ill. by Merle Nacht. Boston: Houghton Mifflin. (page 12)

"Fom Arithmetic" by Carl Sandburg in: de Regniers, B. S. and others. (1988). *Sing a Song of Popcorn*. Ill. by nine Caldecott Medal artists. New York: Scholastic. (page 93)

"Math Class" by Myra Cohn Livingston in:
Farber, N. and Livingston, M. C. (1987). *These Small Stones*. New York: Harper & Row. (page 32)

Katz, M. J. (1990). *Ten Potatoes in a Pot*. Ill. by June Otani. New York: Harper & Row.

"Census Nonsense" in:
Kennedy, X. J. (1975). *One Winter Night in August*. Ill. by David McPhail. New York: Atheneum. (page 26)

"Arithmetic Test" in:
Simmie, L. (1984) *Auntie's Knitting a Baby*. Ill. by Anne Simmie. New York: Orchard. (page 52)

■ Resource Book:

Danielson, K. E. (1990). *Counting on Literature: Primary Math with Picture Books*. Ill. by Robin Sitton. O'Fallon, MO: Book Lures.

Activities for Extension:

1. Encourage students to take a census of the school. Keep track of the number of students in each class, number of teachers, support staff, etc. Chart and display the results.

2. Encourage students to take a census of pets in the neighborhood. Discuss strategies.

3. Allow students to participate in a class discussion about the importance of taking a census.

4. Using the book, *What Comes in 2's, 3's, & 4's* (Aker, 1990), invite students to make their own number books. For example, what comes in 5's, 6's, 7's (days of the week).

5. Encourage students to design and make their own domino cards. Play the game.

6. Ask students to estimate the number of candy pieces in a glass jar. Discuss different strategies.

A·P·R·I·L 7

■ **Date:** April 7

■ **This date is special because:**
It is World Health Day.

Books that relate to this date

■ Picture Books:

Ardley, N. (1982). *Health and Medicine*. New York: Watts.

Baldwin, D. (1987). *Health and Drugs*. Vero Beach, FL: Rourke.

Baldwin, D. (1987). *Health and Exercise*. Vero Beach, FL: Rourke.

Baldwin, D. (1987). *Health and Food*. Vero Beach, FL: Rourke.

Baldwin, D. (1987). *Health and Hygiene*. Vero Beach, FL: Rourke.

Barnes, C. (1989). *It's No Fun to Be Sick!* New York: Western.

Berger, M. (1985). *Germs Make Me Sick!* Ill. by Marilyn Hafner. New York: Crowell.

Brown, L. K. and Brown, M. (1990). *Dinosaurs Alive and Well*. Boston: Little, Brown.

Burstein, J. (1983). *The Healthy Habits Handbook*. Photos by Bruce Curtis. Ill. by Nurit Karlin. New York: Coward-McCann.

Cole, J. (1989). *The Magic School Bus: Inside the Human Body*. Ill. by Bruce Degen. New York: Scholastic.

Davison, M. (1992). *Robby Visits the Doctor*. Ill. by Nancy Stevenson. New York: Random House.

Eyewitness Visual Dictionaries. *The Visual Dictionary of the Human Body*. London: Dorling Kindersley.

Girard, L. W. (1990). *Alex, the Kid with Aids*. Ill. by Abby Levine & Blanche Sims. New York: A Whitman.

Isenberg, B. and Jaffe, M. (1984). *Albert the Running Bear's Exercise Book*. Ill. by Dian de Groat. New York: Clarion.

Iveson-Iveson, J. (1986). *Your Health*. Ill. by Bill Donohue. New York: Bookwright.

Roddie, S., and F. Cony. (1993). *Chicken Pox: A Touch-and-Feel Pull-Tab Pop-Up Book*. Boston: Little, Brown.

Showers, P. (1991). *Your Skin and Mine*. Ill. by Kathleen Kuchera. New York: HarperCollins.

Ward, B. R. (1988). *Health and Hygiene*. New York: Watts.

Wolde, G. (1990). *Betsy and the Chicken Pox*. New York: Random House.

■ Poetry:

"No More Medicine" in: Carlstrom, N. W. (1990). *It's About Time, Jesse Bear*. Ill. by Bruce Degen. New York: Macmillan.

"Boots Have Tongues" in: Prelutsky, J. (1989). *Poems of A. Nonny Mouse*. Ill. by Henrik Drescher. New York: Knopf.

"Sick" in: Silverstein, S. (1974). *Where the Sidewalk Ends*. New York: Harper & Row. (page 58)

"Germs" in:
Simmie, L. (1984). *Auntie's Knitting A Baby*. Ill. by Anne Simmie. New York: Orchard. (page 9)

"My-Oh Wow!-Book" in:
Viorst, J. (1981). *If I Were In Charge of the World and Other Worries*. Ill. by Lynne Cherry. New York: Atheneum. (page 55)

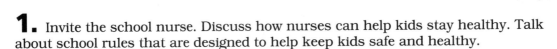

Activities for Extension:

1. Invite the school nurse. Discuss how nurses can help kids stay healthy. Talk about school rules that are designed to help keep kids safe and healthy.

2. Start an "I Went to the doctor to..." class pattern book. Make photo copies of this sentence starter and bind pages to make a book. Place at your writing center and invite children to tell (or dictate) their stories of visits to the doctor. Take a field trip to a doctor's office or hospital. Add a class story to the book about the experience.

3. Invite the P. E. teacher to explain why exercise is an important part of staying healthy. Together, develop a daily routine that students can perform for a healthy break during the school day.

4. Have children take each other's pulses. Exercise and take pulses again. Chart and discuss the differences.

5. Talk about how food helps people stay healthy. Have children cut out pictures of foods from magazines. Place pictures in a paper bag then let children take turns picking pictures and telling what food groups they belong to.

6. Plan parties featuring the five major food groups (fruits, vegetables, breads, milk, fats). With vegetables, for example, you could throw a Great Greens party and provide tastes of different kinds of lettuce, broccoli, green peppers, kale, spinach, and so on.

A·P·R·I·L 8

■ Date: April 8

■ This date is special because:
It is Trina Shart Hyman's birthday (1939).

Books that relate to this date

■ Picture Books:

Alexander, L. (1992). *The Fortune-Tellers*. Ill. by Trina Shart Hyman. New York: Dutton.

Barrie, J. M. (1980). *Peter Pan*. Ill. by Trina Shart Hyman. New York: Scribner.

Cohen, B. (1988). *The Canterbury Tales*. Ill. by Trina Shart Hyman. New York: Lothrop.

Clemens, S. (1988). *A Connecticut Yankee in King Arthur's Court*. Ill. by Trina Shart Hyman. New York: Morrow.

de Regniers, B. (1988). *Sing a Song of Popcorn*. Ill. by Trina Shart Hyman. New York: Scholastic.

Dickens, C. (1983). *A Christmas Carol*. Ill. by Trina Shart Hyman. New York: Holiday.

Durrell, A., and Sachs, M. (1990). The *Big Book for Peace*. Ill. by Trina Shart Hyman. New York: Dutton.

Espeland, P. (1984). *The Cat Walked Through the Casserole*. Ill. by Trina Shart Hyman. Minneapolis: Carolrhoda.

Fonteyn, M. (1989). *Swan Lake*. Ill. by Trina Shart Hyman. New York: Harcourt Brace Jovanovich.

Fritz, J. (1981). *The Man Who Loved Books*. Ill. by Trina Shart Hyman. New York: Putnam.

Grimm, J. (1982). *Rapunzel*. Ill. by Trina Shart Hyman. New York: Holiday House.

Grimm, J. (1977). *The Sleeping Beauty*. Ill. by Trina Shart Hyman. Boston: Little, Brown.

Grimm, J. (1974). *Snow White*. Ill. by Trina Shart Hyman. Boston: Little, Brown.

Grimm, J. (1986). *The Water of Life*. Ill. by Trina Shart Hyman. New York: Holiday.

Hodges, M. (1990). *The Kitchen Knight*. Ill. by Trina Shart Hyman. New York: Holiday.

Hodges, M. (1984). *Saint George and the Dragon*. Ill. by Trina Shart Hyman. Boston: Little, Brown.

Hyman, T. S. (1991). *How Six Found Christmas*. New York: Holiday.

Hyman, T. S. (1980). *A Little Alphabet*. Boston: Little, Brown.

Hyman, T. S. (1981). *Self-Portrait*. Reading, MA: Addison-Wesley.

Hyman, T. S. (1983). *Little Red Riding Hood*. New York: Holiday.

Kimmel, E. (1989). *Hershel and the Hanukkah Goblins*. Ill. by Trina Shart Hyman. New York: Holiday.

Lasky, K. (1981). *The Night Journey*. Ill. by Trina Shart Hyman. New York: Warne.

Livingston, M. C. (1987). *Cat Poems*. Ill. by Trina Shart Hyman. New York: Holiday.

Livingston, M. C. (1984). *Christmas Poems*. Ill. by Trina Shart Hyman. New York: Holiday.

Thomas, D. (1985). *A Child's Christmas in Wales*. Ill. by Trina Shart Hyman. New York: Holiday.

Wallace, D. (1980). *Fairy Poems*. Ill. by Trina Shart Hyman. New York: Holiday.

Winthrop, E. (1985). *The Castle in the Attic*. Ill. by Trina Shart Hyman. New York: Holiday.

■ Resource Book:

Kovacs, D. and Preller, J. (1991). *Meet the Authors and Illustrators: 60 Creators of Favorite Children's Books Talk About Their Work*. New York: Scholastic. (an interview with Hyman) (pages 36–37)

Activities for Extension:

1. Compare Hyman's traditional books with other versions of the same illustrated works.

2. Ask students to make paper sack puppets of the characters in one of Hyman's books. Put on a puppet show.

3. Using the Hyman version as a pattern, students can write and illustrate their own self-portraits.

4. Trina Shart Hyman uses all three of her names. Ask them to brainstorm other famous people who do the same.

5. Read some of Hyman's books. Allow students to vote on their favorites and share with the class.

A·P·R·I·L 14

■ **Date:** April 14

■ **This date is special because:**
It is National Dream Day.

Books that relate to this date

■ **Picture Books:**

Ahlberg, A. (1991). *Dinosaur Dreams*. Ill. by Andre Amstutz. New York: Greenwillow.

Beck, I. (1992). *Emily and the Golden Acorn*. New York: Simon.

Bottner, B. (1992). *Bootsie Barker Bites*. Ill. by Peggy Rathmann. New York: Putnam.

Clifton, L. (1990). *Three Wishes*. New York: Bantam Doubleday Dell.

Collington, P. (1987). *The Angel and the Soldier Boy*. New York: Knopf.

Collins, J. (1989). *My Father*. Ill. by Jane Dyer. Boston: Houghton Mifflin.

Duncan, L. (1985). *Horses of Dreamland*. Ill. by Donna Diamond. Boston: Little, Brown.

Gervais, B. (1992). *Voyage under the Stars*. New York: Lothrop.

James, B. (1990). *The Dream Stair*. Ill. by Richard Jesse Watson. New York: Harper & Row.

Koontz, R. M. (1988). *Dinosaur Dream*. New York: Putnam.

Larrick, N. (1983). *When the Dark Comes Dancing*. Ill. by John Wallner. New York: Philomel.

Lester, A. (1988). *Ruby*. Boston: Houghton Mifflin.

Mayhew, J. (1988). *Katie and the Dinosaurs*. New York: Bantam Doubleday Dell.

Mayher, J. (1989). *Katie's Picture Show*. New York: Bantam Doubleday Dell.

McLerran, A. (1992). *Dreamsong*. Ill. by Valery Vasilier. New York: Tambourine.

Nightingale, S. (1991). *A Giraffe on the Moon*. San Diego: Harcourt Brace Jovanovich.

Nolan, D. (1990). *Dinosaur Dream*. New York: Macmillan.

Nunes, S. (1988). *Coyote Dreams*. Ill. by Ronald Himler. New York: Atheneum.

Osofsky, A. (1992). *Dreamcatcher*. Ill. by Ed Young. New York: Orchard.

Polacco, P. (1991). *Appelemando's Dreams*. New York: Philomel.

Pryor, B. (1992). *Lottie's Dream*. Ill. by Mark Graham. New York: Simon & Schuster.

Say, A. (1988). *A River Dream*. Boston: Houghton Mifflin.

Van Allsburg, C. (1990). *Just a Dream*. Boston: Houghton Mifflin.

Wiesner, D. (1988). *Freefall*. New York: Lothrop.

Zemach, K. (1988). *The Funny Dream*. New York: Greenwillow.

■ Short Stories:

Aiken, J. (1986). *Past Eight O'Clock Goodnight Stories*. Ill. by Jan Pienkowski. New York: Viking.

■ Poetry:

"I Picked a Dream Out of My Head" in: Ciardi, J. (1985). *Doodle Soup*. Ill. by Merle Nacht. Boston: Houghton Mifflin. (page 29)

"Dream Boogie" by Langston Hughes in:
Jabar, C. (1992). *Shimmy Shake Earthquake*. Boston: Little, Brown. (page 4)

"Dreams" by Langston Hughes in: Prelustky, J. (1983). *The Random House Book of Poetry for Children*. Ill. by Arnold Lobel. New York: Random House. (page 225)

"Pretending" by Bobbi Katz in: Prelutsky, J. (1986). *Read-Aloud Rhymes*. Ill. by Marc Brown. New York: Knopf. (page 66)

"Frozen Dream: in: Silverstein, S. (1981). *A Light in the Attic*. New York: Harper & Row. (page 150)

"Invitation" in: Silverstein, S. (1974). *Where the Sidewalk Ends*. New York: Harper & Row. (page 9)

"The Dream" in: Simmie, L. (1984). *Auntie's Knitting a Baby*. Ill. by Anne Simmie. New York: Orchard. (page 18)

Activities for Extension:

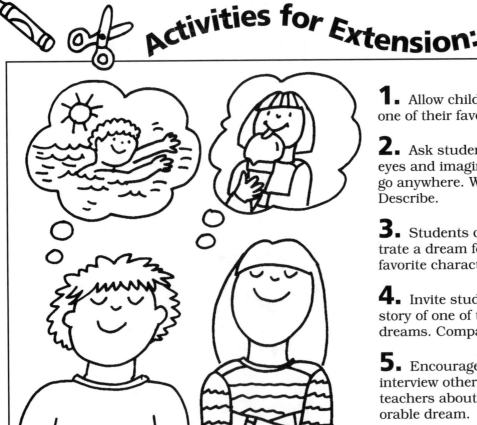

1. Allow children to illustrate one of their favorite dreams.

2. Ask students to close their eyes and imagine they can do or go anywhere. Where are they? Describe.

3. Students can write or illustrate a dream for one of their favorite characters in a book.

4. Invite students to tell the story of one of their scariest dreams. Compare with others.

5. Encourage students to interview other students and teachers about their most memorable dream.

A·P·R·I·L 21

■ **Date:** April 21

■ **This date is special because:**
It is Friedrich Froebel's birthday (1782).

Friedrich Froebel is the man who invented kindergarten.

Books that relate to this date

■ Picture Books:

Calmenson, S. (1983). *The Kindergarten Book*. Ill. by Beth Lee Weiner. New York: Grosset & Dunlap.

Caseley, J. (1991). *Hurricane Harry*. New York: Greenwillow.

de Paola, T. (1989). *The Art Lesson*. New York: Putnam.

Hamilton-Merritt, J. (1982). *My First Days of School*. New York: Messner.

Howe, J. (1986). *When You Go to Kindergarten*. Photos by Betsy Imershein. New York: Knopf.

Hurwitz, J. (1993). *Make Room for Elisa*. Ill. by Lillian Hoban. New York: Morrow.

Jabar, C. (1989). *Alice Ann Gets Ready for School*. Boston: Little, Brown.

Kunhardt, E. (1992). *Red Day, Green Day*. Pictures by Marylin Hafner. New York: Greenwillow.

Marlin, A. (1992). *Rachel Parker, Kindergarten Show-Off*. Ill. by Nancy Poydar. New York: Holiday.

Park, B. (1993). *Junie B. Jones and a Little Monkey Business*. Ill. by Denise Brunkus. New York: Random House.

Pryor, Bonnie. (1992). *Jumping Jenny*. Ill. by Anita Riggio. New York: Morrow.

Schwartz, A. (1991). *Annabelle Swift, Kindergartner*. New York: Orchard.

Schwartz, A. (1982). *Bea and Mr. Jones*. New York: Bradbury.

Serfozo, M. (1993). *Benjamin Bigfoot*. Ill. by Jos Smith. New York: Macmillan.

■ German Heritage Books:

Amos, J. (1993). *Getting to Know Germany and German*. Ill. by Kim Woolley. Hauppauge, NY: Barron's.

Croll, C. (1991). *The Three Brothers: A German Folk Tale*. New York: Putnam.

Harrap. (1990). *My First Vocabulary: English-German*. Kent, England: Harrap Books.

Hodges, M. (1993). *The Hero of Bremen*. Ill. by Charles Mikolaycak. New York: Holiday House.

Irving, N. (1992). *Learn German*. Ill. by Ann Johns. London: Usborne.

■ Poetry:

Dakos, K. (1990). *If You're Not Here, Please Raise Your Hand*. Ill. by G. Brian Kara. New York: Macmillan.

"Five Years Old" by Marie Louise Allen in:
Prelutsky, J. (1986). *Read-Aloud Rhymes for the Very Young*. Ill. by Marc Brown. New York: Knopf. (page 29)

1. Ask students to write their favorite kindergarten memory.

2. Students might want to interview parents about their kindergarten memories. Discuss the differences.

3. Invite a kindergarten class and their teacher to your room. Read to each other from the suggested reading list and illustrate responses to the literature. Maintain a pen-pal relationship with these students.

4. Invite students to volunteer to be aides in a kindergarten class for an hour. Ask students to write about their experiences.

5. Encourage students to learn about Germany. Ask them to share an interesting fact from a book.

A·P·R·I·L 22

■ Date: April 22

■ This date is special because:
It is Arbor Day.

Books that relate to this date
■ Picture Books:

Arnosky, J. (1992). *Crinkleroot's Guide to Knowing the Trees*. New York: Macmillan.

Bash, B. (1989). *Tree of Life: The World of the African Baobab*. Boston: Little, Brown.

Brandt, S. R. (1992). *State Trees*. New York: Watts.

Bunting, E. (1991). *Night Tree*. Ill. by Ted Rand. New York: Harcourt Brace Jovanovich.

Bunting, E. (1993). *Someday a Tree*. Ill. by Ronald Himler. Boston: Houghton Mifflin.

Cherry, L. (1990). *The Great Kapok Tree*. San Diego: Harcourt Brace Jovanovich.

Climo, S. (1988). *King of the Birds*. Ill. by Ruth Heller. New York: Harper.

Davol, M. W. (1992). *The Heart of the Wood*. Ill. by Sheila Humanaka. New York: Simon & Schuster.

De Bourgoing, P. (1992). *Tree*. Ill. by P. M. Valat & Sylvie Perols. New York: Scholastic.

Edwards, R. (1993). *Ten Tall Oak Trees*. Ill. by Caroline Crossland. New York: Tambourine.

Himmelman, J. (1986). *The Talking Tree: Or Don't Believe Everything You Hear*. New York: Viking Kestrel.

Hiscock, B. (1991). *The Big Tree*. New York: Atheneum.

Izen, M. and West, J. (1992). *Why the Willow Weeps: A Story Told with Hands*. New York: Doubleday.

Jeunesse, G. and de Bourgoing, P. (1992). *The Tree: A First Discovery Book*. Ill. by Christian Broutin. New York: Scholastic.

Levine, A. A. (1993). *Pearl Moscowitz's Last Stand*. Ill. by Robert Roth. New York: Tambourine.

Lyon, G.E. (1989). *A B Cedar: An Alphabet of Trees*. Ill. by Tom Parker. New York: Orchard.

Markle, S. (1993). *Outside and Inside Trees*. New York: Bradbury.

Quinn, G.H. (1994). *The Gift of a Tree*. Ill. by Ronder Krum. New York: Scholastic.

Rockwell, A. (1992). *Our Own Yard Is Full of Birds*. Ill. by Lizzy Rockwell. New York: Macmillan.

Ryder, J. (1991). *Hello, Tree!* Ill. by Michael Hays. New York: Dutton.

Silverstein, S. (1964). *The Giving Tree*. New York: Harper & Row.

Singer, A. and Singer, A. (1986). *State Birds*. New York: Dutton.

Tresselt, A. (1992). *The Gift of the Tree.* Ill. by Henri Sorensen. New York: Lothrop.

■ Poetry:

Behn, H. (1992). *Trees.* Ill. by James Endicott. New York: Holt.

"Tell Me" in:
Esbensen, B. (1992). *Who Shrank My Grandmother's House?* Ill. by Eric Beddows. New York: HarperCollins. (page 39)

Frost, R. (1988). *Birches.* Ill. by Ed Young. New York: Henry Holt.

Manson, C. (1993). *The Tree in the Wood.* New York: North-South Books.

Activities for Extension:

1. Ask students to keep a class scrapbook of different tree leaves. Include pictures and illustrations.

2. Visit a local tree nursery. Take a small amount of money per child for purchase of a seedling.

3. Plant a tree in your school yard and keep a class observational diary of the tree. Note changes throughout the year.

4. Adopt a tree on the school grounds.

A·P·R·I·L 26

■ **This date is special because:**
It is John J. Audubon's birthday (1785).

Books that relate to this date

■ Picture Books:

Arnosky, J. (1992). *Crinkeroot's Guide to Knowing the Birds*. New York: Bradbury.

Baker, J. (1984). *Home in the Sky*. New York: Greenwillow.

Bash, B. (1990). *Urban Roosts: Where Birds Nest in the City*. San Francisco: Sierra Books.

Climo, S. (1988). *King of the Birds*. Ill. by Ruth Heller. New York: Crowell.

Ehlert, L. (1990). *Feathers for Lunch*. San Diego: Harcourt Brace Jovanovich.

Flora, D. (1989). *Feathers Like a Rainbow: An Amazon Indian Tale*. New York: Harper & Row.

Guiberson, B. Z. (1991). *Cactus Hotel*. Ill. by Megan Lloyd. New York: Henry Holt.

Keller, H. (1992). *Island Baby*. New York: Greenwillow.

Kleven, E. (1992). *The Lion and the Little Red Bird*. New York: Dutton.

Oppenheim, J. (1986). *Have You Seen Birds?* Ill. by Barbara Reid. New York: Scholastic.

Pearson, S. (1992). *Lenore's Big Break*. Ill. by Nancy Carlson. New York: Viking.

Pedersen, J. (1989). *The Tiny Patient*. New York: Knopf.

Pomerantz, C. (1989). *Flap Your Wings and Try*. Ill. by Nancy Tafuri. New York: Greenwillow.

Rockwell, A. (1992). *Our Yard Is Full of Birds*. Ill. by Lizzy Rockwell. New York: Macmillan.

Ross, M. E. (1992). *Became and Bird and Fly*. Ill. by Peter Parnall. Brookfield, CT: Millbrook.

Selsam, M. (1984). *A First Look at Bird Nests*. New York: Walker.

Singer, A. and A. Singer. (1986). *State Birds*. New York: Lodestar.

Stanley, D. (1985). *Birdsong Lullaby*. New York: Morrow.

Van Laan, N. (1987). *The Big Fat Worm*. Ill. by Marisabina Russo. New York: Knopf.

■ Novels:

James, M. (1993). *The Shuteyes*. New York: Scholastic.

Kastner, J. (1992). *John James Audubon*. New York: Abrams.

■ Poetry:

"Robin" by Iain Crichton Smith in: Bennett, J. (1991). *A Cup of Starshine.* Ill. by Graham Percy. San Diego: Harcourt Brace Jovanovich. (page 33)

"Sparrow Dreaming" in: Esbensen, B. (1992). *Who Shrank My Grandmother's House? Poems of Discovery.* Ill. by Eric Beddows. New York: HarperCollins. (page 23)

"Little Bird" by Julie Cunningham in: Farber, N. and Livingston, M. C. (1997). *These Small Stones.* New York: Harper & Row. (page 31)

"The Vultures and the Warblers" in: Hubbell, P. (1988). *The Tigers Brought Pink Lemonade.* Ill. by Ju-Hong Chen. New York: Atheneum. (page 25)

Prelutsky, J. (1983). *The Random House Book of Poetry For Children.* Ill. by Arnold Lobel. New York: Random House. (pages 83–87)

Prelutsky, J. (1986). *Read-Aloud Rhymes For the Very Young.* Ill. by Marc Brown. New York: Knopf. (page 23)

Yolen, J. (1990). *Bird Watch.* Ill. by Ted Lewin. New York: Philomel.

  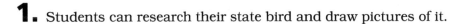

Activities for Extension:

1. Students can research their state bird and draw pictures of it.

2. Ask students to keep a class diary of birds seen during the day/week/month.

3. Allow students to write about their favorite bird, real or imaginary.

4. Using the above books, encourage students to draw various birds and make a class book.

5. Purchase a model of a bird and ask the class to assemble and research the bird.

6. Students can write for a booklet on vital information about pet birds. Enclose $1.00 and send to:

> American Cage-Bird Magazine
> Department M
> One Glamore Court
> Smithtown, NY 11787

(from *Free Stuff for Kids*, Meadowbrook Press, 1993, page 51)

■ **This month is special because:** It is Garden Planting Month.

Books that relate to this month
■ Picture Books:

Bjork, C. (1987). *Linnea in Monet's Garden*. Ill. by Lena Anderson. New York: Farrar, Strauss & Giroux.

Bolton, F. and Snowball, D. (1986). *Growing Radishes and Carrots*. Ill. by Donna Rawlins. New York: Scholastic.

Brown, M. (1981). *Your First Garden* Book. New York: Little, Brown.

Butterworth, N. (1993). *Jasper's Beanstalk*. Ill. by Mick Inkpen. New York: Bradbury.

Carle, E. (1987). *The Tiny Seed*. New York: Scholastic.

Carlson, N. (1982). *Harriet and the Gardner*. Minneapolis: Carolrhoda.

Caseley, J. (1990). *Grandpa's Garden Lunch*. New York: Greenwillow.

Coats, L. J. (1993). *Alphabet Garden*. New York: Macmillan.

Ehlert, L. (1989). *Eating the Alphabet*. San Diego: Harcourt Brace Jovanovich.

Ehlert, L. (1987). *Growing Vegetable Soup*. San Diego: Harcourt Brace Jovanovich.

Ehlert, L. (1988). *Planting a Rainbow*. San Diego: Harcourt Brace Jovanovich.

Ernst, L. C. (1991). *Miss Penny and Mr. Grubbs*. New York: Bradbury.

Gibbons, G. (1991). *From Seed to Plant*. New York: Holiday House.

Howard, E. (1993). *The Big Seed*. Ill. by Lillian Hoban. New York: Simon & Schuster.

Lobel, A. (1985). *The Rose in My Garden*. Ill. by Anita Lobel. New York: Scholastic.

Markmann, E. (1991). *Grow It! An Indoor-Outdoor Gardening Guide for Kids*. Ill. by Gisela Konemund. New York: Random House.

Maris, M. (1988). *In My Garden*. New York: Greenwillow.

Marston, E. (1993). *A Griffin in the Garden*. Il. by Larry Daste. New York: Tambourine.

McMillan, B. (1988). *Growing Colors*. New York: Lothrop.

Merrill, C. (1973). *A Seed Is a Promise*. Ill. by Susan Swan. New York: Scholastic.

Muller, G. (1991). *The Garden in the City*. New York: Dutton.

Oechsli, H. & Oechsli, K. (1985). *In My Garden: A Child's Gardening Book*. New York: Macmillan.

Palmisciano, D. (1989). *Garden Partners*. New York: Atheneum.

Rockwell, A. and Rockwell, H. (1982). *How My Garden Grew*. New York: Macmillan.

Rylant, C. (1987). *This Year's Garden*. Ill. by Mary Szilagyi. New York: Macmillan.

Stevenson, J. (1989). *Grandpa's Too-Good Garden*. New York: Greenwillow.

Wexler, J. (1987). *Flowers, Fruits, and Seeds*. New York: Prentice-Hall.

Wilkes, A. (1992). *My First Garden Book*. New York: Knopf.

Wolf, J. (1990). *The Rosy Fat Magenta Radish*. Boston: Little, Brown.

■ Poetry:

"In My Garden" in:
Causley, C. (1986). *Early in the Morning: A Collection of New Poems*. Ill. by Michael Foremen. New York: Viking. (page 23)

Florian, D. (1991). *Vegetable Garden*. San Diego: Harcourt Brace Jovanovich.

"The Garden" in:
Silverstein, S. (1974). *Where the Sidewalk Ends*. New York: Harper & Row. (page 61)

Steele, M. Q. (1989). *Anna's Garden Songs*. Ill. by Lena Anderson. New York: Greenwillow.

Activities for Extension:

1. Using the books above, help students plan and plant a garden.

2. Make vegetable soup, using the recipe in *Growing Vegetable Soup* (Ehlert, 1987).

3. Encourage students to make a schedule for daily garden duties: weeding, watering, fertilizing, planting, harvesting, thinning, cultivating. Help them sequence these chores in logical order.

4. Allow students to write poems about growing. What else grows besides plants?

5. Invite a gardener to discuss gardening, show tools, and talk about the rewards of gardening.

M·A·Y 1

Date: May 1

This date is special because:
It is Mother Goose Day.

Books that relate to this date

Picture Books:

Alderson, B. (1986). *The Helen Oxenbury Nursery Rhyme Book*. New York: Morrow.

Aylesworth, J. (1992). *The Cat and the Fiddle and More*. New York: Atheneum.

Aylesworth, J. (1990). *The Completed Hickory Dickory Dock*. New York: Atheneum.

Calmenson, S. (1989). *The Principal's New Clothes*. New York: Scholastic.

Cole, B. (1986). *Princess Smartypants*. New York: Putnams.

de Paola, T. (1985). *Tomie de Paola's Mother Goose*. New York: Putnam.

Edens, C. (1988). *Glorious Mother Goose*. New York: Macmillan.

Gammell, Stephen. (1981). *Once Upon MacDonald's Farm*. New York: Four Winds.

Greenaway, K. (1988). *Kate Greenaway's Mother Goose*. New York: Dial.

Gwynne, F. (1990). *Pondlarker*. New York: Simon & Schuster.

Hale, S. (1990). *Mary Had a Little Lamb*. New York: Scholastic.

Hannant, J. S. (1991). *The Doornob Collection*. Boston: Little, Brown.

Hennessy, B. G. (1989). *The Missing Tarts*. New York: Viking.

Kimmel, E. (1992). *The Old Woman and Her Pig*. New York: Holiday House.

Koontz, R. M. (1987). *Pussycat Ate the Dumplings*. New York: Dodd.

Lamont, P. (1990). *Ring-A-Round-A-Rosy: Nursery Rhymes, Action Rhymes and Lullabies*. Boston: Little, Brown.

Lewis, B. (1984). *Home Before Midnight*. New York: Lothrop.

Lines, K. (1987). *Lavender's Blue: A Book of Nursery Rhymes*. New York: Oxford University Press.

Lobel, A. (1986). *The Random House Book of Mother Goose*. New York: Random House.

Loomans, D. and Loomans, J., and Kolberg, K. (1991). *Positively Mother Goose*. New York: Tiburoni.

MacDonald, S. (1990). *Once Upon Another/ The Tortoise and the Hare*. New York: Dial.

Marcus, L., and Schwartz, A. (1990). *Mother Goose's Little Misfortunes*. New York: Bradbury.

Marshall, J. (1986). *James Marshall's Mother Goose*. New York: Farrar, Straus & Giroux.

O'Brien, John. (1989). *The Calico Mother Goose Book of Games, Riddles, and Tongue* Twisters. Chicago: Contemporary Books.

Opie, I. (1988). *Tail Feathers from Mother Goose: The Opie Rhyme Book*. Boston: Little, Brown.

Rader, L. (1993). *Mother Hubbard's Cupboard*. New York: Tambourine.

Reid, Barbara. (1987). *Sing a Song of Mother Goose*. New York: Scholastic.

Scieszka, J. (1991). *The Frog Prince Continued*. New York: Viking.

Sutherland, Zena. (1989). *Orchard Book of Nursery Rhymes*. New York: Orchard.

Tudor, T. (1989). *Mother Goose*. New York: Random House.

Voake, Charlotte. (1985). *Over the Moon*. New York: Crown.

Weil, Lisl. (1981). *Mother Goose Picture Riddles*. New York: Holiday House.

Wright, Barbara. (1916). *The Real Mother Goose*. New York: Macmillan.

■ **Poetry:**

Glazer, Tom. (1990). *The Mother Goose Songbook*. New York: Doubleday.

Yolen, J. (1992). *Jane Yolen's Mother Goose Songbook*. Ill. by Rosekrans Hoffman. Honesdale, PA: Boyd Mills.

Activities for Extension:

1. Invite students to illustrate and write appropriate greeting cards for rhymes (e.g., "Sorry to Hear of Your Accident" sent to Humpty Dumpty).

2. Invite students to create props for various rhymes (e.g., plastic spider, bowl, spoon, and bonnet for Little Miss Muffet).

3. Students might want to write a riddle for a Mother Goose character rhyme, such as: I was going to get water. I fell down and hurt my head. Who am I?

4. Allow students to dress up as nursery rhyme characters and have a party.

5. Make a list of all the occupations found in Mother Goose rhymes.

M·A·Y 5

■ **Date:** May 5

■ **This date is special because:**
It is Cinco de Mayo.

Books that relate to this date

■ **Picture Books:**

Behrens, J. (1985). *Fiesta! Cinco de Mayo, Dias de Fiesta*. Ill. by Scott Taylor. Chicago: Childrens Press.

Brown, T. (1986). *Hello, Amigos!* Ill. by Fran Ortiz. New York: Henry Holt.

Bulmer-Thomas, B. (1991). *Journey Through Mexico*. Mahwah, NJ: Troll.

Coronado, R. (1982). *Cooking the Mexican Way*. Minneapolis: Lerner.

Czernecki, S. and Rhodes, T. (1992). *Pancho's Pinata*. New York: Hyperion.

Delacre, L. (1993). *Vejigante Masquerader*. New York: Scholastic. (written in Spanish and English)

Dorros, A. (1993). *Abuela*. Ill. by Elisa Kleven. New York: Dutton.

Emberley, R. (1990). *My House, Mi Casa: A Book in Two Languages*. Boston: Little, Brown.

Emberley, R. (1990). *Taking a Walk, Caminando: A Book in Two Languages*. New York: Scholastic.

Ets, M. and Labastida, A. (1959). *Nine Days to Christmas*. New York: Viking.

Fisher, L. E. (1988). *Pyramid of the Sun: Pyramid of the Moon*. New York: Macmillan.

Gleiter, J. (1990). *Benito Juarez*. Milwaukee: Raintreee.

Gray, G. (1978). *How Far, Felipe?* Ill. by Ann Grifalconi. New York: Harper.

Haskins, J. (1989). *Count Your Way Through Mexico*. Ill. by Helen Byers. Minneapolis: Carolrhoda.

Havill, J. (1992). *Treasure Nap*. Ill. by Elivia Savadier. Boston: Houghton Mifflin.

Hewett, J. (1990). *Hector Lives in the U.S. Now: The Story of a Mexican-American Child*. Ill. by Richard Hewett. New York: HarperCollins.

Ian, J. (1989). *Mexico*. New York: Watts.

Jacobsen, P. O. & Kristensen, P. S. (1984). *A Family in Mexico*. New York: Bookwright.

James, I. (1989). *Mexico*. New York: Watts.

Kimmel, E. A. (1993). *The Witch's Face: A Mexican Tale*. Ill. by Fabricio Vanden Broeck. New York: Holiday House.

Lattimore, D. N. (1987). *The Flame of Peace: A Tale of the Aztecs*. New York: Harper & Row.

Lewis, T. P. (1971). *Hill of Fire*. Ill. by Joan Sandin. New York: Harper.

Lye, K. (1982). *Take a Trip to Mexico*. New York: Watts.

Mora, P. (1992). *A Birthday Basket for Tia*. Ill. by Cecily Lang. New York: Macmillan.

Moran, T. (1987). *A Family in Mexico*. Minneapolis: Lerner.

My First Phrases in Spanish and English. (1993). New York: Simon & Schuster.

Poulet, V. (1988). *Azulin Encontro' Algo.* Chicago: Childrens Press.

Poulet, V. (1985). *Azulin Va a La Escuela.* Ill. by Peggy Perry Anderson. Chicago: Childrens Press.

Poulet, V. (1990). *Azulin Visita a Mexico: Blue Bug Visits Mexico.* Ill. by Peggy P. Anderson. Chicago: Childrens Press.

Poulet, V. (1981). *El Libro de Colores de Azulin.* Chicago: Childrens Press.

Poulet, V. (1988). *El Tesoro de Azulin.* Chicago: Childrens Press.

Roe, E. (1992). *Con Mi Hermano/With My Brother.* Ill. by Robert Casilla. New York: Scholastic.

Shalant, P. (1992). *Look What We've Brought You from Mexico.* New York: Messner.

Singer, I. B. (1991). *Por Que' Noe' Eligio' La Palamo.* Ill. by Eric Carle. New York: Farrar, Straus & Giroux.

Taha, K. T. (1986). *A Gift for Tia Rosa.* Ill. by Dee deRosa. Minneapolis: Dillon.

Wepman, D. (1986). *Benito Juarez.* New York: Chelsea House.

Williams, L. (1991). *Getting to Know Mexico.* Lincolnwood, IL: Passport Books.

■ Poetry:

Dabcovich, L. (1992). *The Keys to My Kingdom: A Poem in Three Languages.* New York: Lothrop. (English, French, Spanish)

De Gerez, T. (1984). *My Song Is a Piece of Jade: Poems of Ancient Mexico in English and Spanish.* Ill. by William Stark. Boston: Little, Brown.

Yolen, J. (1992). *Street Rhymes Around the World.* Honesdale, PA: Wordsong. (pages 6–7, 18–19)

1. Celebrate a fiesta with foods from Mexico.

2. Help students make a piñata depicting something from the Mexican culture. Fill it with candy and take outside to swing at and break.

3. Use a pocket chart to collect information learned about Mexico. Put the words on the left in the pocket chart and invite students to find examples from the above books.

Volcanoes/Mountains: Popocatapetl, Ixtaccihuatl
Cities: Mexico City, Chihuahua, Fresnillo, Pachuca, Taxco, Oaxaca, Acapulco, Puerto Vallarta
Foods: tortilla, masa, memela, cafe' de ollita, tacos, menudo, cochinita pibil

4. Match the Spanish words to the English symbols in a pocket chart.

1. Uno (OO-no)
2. Dos (dohs)
3. Tres (trace)
4. Cuatro (KWA-tro)
5. Cinco (SIN-ko)
6. Seis (sace)
7. Siete (see-EH-tay)
8. Ocho (O-cho)
9. Nueve (noo-EH-vay)
10. Diez (dee-ES)

5. Other words to be matched in a pocket chart:

COLORS:

red: rojo
pink: rosado or rosa
orange: anaranjado
yellow: amarillo
green: verde
blue: azul
purple: morado
gray: gris
black: negro
white: blanco

SHAPES:

circle: el círculo
square: el cuadro
triangle: el triángulo
diamond: el rombo
rectangle: el rectángulo
octagon: el octagonol
oval: el ovalo

WORDS ASSOCIATED WITH SCHOOL:

nombre: name
alfabeto: alphabet
escuela: school
números: numbers
creyones: crayons

M·A·Y 9

■ Date: May 9

■ This date is special because:
It is the day that the first Mother's Day was celebrated (1914).

Books that relate to this date
■ Picture Books:

Blaine, M. (1983). *The Terrible Thing That Happened at Our House*. Ill. by John Wallner. New York: Scholastic.

Bunting, E. (1986). *The Mother's Day Mice*. Ill. by Jan Brett. New York: Clarion.

Cole, B. (1984). *The Trouble with Mom*. New York: Putnam.

Cowen-Fletcher, J. (1993). *Mama Zooms*. New York: Scholastic.

Fox, M. (1987). *Koala Lou*. Ill. by Patricia Mullin. New York: Bradbury.

Goode, D. (1991). *Where's Our Mama?* New York: Scholastic.

Hest, A. (1991). *The Mommy Exchange*. Ill. by Dyanne DiSalvo-Ryan. New York: Macmillan.

Joose, B. M. (1992). *Mama, Do You Love Me?* Ill. by Barbara Lavallee. New York: Scholastic.

Levine, A. (1990). *What Did Mommy Do Before You?* New York: Puffin.

MacLachlan, P. (1982). *Mama One, Mama Two*. Ill. by Ruth Bornstein. New York: Harper.

Mahy, M. (1985). *The Man Whose Mother Was a Pirate*. Ill. by Margaret Chamberlain. New York: Viking.

Martin, A. M. (1989). *Kristy and the Mother's Day Surprise*. New York: Scholastic.

McGraw, S. and Cline, P. (1991). *My Mother's Hands*. Ill. by Sheila McGraw. New York: Green Tiger Press.

Merriam, E. (1991). *Mommies at Work*. New York: Simon & Schuster.

Munsch, R. (1989). *Love You Forever*. Ill. by Sheila McGraw. Ontario, Canada: Firefly.

Rosenberg, L. (1993). *Monster Mama*. Ill. by Stephen Gammell. New York: Philomel.

Russo, M. (1993). *Trade-In-Mother*. New York: Greenwillow.

Sharmat, M. J. (1986). *Hooray for Mother's Day!* Ill. by John Wallner. New York: Holiday House.

Wells, R. (1989). *Hazel's Amazing Mother*. New York: Dial.

Wynot, J. (1990). *The Mother's Day Sandwich*. Ill. by Maxie Chambliss. New York: Orchard.

Zolotow, C. (1980). *Say It!* Ill. by James Stevenson. New York: Greenwillow.

Zolotow, C. (1992). *This Quiet Lady*. Ill. by Anita Lobel. New York: Greenwillow.

■ Novels:

Cleary, B. (1979). *Ramona and Her Mother*. New York: Morrow.

Clymer, E. (1982). *My Mother Is the Smartest Woman in the World*. New York: Macmillan.

Delton, J. (1986). *Angel's Mother's Boyfriend*. Ill. by Margot Apple. Boston: Houghton Mifflin.

Delton, J. (1990). *Angel's Mother's Wedding*. New York: Dell.

■ Poetry:

"Mother's Nerves" in:
Kennedy, X. J. (1975). *One Winter Night in August*. Ill. by David McPhail. New York: Atheneum. (page 4)

Livingston, M. C. (1988). *Poems for Mothers*. Ill. by Deborah Kogan Ray. New York: Holiday House.

"On Mother's Day" by Aileen Fisher in: Prelutsky, J. (1983). *Random House Book of Poetry for Children*. Ill. by Arnold Lobel. New York: Random House. (page 43)

"Happy Birthday, Mother Dearest" in: Prelutsky, J. (1990). *Something BIG Has Been Here*. Ill. by James Stevenson. New York: Greenwillow. (page 10)

Activities for Extension:

1. Brainstorm the characteristics that make a good mother.

2. Ask students to write a want ad using the characteristics in Activity 1.

3. Ask students to write a Mother's Day poem for their mothers or caregivers.

4. Invite students to interview a mother about motherhood. Ask them to report back to the class.

5. Brainstorm and keep a chart of famous mothers, such as Mother Goose, Whistler's Mother, and so on.

M·A·Y 14

■ **This date is special because:**
It is Gabriel Fahrenheit's birthday (1686).

Gabriel Farenheit introduced the use of mercury in thermometers and improved their accuracy.

Books that relate to this date
■ **Picture Books:**

Ardely, N. (1983). *Hot and Cold*. New York: Watts.

Barrett, J. (1978). *Cloudy with a Chance of Meatballs*. New York: Macmillan.

Bauer, C. F. (1986). *Rainy Day Stories and Poems*. New York: Lippincott.

Bauer, C. F. (1988). *Windy Day Stories and Poems*. New York: Lippincott.

Berger, M. (1991). *Make Your Own Weather Station*. New York: Scholastic.

Borden, L. (1989). *Caps, Hats, Socks, and Mittens*. New York: Scholastic.

Branley, F. (1985). *Flash, Crash, Rumble, and Roll*. New York: Crowell.

Branley, F. (1985). *Hurricane Watch*. New York: Crowell.

Branley, F. (1987). *It's Raining Cats and Dogs*. Boston: Houghton Mifflin.

Branley, F. (1983). *Rain and Hail*. New York: Crowell.

Branley, F. (1984). *Shivers and Goose Bumps: How We Keep Warm*. New York: Crowell.

Briggs, R. (1978). *The Snowman*. New York: Random House.

Caple, K. (1990). *The Coolest Place in Town*. Boston: Houghton Mifflin.

de Paola, T. (1975). *The Cloud Book*. New York: Holiday House.

DeWitt, L. (1991). *What Will the Weather Be?* New York: HarperCollins.

Dorros, A. (1989). *Feel the Wind*. New York: Crowell.

Dupasquier, P. (1988). *Our House on the Hill*. New York: Viking.

Gibbons, G. (1987). *Weather Forecasting*. New York: Macmillan.

Gibbons, G. (1990). *Weather Words and What They Mean*. New York: Holiday House.

Jeunesse, G. and de Bourgoing, P. (1991). *Weather*. New York: Scholastic.

Kahl, J. D. (1992). *Weatherwise: Learning about the Weather*. Minneapolis: Lerner.

Kahl, J. (1992). *Wet Weather: Rain Showers and Snowfall*. Minneapolis: Lerner.

Knutson, K. (1992). *Muddigush*. New York: Macmillan.

Leslie, C. W. (1991). *Nature All Year Long*. New York: Greenwillow.

Lyon, G.E. (1990). *Come a Tide*. New York: Orchard.

Maass, R. (1990). *When Autumn Comes*. New York: Holt.

Maestro, B. and Maestro, G. (1990). *Temperature and You*. New York: Lodestar.

Pearson, S. (1988). *My Favorite Time of the Year*. New York: Harper & Row.

Pettigrew, M. (1987). *Science Today: Weather*. New York: Gloucester.

Polacco, P. (1990). *Thunder Cake*. New York: Philomel.

Provensen, A. and Provensen, M. (1978). *The Year at Maple Hill Farm*. New York: Atheneum.

Rogers, P. (1989). *What Will the Weather Be Like Today?* New York: Scholastic.

Serfozo, M. (1990). *Rain Talk*. New York: McElderry.

Seymour, P. (1985). *How the Weather Works*. Ill. by Sally Springer. New York: Macmillan.

Simon, S. (1989). *Storms*. New York: Morrow.

Spier, P. (1982). *Rain*. Garden City, NY: Doubleday.

Wilson, F. (1987). *The Weather Pop-Up Book*. Ill. by Philip Jacobs. New York: Simon & Schuster.

Wyler, R. (1989). *Raindrops and Rainbows*. Englewood Cliffs, NJ: Messner.

■ Novels:

Lawson, L. (1989). *Addie's Dakota Winter*. New York: Whitman.

Ruckman, I. (1984). *Night of the Twisters*. New York: Crowell.

■ Poetry:

Adoff, A. (1991). *In for Winter, Out for Spring*. San Diego: Harcourt Brace Jovanovich.

Adoff, A. (1977). *Tornado Poems*. New York: Delacorte.

Lewis, J. P. (1991). *Earth Verses and Water Rhymes*. New York: Atheneum.

Martin, B., and Archambault, J. (1988). *Listen to the Rain*. New York: Holt.

Prelutsky, J. (1984). *It's Snowing*. New York: Greenwillow.

Yolen, J. (1986). *Ring of Earth*. San Diego: Harcourt Brace Jovanovich.

Yolen, J. (1993). *Weather Report*. Ill. by Annie Gusman. Honesdale, PA: Wordsong.

Activities for Extension:

1. Make a chart of the four seasons of the year. Ask students which is their favorite.

2. Keep a calendar of special events that are related to weather: the first snowfall, when the first leave turns gold in the fall, and so on.

3. Invite students to make a list of sound words related to weather.

4. Ask students to write or tell weather-related experience stories or poems.

5. Compare temperatures in different locales across the nation. Use the newspaper to chart the high and low temperatures.

M·A·Y 25

■ **Date:** May 25

■ **This date is special because:**

It is African Freedom Day.

Some African states commemorate their independence from colonial rule on this day.

Books that relate to this date

■ **Picture Books:**

Aardema, V. (1992). *Anansi Finds a Fool: An Ashanti Tale.* New York: Dial.

Aardema, V. (1985). *Bimwili and the Zimwi: A Tale from Zanzibar.* Ill. by Susan Meddaugh. New York: Dial. (Zanzibar)

Alexander, L. (1992). *The Fortune-Tellers.* Ill. by Trina Schart Hyman. New York: Dutton.

Anderson, D. A. (1993). *The Origin of Life on Earth.* Ill. by Kathleen Atkins Wilson. Mt. Airy, MD: Sights Productions.

Barker, C. (1985). *A Family in Nigeria.* Minneapolis: Lerner. (Nigeria)

Daly, B. (1985). *My Village in Morocco: Mokhtar of the Atlas Mountains.* Morristown, NJ: Silver Burdett. (Morocco)

Daly, B. (1985). *My Village in the Sahara: Tarlift, Tuareg Boy.* Morristown, NJ: Silver Burdett.

Daly, N. (1986). *Not So Fast, Songololo.* New York: Atheneum. (South Africa)

Feelings, T. (1974). *Jambo Means Hello.* New York: Dial. (Swahili)

Feelings, T. (1971). *Moja Means One.* New York: Dial. (Swahili)

French, F. (1993). *King of Another Country.* New York: Scholastic.

Gray, N. (1988). *A Country Far Away.* Ill. by Peter Dupasquier. New York: Orchard.

Grifalconi, A. (1987). *Darkness and the Butterfly.* Boston: Little, Brown.

Grifalconi, A. (1986). *Village of Round and Square Houses.* Boston: Little, Brown. (Cameroon)

Griffin, M. (1988). *A Family in Kenya.* Photos by Liba Taylor. Minneapolis: Lerner. (Kenya)

Heide, F. P. and Gilliland, J. H. (1990). *The Day of Ahmed's Secret.* Ill. by Ted Lewin. New York: Lothrop. (Egypt)

Isadora, R. (1991). *At the Crossroads.* New York: Greenwillow.

Isadora, R. (1992). *Over the Green Hills.* New York: Greenwillow. (Transkei)

Jacobsen, P. O. and Kristensen, P. S. (1985). *A Family in West Africa.* New York: Bookwright.

Kroll, V. (1993). *Africa Brothers and Sisters.* Ill. by Vanessa French. New York: Four Winds. (many cultures)

Kroll, V. (1992). *Masai and I.* Ill. by Nancy Carpenter. New York: Four Winds. (Masai)

Leigh, N. K. (1993). *Learning to Swim in Swaziland: A Child's Eye View of a Southern African Country.* New York: Scholastic. (Swaziland)

Lerner Publications. (1988). *Tanzania in Pictures.* Minneapolis: Lerner.

Lewin, H. (1981). *Jafta and the Wedding.* Ill. by Lisa Kopper. Minneapolis: Carolrhoda.

Lewin, H. (1983). *Jafta: The Town*. Ill. by Lisa Kopper. Minneapolis: Carolrhoda.

Lye, K. (1983). *Take a Trip to Nigeria*. New York: Watts. (Nigeria)

Margolies, B. A. (1990). *Rehema's Journey: A Visit in Tanzania*. New York: Scholastic. (Tanzania)

McDermott, G. (1992). *Zomo the Rabbit: A Trickster Tale from West Africa*. New York: Dial.

McKenna, N. D. (1986). *A Zulu Family*. Minneapolis: Lerner. (South Africa)

Mennen, I. and Dale, N. (1990). *Somewhere in Africa*. Ill. by Nicolaas Martiz. New York: Dutton. (South Africa)

Mollel, T. M. (1990). *The Orphan Boy*. Ill. by Paul Morin. New York: Clarion. (Masaii folktale)

O'Toole, T. (1988). *Malawi in Pictures*. Minneapolis: Lerner. (Malawi)

Peters, L. W. (1989). *Serengeti*. New York: Crestwood House. (Tanzania)

Sierra, J. (1992). *The Elephant's Wrestling Match*. Ill. by Brian Pinkney. New York: Lodestar.

Stelson, C. B. (1988). *Safari*. Photos by Kim A. Stelson. Minneapolis: Carolrhoda. (Tanzania)

Steptoe, J. (1987). *Mufaro's Beautiful Daughters*. New York: Lothrop. (Zimbabwe)

Stewart, D. (1993). *The Dove*. Ill. by Jude Daly. New York: Greenwillow. (Durban, South Africa)

Stewart, J. (1986). *A Family in Morocco*. Photos by Jenny Matthews. Minneapolis: Lerner. (Morrocco)

Watson, R. L. (1988). *South Africa in Pictures*. Minneapolis: Lerner.

Williams, K. (1991). *Galimoto*. Ill. by Katherine Stock. New York: Lothrop. (Malawi)

Williams, K. (1991). *When Africa Was Home*. Ill. by Floyd Cooper. New York: Orchard.

Wisniewski, D. (1992). *Sundiata: Lion King of Mali*. New York: Clarion. (Mali).

■ Novel:

Fairman, T. (1992). *Bury My Bones but Keep My Words*. Ill. by Meshack Asare. New York: Henry Holt.

■ Poetry:

Hudson, W. (1993). *Pass It On: African American Poetry for Children*. Ill. by Floyd Cooper. New York: Scholastic.

Johnson, J. W. (1993). *Lift Every Voice and Sing*. Ill. by Elizabeth Catlett. New York: Walker.

Yolen, J. (1992). *Street Rhymes Around the World*. Honesdale, PA: Wordsong. (pages 26–27)

 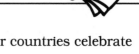

Activities for Extension:

1. Discuss the meaning of independence or freedom. What other countries celebrate their independence?

2. After reading *Rehema's Journey* (Margolies, 1990), students can write their own travelogue of the city, state, or region they live in.

3. African Freedom Day is celebrated with sports contests. Invite children to hold a "class olympics."

M·A·Y 26

■ **Date:** May 26

■ **This date is special because:**
It is Sally Ride's birthday (1951).

Books that relate to this date

■ **Picture Books:**

Barton, B. (1988). *I Want to Be an Astronaut*. New York: Harper.

Behrens, J. (1984). Sally Ride, Astronaut: An American First. Chicago: Childrens Press.

Blacknall, C. (1984). *Sally Ride: America's First Woman in Space*. New York: Macmillan.

Embury, B. (1990). *The Dream Is Alive*. New York: Harper & Row.

Gibbons, G. (1992). *Stargazers*. New York: Holiday House.

Goodman, S. (1993). *Amazing Space Facts*. New York: Peter Bedrick.

Mauerer, R. (1989). *Junk in Space*. New York: Simon & Schuster.

O'Connor, K. (1983). *Sally Ride and the New Astronauts*. New York: Watts.

Stott, C. (1989). *Into the Unknown*. New York: Hampstead Press.

■ **Poetry:**

"Last Laugh" by Lee Bennett Hopkins in:
Hopkins, L. B. (1973). *Surprises*. Ill. by Megan Lloyd. New York: Harper & Row. (page 26)

"To an Aviator" by Daniels Whitehead Hicky:
Prelutsky, J. (1983). *Random House Book of Poetry for Children*. Ill. by Arnold Lobel. New York: Random House. (page 223)

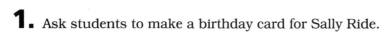

Activities for Extension:

1. Ask students to make a birthday card for Sally Ride.

2. Encourage students to write a song about space.

3. Ask students to pretend they are going into space. What would they pack? Why?

4. Challenge students to research other astronauts.

5. Students can write to NASA for information about the space program. Write to: National Aeronautics & Space Administration, 600 Independence Ave. SW, Washington, DC 20546. Phone: (202) 453-1000.

JUNE

■ **This month is special because:** It is Zoo and Aquarium Month.

Books that relate to this month
■ **Picture Books:**

Ancona, G. and Beth, M. (1989). *Handtalk Zoo*. New York: Macmillan.

Borlenchi, P. (1992). *From Albatross to Zoo: An Alphabet Book in Five Languages*. Ill. by Pers Harper. New York: Scholastic.

Brennan, J. and Keaney, L. (1989). *Zoo Day*. Minneapolis: Carolrhoda.

Broekel, R. (1982). *Aquariums and Terrariums*. New York: Childrens.

Browne, A. (1992). *Zoo*. New York: Knopf.

Buehner, C. and Buehner, M. (1992). *The Escape of Marvin the Ape*. New York: Dial.

Butterworth, N. and Inkpen, M. (1987). *I Wonder at the Zoo*. New York: Zondervan.

Carle, E. (1989). *One, Two, Three to the Zoo*. New York: Putnam.

Cohen, D. and Cohen S. (1989). *Zoos*. New York: Bantam Doubleday.

Cole, J. (1993). *The Magic School Bus on the Ocean Floor*. Ill. by Bruce Degen. New York: Scholastic.

Demi. (1985). *Demi's Find the Animal A-B-C*. New York: Putnam.

Ehlert, L. (1990). *Fish Eyes: A Book You Can Count On*. San Diego: Harcourt Brace Jovanovich.

Ehlert, L. (1989). *Color Zoo*. New York: Lippincott.

Gibbons, G. (1987). *Zoo*. New York: HarperCollins.

Goennel, H. (1993). *Heidi's Zoo: An Un-Alphabet Book*. New York: Tambourine.

Knowles, S. (1990). *Edward the Emu*. Ill. by Rod Clement. New York: HarperCollins.

Lacome, J. (1993). *Walking Through the Jungle*. New York: Candlewick.

Lauber, P. (1990). *An Octopus Is Amazing*. Ill. by Holly Keller. New York: Crowell.

MacCarlky, P. (1990). *Ocean Parade: A Counting Book*. New York: Dial.

Maestro, B. (1990). A *Sea Full of Sharks*. Ill. by Gialio Maestro. New York: Scholastic.

Marshall, J. P. (1989). *My Camera at the Zoo*. Boston: Little, Brown.

McMillan, B. (1992). *The Baby Zoo*. New York: Scholastic.

Moss, M. (1987). *Zoos*. New York: Bookwright.

Ormerod, J. (1991). *When We Went to the Zoo*. New York: Lothrop.

Parramon, J. M. (1990). *My First Visit to the Aquarium*. Ill. by G. Sales. New York: Barron.

Pfister, M. (1992). *The Rainbow Fish*. New York: North-South Books.

Roffey, M. (1988). *I Spy at the Zoo*. New York: Macmillan.

Sadler, M. (1988). *Alistair Underwater*. Ill. by Roger Bollen. New York: Simon & Schuster.

Spencer, E. (1990). *Animal Babies 1, 2, 3*. Ill. by Susan David. Milwaukee: Raintree.

Wilson, A. (1990). *Look! The Ultimate Spot the Difference Book*. New York: Dial.

Wood, J. (1993). *Animal Parade*. New York: Macmillan.

Wu, N. (1993). *Fish Faces*. New York: Holt.

Ziefert, H. (1991). *Zoo Parade!* Ill. by Simms Taback. New York: HarperCollins.

■ Poetry:

Carle, E. (1989). *Animals, Animals*. New York: Scholastic.

Edwards, R. (1993). M*oon Frog*. Ill. by Sarah Fox-Davies. New York: Candlewick.

Hooper, P. (1987). *A Bundle of Beasts*. Ill. by Mark Steele. Boston: Houghton Mifflin.

Lewis, J. P. (1990). A *Hippopatamusn't*. Ill. by Victoria Chess. New York: Dial.

Martin, B. (1991). *Polar Bear, Polar Bear, What Do You Hear?* Ill. by Eric Carle. New York: Holt.

Prelutsky, J. (1983). *Zoo Things*. Ill. by Paul O. Zelinsky. New York: Greenwillow.

"The Zoo Was in an Uproar" in: Prelutsky, J. (1990). *Something BIG Has Been Here*. Ill. by James Stevenson. New York: Greenwillow. (page 62)

Yolen, J. (1980). *How Beastly! A Menagerie of Nonsense* Poems. Ill. by James Marshall. New York: Collins.

Activities for Extension:

1. Brainstorm the type of animals students will see on a zoo visit.

2. Arrange a visit to the zoo.

3. Help students make a class scrapbook of memories of the zoo.

J·U·N·E 6

■ **Date:** June 6

■ **This date is special because:**
It is Recycling Day.

Books that relate to this date

■ Picture Books:

Bailey, D. (1991). *What Can We Do about Recyling Garbage?* New York: Watts.

Base, G. (1992). *The Sign of the Seahorse.* New York: Abrams.

Bellamy, D. (1991). *How Green Are You?* Ill. by Danna Penny. New York: Crown.

Bellamy, D. (1992). *Tomorrow's Earth.* Ill. by Benoit Jacques. Philadelphia: Courage Books.

Bogart, A. (1993). *Thinking Green in My Home.* New York: Smithmark.

Bogart, A. (1993). *Thinking Green in My Neighborhood.* New York: Smithmark.

Bowden, J. (1990). *Where Does Our Garbage Go?* New York: Bantam Doubleday.

Bright, M. (1991). *The Ozone Layer.* New York: Watts.

Brown, L. K. and Brown, M. (1992). *Dinosaurs to the Rescue: A Guide to Protecting Our Planet.* Ill. by Marc Brown. Boston: Little, Brown.

Elkington, J., Hailes, J., Hill, D. and Makower, J. (1990). *The Green Consumer.* Ill. by Tony Ross. New York: Puffin.

Ernst, L. C. (1993). *Squirrel Park.* New York: Bradbury.

Fife, D. H. (1991). *The Empty Lot.* Ill. by Jim Arnosky. San Francisco: Sierra Club.

Gore, W. W. (1992). *Earth Day.* Hillside, NJ: Enslow.

Greenblat, R. A. (1991). *Aunt Ippy's Museum of Junk.* New York: HarperCollins.

Greene, C. (1991). *Caring for Our Air.* New York: Enslow.

Jeffers, S. (1991). *Brother Eagle, Sister Sky: A Message from Chief Seattle.* New York: Dial.

Lambert, D. (1986). *Pollution and Conservation.* New York: Watts.

Lowry, L. (1992). *Earthwise at Home: A Guide to the Care and Feeding of Your Planet.* Minneapolis: Carolrhoda.

Lowry, L. (1993). *Earthwise at Play: A Guide to the Care and Feeding of Your Planet.* Ill. by David Mataya. Minneapolis: Carolrhoda.

Lowry, L. (1993). *Earthwise at School: A Guide to the Care and Feeding of Your Planet.* Ill. by David Mataya. Minneapolis: Carolrhoda.

McQueen, K. and Fassler, D. (1991). *Let's Talk Trash: The Kids' Book about Recycling.* New York: Waterfront.

Newton-John, O. and Hurst, B. (1993). *A Pig Tale.* Ill. by Sal Murdocca. New York: Simon & Schuster.

Rosenburg, H. (1991). *Joey's Cabbage Patch*. New York: Go Jolly.

Snow, T. (1990). *Global Change*. New York: Childrens.

■ Novel:

Conford, E. (1991). *Can Do, Jenny Archer*. Ill. by Diane Palmisciano. Boston: Little, Brown.

■ Poetry:

"Mama Drives. . ." in:
Adoff, A. (1988). *Greens*. Ill. by Betsy Lewin. New York: Lothrop, Lee & Shepard. (page 18)

"Cacophony" in:
Merriam, E. (1981). *Chortles*. Ill. by Sheila Mamanaka. New York: Morrow. (page 11)

Moon, P. (1993). *Earth Lines: Poems for the Green Age*. New York: Greenwillow.

■ Resource Book:

Fleming, M. (1992). *Garbage*. New York: Scholastic.

Activities for Extension:

1. Organize or support a school recycling center. Ask individual grades to bring in recyclable items.

2. Encourage students to have a class competition for the most aluminum cans collected.

3. Establish a class recycling club. Collect dues and form club rules.

4. Students can write and put on a play, setting forth their recycling goals and objectives for the whole school.

5. Ask students to pick up recyclables around the community.

6. Visit a recycling center.

7. Brainstorm items that are made from recycled products.

JUNE 11

■ **Date:** June 11

■ **This date is special because:**
It is King Kamehameha's birthday (1737).

King Kamehameha was a Hawaiian king.

Books that relate to this date

■ Picture Books:

Feeney, S. (1985). *A is for Aloha*. Photos by Jeff Reese. Honolulu: University of Hawaii Press.

Feeney, S. (1980). *Hawaii Is a Rainbow*. Ill. by Hella Hammid. Honolulu: University of Hawaii Press.

Feeney, S. (1989). *Sand to Sea: Marine Life of Hawaii*. Photos by Ed Robinson & others. Honolulu: University of Hawaii Press.

Kawai'ae'a, K. C. (1988). *Let's Learn to Count in Hawaiian*. Ill. by Cliff Tanaka. Hawaii: Island Heritage.

Marsh, C. (1992). *Hawaii Timeline: A Chronology of Hawaii History, Mystery, Trivia, Legend, Lore and More*. New York: Gallopade.

Marsh, C. (1992). *My First Book about Hawaii*. New York: Gallopade.

McNair, S. (1990) *Hawaii*. Chicago: Childrens Press.

Murray, P. (1987). *Let's Learn the Hawaiian Alphabet*. Ill. by Cliff Tanaka. Hawaii: Island Heritage.

Stanley, F. (1991). *The Last Princess: The Story of Princess Ka'iulani of Hawaii*. Ill. by Diane Stanley. New York: Macmillan.

■ Poetry:

"I Left My Book in Hawaii" in: Dakos, K. (1990). *If You're Not Here, Please Raise Your Hand*. Ill. by G. Brian Kara. New York: Macmillan.

"Lulu" in: Lee, D. (1991). *The Ice Cream Store*. Ill. by David McPhail. New York: Scholastic.

 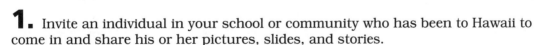

Activities for Extension:

1. Invite an individual in your school or community who has been to Hawaii to come in and share his or her pictures, slides, and stories.

2. Invite students to create a pocket chart of Hawaii. They may include islands, cities, volcanoes, and other names taken from the above titles.

3. Encourage students to design a crown for King Kamehameha.

J·U·N·E 14

■ Date: June 14

■ This date is special because:
It is Flag Day.

Books that relate to this date
■ Picture Books:

Armbruster, A. (1991). *The American Flag*. New York: Watts.

Ayer, E. (1992). *Our Flag*. New York: Millbrook.

Brandt, S. R. (1992). *State Flags*. New York: Watts.

Crampton, W. G. (1989). *Flag*. New York: Knopf.

DeBarr, C. M. (1990). *Saga of the American Flag*. Ill. by Barbara Schiefer. Tucson, AZ: Harbinger.

Fisher, L. E. (1993). *Stars and Stripes: Our National Flag*. New York: Holiday House.

Fradin, D. B. (1988). *The Flag of the United States*. New York: Childrens.

Gross, R. B. (1991). *You Don't Need Words! A Book about Ways People Talk Without Words*. Ill. by Susannah Ryan. New York: Scholastic.

Haban, R. D. (1989). *How Proudly They Wave: Flags of the Fifty States*. New York: Lerner.

Jefferis, D. (1985). *Flags*. New York: Watts.

Rowland-Entwistle, T. (1988). *Flags*. New York: Bookwright.

Swanson, J. (1990). *I Pledge Allegiance*. Ill. by Rick Hanson. Minneapolis: Carolrhoda.

■ Poetry:

"Flag" in:
Silverstein, S. (1974). *Where The Sidewalk Ends*. New York: Scholastic. (page 24)

Activities for Extension:

1. Ask students to research the state flag and make a replica for the classroom.

2. Challenge students to design a flag for the school.

3. Ask students to design a flag for the classroom, or an individual flag depicting themselves.

4. Challenge the class to research flags around the world. Let students vote on their favorites and chart the results.

J·U·N·E 19

■ **Date:** June 19

■ **This date is special because:**
It is the day that the first Father's Day was celebrated (1910).

Books that relate to this date

■ **Picture Books:**

Asch, F. (1984). *Just Like Daddy*. New York: Simon & Schuster.

Bayton, M. (1990). *Why Do You Love Me?* New York: Greenwillow.

Bunting, E. (1991). *A Perfect Father's Day*. Ill. by Susan Meddaugh. Boston: Houghton Mifflin.

Friend, D. (1990). *Baseball, Football, Daddy & Me*. Ill. by Rick Brown. New York: Viking.

Greenfield, E. (1991). *My Daddy and I*. Ill. by Jan S. Gilchrist. New York: Writers & Readers.

Hallinan, P. K. (1989). *We're Very Good Friends, My Father and I*. New York: Childrens.

Hines, A. (1986). *My Daddy Makes the Best Spaghetti*. Ill. by Anna G. Hines. Boston: Houghton Mifflin.

Isadora, R. (1991). *At the Crossroads*. New York: Greenwillow.

Kidd, N. (1991). *June Mountain Secret*. Ill. by Nina Kidd. New York: HarperCollins.

Kroll, S. (1988). *Happy Father's Day*. Ill. by Marylin Hafner. New York: Holiday.

Lewin, H. (1989). *Jafta's Father*. Ill. by Lisa Kopper. New York: Lerner.

Lindenbaum, P. (1991). *Else-Marie and Her Seven Little Daddies*. New York: Henry Holt.

McGraw, S. (1990). *My Father's Hands*. Ill. by Sheila McGraw. New York: Green Tiger Press.

Merriam, E. (1991). *Daddies at Work*. Ill. by Eugenie Fernandes. New York: Simon & Schuster.

Mills, L. (1991). *The Rag Coat*. Boston: Little, Brown.

Parker, K. (1987). *My Dad the Magnificent*. Ill. by Lillian Hoban. New York: Dutton.

Ray, D. (1990). *My Daddy Was a Soldier: A World War Two Story*. New York: Holiday.

Steele, D. (1989). *Martha's New Daddy*. Ill. by Jacqueline Rogers. New York: Delacorte.

Waddell, M. (1993). *Let's Go Home, Little Bear*. Ill. by Barbara Firth. New York: Candlewick.

Watanabe, S. (1991). *Where's My Daddy?* New York: Putnam.

Wetzel, J. S. (1992). *The Christmas Box*. Ill. by Barry Root. New York: Knopf.

Yolen, J. (1991). *All Those Secrets of the World*. Boston: Little, Brown.

Best Dad Day

"Ziefert, H. (1991). *When Daddy Had the Chicken Pox*. Ill. by Lionel Kalish. New York: HarperCollins.

■ Poetry:

"Piggyback Dad" in:
Chandra, D. (1988). *Balloons and Other Poems*. New York: Farrar, Straus & Giroux. (page 15)

Collins, J. (1989). *My Father*. Ill. by Jane Dyer. Boston: Little, Brown.

Lauture, D. (1992). *Father and Son*. Ill. by Jonathan Green. New York: Philomel.

"My Father's Words" in:
Lewis, C. (1991). *Up in the Mountains*. Ill. by Joel Fontaine. New York: HarperCollins. (page 4)

Livingston, M. C. (1989). *Poems for Fathers*. Ill. by Robert Casilla. New York: Holliday House.

"My Father" in:
Zolotow, C. (1987). *Everything Glistens and Everything Sings*. Orlando, FL: Harcourt Brace Jovanovich. (page 46)

 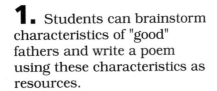 Activities for Extension:

1. Students can brainstorm characteristics of "good" fathers and write a poem using these characteristics as resources.

2. Encourage the class to make a list of famous fathers.

3. Ask volunteers to interview a father about the joys of fatherhood. Students might wish to record the interview and report back to the class.

4. Brainstorm activities children do with their fathers, or primary caregiver. Make a class book with illustrations.

J·U·N·E 25

Date: June 25

This date is special because:
It is Eric Carle's birthday (1929).

Books that relate to this date

Picture Books:

Carle, E. (1974). *Arthur (An Absolutely Absurd Ape)*. New York: Watts.

Carle, E. (1989). *Animals, Animals*. New York: Philomel.

Carle, E. (1971). *Do You Want to Be My Friend?* New York: Crowell.

Carle, E. (1991). *Dragons, Dragons and Other Creatures That Never Were*. New York: Philomel.

Carle, E. (1992). *Draw Me A Star*. New York: Philomel.

Carle, E. (1976). *Eric Carle's Storybook: Seven Tales by the Brothers Grimm*. New York: Watts.

Carle, E. (1973). *Have You Seen My Cat?* New York: Watts

Carle, E. (1987). *A House for Hermit Crab*. New York: Picture Book Studio.

Carle, E. (1973). *I See a Song*. New York: Crowell.

Carle, E. (1989). *La Oruga Muy Hambrienta*. New York: Philomel.

Carle, E. (1984). *The Mixed-up Chameleon*. New York: Crowell.

Carle, E. (1986). *My Very First Book of Food*. New York: HarperCollins.

Carle, E. (1968). *1, 2, 3 to the Zoo*. New York: Philomel.

Carle, E. (1986). *My Very First Book of Heads and Tails*. New York: HarperCollins.

Carle, E. (1986). *My Very First Book of Tools*. New York: HarperCollins.

Carle, E. (1972). *Rooster's Off to See the World*. New York: Picture Book Studio.

Carle, E. (1972). *The Secret Birthday Message*. New York: Crowell.

Carle, E. (1970). *The Tiny Seed*. New York: Crowell.

Carle, E. (1993). *Today Is Monday*. New York: Philomel.

Carle, E. (1988). *Treasury of Classic Stories for Children: Aesop, Hans Christian Andersen, and the Brothers Grimm*. New York: Orchard.

Carle, E. (1984). *The Very Busy Spider*. New York: Philomel.

Carle, E. (1969). *The Very Hungry Caterpillar*. New York: World/Collins & World/Philomel.

Carle, E. (1990). *The Very Quiet Cricket*. New York: Philomel.

Carle, E. (1974). *The Hole in the Dike*. New York: Crowell.

Carle, E. (1982). *Otter Nonsense*. New York: Philomel.

Martin, B. (1983). *Brown Bear, Brown Bear, What Do You See?* New York: Holt & Rinehart.

Martin, B. (1991). *Polar Bear, Polar Bear, What Do You Hear?* New York: Holt.

McLerran, A. (1985). *The Mountain That Loved a Bird*. New York: Picture Book Studio.

■ Resource Book:

Kovacs, D. and Preller, J. (1991). *Meet the Authors and Illustrators: 60 Creators of Favorite Children's Books Talk About Their Work*. New York: Scholastic. (additional information about Eric Carle) (pages 20–21).

Activities for Extension:

1. Encourage students to make collages of their favorite things. Then ask them to explain their collages to the class.

2. Students can paint a picture using sponges for brushes.

3. Students can write their own class pattern book using the books *Brown Bear, Brown Bear, What Do You See?* (Martin, 1983) and *Polar Bear, Polar Bear, What Do You Hear?* (Martin, 1991) as a model.

4. Ask the class to design a birthday card for Eric Carle.

5. You might want to bake a cake for Eric Carle in the shape of the students' favorite Carle animal.

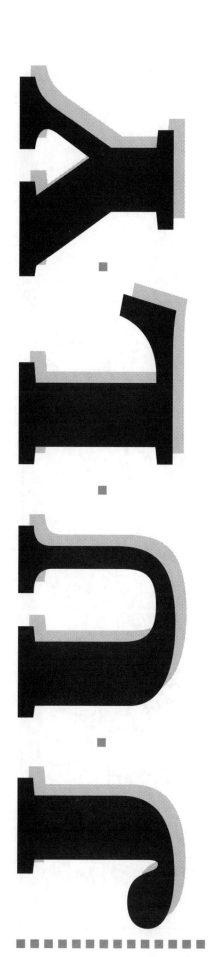

■ **This month is special because:** It is National Picnic Month.

Books that relate to this month
■ Picture Books:

Baer, G. (1988). *The Eleventh Hour: A Curious Mystery*. New York: Abrams.

Brown, M. (1991). *Pickle Things*. New York: Putnam.

Brown, R. (1992). *The Picnic*. New York: Dutton.

Darling, A. (1991). *Teddy Bears' Picnic Cookbook*. Ill. by Alexandra Day. New York: Viking.

Dubanevich, A. (1985). *Pig William*. New York: Bradbury.

DuQuette, K. (1990). *A Ripping Day for a Picnic*. New York: Viking.

Ernst, L. C. (1986). *Up to Ten and Down Again*. New York: Lothrop.

Gackenbach, D. (1993). *Claude Has a Picnic*. New York: Clarion.

Hayes, S. (1988). *This Is Bear and Picnic Lunch*. Ill. by Helen Craig. Boston: Little-Brown.

Hill, E. (1987). *Spot's First Picnic*. New York: Putnam.

Keller, H. (1985). *Henry's Fourth of July*. New York: Greenwillow.

Kennedy, J. (1987). *The Teddy Bear's Picnic*. Ill. by Prue Theobalds. New York: Bedrick.

McCully, E. A. (1984). *Picnic*. New York: Harper & Row.

Novak, M. (1990). *Mr. Floop's Lunch*. New York: Orchard.

Polacco, P. (1992). *Picnic at Mudsock Meadow*. New York: Putnam.

Vincent, G. (1982). *Ernest and Celestine's Picnic*. New York: Greenwillow.

Yeoman, J. (1987). *The Bear's Water Picnic*. Ill. by Quentin Blake. New York: Atheneum.

Yolen, J. (1988). *Picnic with Piggins*. Ill. by Jane Dyer. San Diego: Harcourt Brace Jovanovich.

■ Poetry:

Benjamin, A. (1982). *A Change of Plans*. Ill. by Steven Kellogg. New York: Four Winds.

Butler, D. (1991). *Higgledy Piggledy Hobbledy Hay*. Ill. by Lyn Kriegler. New York: Greenwillow.

Hines, A. G. (1991). *The Greatest Picnic*. New York: Clarion.

"The Picnic" by Dorothy Aldis and "Picnic Day" by Rachel Field in: Prelutsky, J. (1986). *Read-Aloud Rhymes for the Very Young*. Ill. by Marc Brown. New York: Knopf. (pages 31, 32)

Activities for Extension:

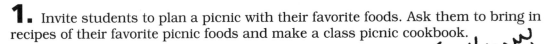

1. Invite students to plan a picnic with their favorite foods. Ask them to bring in recipes of their favorite picnic foods and make a class picnic cookbook.

2. Walk to a nearby park and have a picnic.

3. Plan some games that would be fun to play at a picnic. Listed below are some examples.

> Red Rover, Red Rover
> Croquet
> Sack Races
> Bubble Gum Blowing Contest
> Baseball

4. Invite students to write stories of memorable picnics they've shared with their families or friends. If they can't remember one, ask them to make one up.

5. Invite students to pretend that some of their favorite book characters went on a picnic. Then ask students to discuss or write about their imaginary picnic. Ask some children to illustrate their stories. Collect and display all stories and illustrations in a classroom book.

J·U·L·Y 4

■ **Date:** July 4

■ **This date is special because:**

It is Independence Day.

Books that relate to this date

■ Picture Books:

Anderson, J. (1986). *The Glorious Fourth at Prairietown.* Photographs by George Ancona. New York: Morrow.

Dalgliesh, A. (1972). *Fourth of July Story.* Ill. by Marie Nonnast. New York: Macmillan.

Giblin, J. C. (1983). *Fireworks, Picnics, and Flags: The Story of the 4th of July Symbols.* Ill. by Ursula Arndt. Boston: Ticknor & Fields.

Joose, B. M. (1985). *Fourth of July.* New York: Knopf.

Keller, H. (1985). *Henry's Fourth of July.* New York: Greenwillow.

Lasky, K. (1991). *4th of July Bear.* Ill. by Helen Cogancherry. New York: Morrow.

"Caddie's Independence Day" by Carol Ryrie Brink in: Low, A. (1991). *The Family Read-Aloud Holiday Treasury.* Ill. by Marc Brown. Boston: Little, Brown. (pages 76–85)

Shachtman, T. (1986). *America's Birthday: The 4th of July.* Photos by Chuck Saat. New York: Macmillan.

Spier, P. (1987). *We the People.* Garden City, NY: Doubleday.

Watson, W. (1992). *Hurray for the Fourth of July.* New York: Clarion.

■ Novel:

Fritz, J. (1987). *Shhh! We're Writing the Constitution.* Ill. by Tomie de Paola. New York: Putnam.

■ Poetry:

"Fireworks" in: Chandra, D. (1990). *Balloons and Other Poems.* Ill. by Leslie Bowman. New York: Farrar, Straus & Giroux. (page 4)

Hopkins, L. B. (1993). *Beat the Drum: Independence Day Has Come.* Ill. by Tomie de Paola. Honesdale, PA: Wordsong.

"Fourth of July" in: Livingston, M. C. (1985). *Celebrations.* Ill. by Leonard Everett Fisher. New York: Holiday House. (page 20)

"Fireworks" in: Livingston, M. C. (1989). *Remembering and Other Poems.* New York: McElderry (page 5)

"Fireworks" by Dorothy Aldis in:
Low, A. (1991). *The Family Read-Aloud Holiday Treasury*. Ill. by Marc Brown. Boston: Little, Brown. (page 74)

"The Fourth" in:
Silverstein, S. (1974). *Where the Sidewalk Ends*. New York: Harper & Row. (page 116)

■ Reference Books:

Greene, C. (1982). *Holidays Around the World*. Chicago: Children's Press.

Van Straalen, A. (1986). *The Book of Holidays Around the World*. New York: Dutton.

 # Activities for Extension:

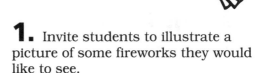
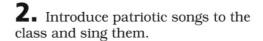

1. Invite students to illustrate a picture of some fireworks they would like to see.

2. Introduce patriotic songs to the class and sing them.

3. Students can write about their favorite Fourth of July memories.

4. Read a class-favorite Fourth of July story and role play the various characters and scenes.

5. Invite students to write about the one thing about the USA that they are most thankful for. Some children might want to write thank you notes to Uncle Sam, Ms. Liberty, or the president.

J·U·L·Y 13

■ Date: July 13

■ This date is special because:
It is Ashley Bryan's birthday (1923).

Books that relate to this date

■ Picture Books:

Bryan, A. (1976). *The Advent of Aku*. New York: Atheneum.

Bryan, A. (1991). All Night, All Day: A Child's First Book of African American Spirituals. New York: Atheneum.

Bryan, A. (1980). *Beat the Story Drum, Pum, Pum*. New York: Atheneum.

Bryan, A. (1985). *The Cat's Purr*. New York: Atheneum.

Bryan, A. (1977). *I'm Going to Sing*. New York: Atheneum.

Bryan, A. (1986). *Lion and the Ostrich Chicks*. New York: Atheneum.

Bryan, A. (1971). *The Ox of the Wonderful Horns and Other African Folktales*. New York: Atheneum.

Bryan, A. (1988). *Sh-Ko and His 8 Wicked Brothers*. New York: Atheneum.

Cooper, S. (1979). *Jethro & Jumbie*. Ill. by Ashley Bryan. New York: Atheneum.

Langstaff, J. M. (1987). *What a Morning!* Ill. by Ashley Bryan. New York: Atheneum.

■ Poems:

Dunbar, P. L. (1978). *I Greet the Dawn*. Ill. by Ashley Bryan. New York: Atheneum.

Tagore, R. (1967). *Moon, for What Do You Want?* Ill. by Ashley Bryan. New York: Atheneum.

■ Resource Book:

Kovacs, D. & Preller, J. (1991). *Meet the Authors and Illustrators: 60 Creators of Famous Children's Books Talk about Their Work*. New York: Scholastic. (pages 18–19) (an interview with Ashley Bryan)

  ## Activities for Extension:

1. Read some of the above books and vote on a class favorite.

2. Invite students to tell a story that has been handed down in their families. Some students might want to add theirs to their writing journal.

3. Invite storytellers into the classroom (older students, professional storytellers, and the like).

J·U·L·Y 16

■ **Date:** July 16

■ **This date is special because:**
It is Shirley Hughes' birthday.

Books that relate to this date

■ Picture Books:

Hughes, S. (1981). *Alfie Gets in First.* New York: Lothrop.

Hughes, S. (1983). *Alfie Gives a Hand.* New York: Lothrop.

Hughes, S. (1982). *Alfie's Feet.* New York: Lothrop.

Hughes, S. (1986). *All Shapes and Sizes.* New York: Lothrop.

Hughes, S. (1989). *Angel Mae: A Tale of Trotter Street.* New York: Lothrop.

Hughes, S. (1987). *Another Helping of Chips.* New York: Lothrop.

Hughes, S. (1985). *Bathwater's Hot.* New York: Lothrop.

Hughes, S. (1989). *The Big Alfie and Annie Rose Storybook.* New York: Lothrop.

Hughes, S. (1992). *The Big Alfie out of Doors Storybook.* New York: Lothrop.

Hughes, S. (1990). *The Big Concrete Lorry: A Tale of Trotter Street.* New York: Lothrop.

Hughes, S. (1993). *Bouncing.* New York: Candlewick.

Hughes, S. (1982). *Charlie Moon and Big Bonanza Bust-Up.* New York: Lothrop.

Hughes, S. (1986). *Chips and Jessie.* New York: Lothrop.

Hughes, S. (1986). *Colors.* New York: Lothrop.

Hughes, S. (1978). *David and Dog.* New York: Lothrop.

Hughes, S. (1984). *An Evening at Alfie's.* New York: Lothrop.

Hughes, S. (1993). *Giving.* New York: Candlewick.

Hughes, S. (1977). *Haunted House.* Englewood Cliffs, NJ: Prentice-Hall.

Hughes, S. (1986). *Here Comes Charlie Moon.* New York: Lothrop.

Hughes, S. (1987). *Lucy and Tom's 123.* New York: Lothrop.

Hughes, S. (1986). *Lucy and Tom's ABC.* New York: Lothrop.

Hughes, S. (1986). *Lucy and Tom's Christmas.* New York: Lothrop.

Hughes, S. (1988). *Moving Molly.* New York: Lothrop.

Hughes, S. (1985). *Noisy.* New York: Lothrop.

Hughes, S. (1988). *Out and About.* New York: Lothrop.

Hughes, S. (1990). *The Snow Lady: A Tale of Trotter Street.* New York: Lothrop.

Hughes, S. (1993). *Stories by Firelight.* New York: Lothrop.

Hughes, S. (1986). *Two Shoes, New Shoes.* New York: Lothrop.

106

Hughes, S. (1979). *Up and Up*. New York: Lothrop.

Hughes, S. (1991). *Wheels: A Tale of Trotter Street*. New York: Lothrop.

Hughes, S. (1985). *When We Went to the Park*. New York: Lothrop

Activities for Extension:

1. Shirley Hughes is from England. Ask students to read some of the following books about this country:

Anno, M. (1982). *Anno's Britain*. New York: Philomel.

Fairclough, C. (1982). *Take a Trip to England*. New York: Watts.

Fairclough, C. (1984). *We Live in Britain*. New York: Bookwright.

James, I. (1988). *Inside Great Britain*. Photos by Chris Fairclough. New York: Watts.

Langley, A. (1986). *Passport to Great Britain*. New York: Watts.

Sproule, A. (1986). *Great Britain*. Morristown, NJ: Silver Burdett.

St. John, J. (1988). *A Family in England*. Photos by Nigel Harvey. Minneapolis: Lerner.

2. Find a map of the world and locate England.

3. Invite someone from England to come and talk to the class.

4. Note the vocabulary differences in Hughes's books. Have students collect different words from the book and do a pocket chart with it. Or use the following:

biscuit—cookie
bonnet—hood of a car
boot—trunk of a car
chips—french fries
flat—apartment

football—soccer
holiday—vacation
lift—elevator
petrol—gasoline
push chair—baby stroller

J·U·L·Y 20

Date: July 20

This date is special because: It is the date of the first moon landing (1969).

Books that relate to this date

Picture Books:

Alexander, M. (1982). *Maggie's Moon*. New York: Dial.

Asch, F. (1988). *Happy Birthday Moon*. New York: Simon & Schuster.

Asch, F. (1993). *Moondance*. New York: Scholastic.

Barrett, N. (1985). *The Moon*. Ill. by Ron Jobson. New York: Watts.

Branley, F. (1987). *The Moon Seems to Change*. New York: Harper.

Branley, F. (1986). *What the Moon Is Like*. Ill. by True Kelley. New York: Harper.

Carle, E. (1986). *Papa, Please Get Me the Moon*. New York: Picture Book Studio.

Gustafson, J. (1992). *Planets, Moons and Meteors*. New York: Messner.

Ingves, G. (1992). *To Pluto and Back: A Voyage in the Milky Way*. New York: R & S Books.

Lankford, M. D. (1991). *Is It Dark? Is It Light?* Ill. by Stacey Schuett. New York: Knopf.

Livingston, M. C. (1988). *Space Songs*. Ill. by Leonard Everett Fisher. New York: Holiday House.

Muirden, J. (1987). *Going to the Moon*. Ill. by Nigel Code. New York: Random House.

Ormerod, J. (1982). *Moonlight*. New York: Lothrop.

Pfister, M. (1990). *Sun and Moon*. New York: North-South Books.

Rosen, S. (1992). *How Far Is a Star?* Ill. by Dean Lindberg. Minneapolis: Carolrhoda.

Rosen, S. (1992). *Where Does the Moon Go?* Ill. by Dean Lindberg. Minneapolis: Carolrhoda.

Simon, S. (1984). *The Moon*. New York: Macmillan.

Simon, S. (1992). *Our Solar System*. New York: Morrow.

Stein, R. C. (1985). *The Story of Apollo 11*. Chicago: Childrens Press.

Stevenson, R. L. (1984). *The Moon*. Ill. by Denise Saldutti. New York: Harper.

Sullivan, G. (1990). *The Day We Walked on the Moon*. New York: Scholastic.

Willard, N. (1983). *The Nightgown of the Sullen Moon*. San Diego: Harcourt Brace Jovanovich.

Poetry:

"The Moon Was but Chin of Gold" in: Ackerman, K. (1990). *Emily Dickinson: A Brighter Garden*. Ill. by Tasha Tudor. New York: Philomel. (page 20)

"Moon-Come-Out" by Eleanor Farjeon, "Full Moon" by Odette Thomas, "I Talk with the Moon" in: Bennet, J. (1991). *A Cup of Starshine*. Ill. by Graham Percy. San Diego: Har-court Brace Jovanovich. (pages 10, 22, 47)

"The Morning Moon" in:
Morrison, L. (1992). *Whistling the Morning In*. Ill. by Joel Cook. Honesdale, PA: Wordsong. (pages 26–27)

"A Path to the Moon" by Nichol in: Booth, D. (1990). *'Tis All the Stars Have Fallen*. Ill. by Kady MacDonald Denton. New York: Viking. (page 21)

"I See the Moon," "Moon Boat" by Charlotte Pomerantz, and "Moon-Come-Out" by Eleanor Farjeon in: Prelutksy, J. (1986). *Read-Aloud Rhymes for the Very Young*. Ill. by Marc Brown. New York: Knopf. (page 71)

Activities for Extension:

1. Keep a class journal or diary of the phases of the moon.

2. "One small step for man, one giant leap for mankind." This sentence was uttered by Neil Armstrong upon first stepping on the moon. Discuss with students what they might have said and chart their ideas.

3. Discuss: Besides a flag, what would you leave on the moon that is indicative of your culture?

4. Ask students to design a house that would exist on the moon. How would it be similar and different from houses on earth?

5. Help students make paper plate puppets of the moon and the sun. Use the puppets to retell *Sun and Moon* (Pfister, 1990).

J·U·L·Y 23

■ Date: July 23

■ This date is special because:
It is the day the ice cream cone was invented.

Books that relate to this date

■ Picture Books:

Cobb, V. (1985). *The Scoop on Ice Cream*. Ill. by Brian Karas. Boston: Little, Brown.

Hall, C. V. (1976). *I Love Ice Cream*. Garden City, NY: Doubleday.

Jaspersohn, W. (1988). *Ice Cream*. New York: Macmillan.

Krensky, S. (1986). *Scoop after Scoop: A History of Ice Cream*. Ill. by Richard Rosenblum. New York: Atheneum.

Mitgutsch, A. (1981). *From Milk to Ice Cream*. Minneapolis: Carolrhoda.

Modell, F. (1988). *Ice Cream Soup*. New York: Greenwillow.

Reece, C. (1985). *What Was It Before It Was Ice Cream?* Ill. by Lois Axwman. New York: Child's World.

Turner, D. (1988). *Milk*. Ill. by John Yates. Minneapolis: Carolrhoda.

■ Novel:

Hurwitz, J. (1981). *Aldo Ice Cream*. Ill. by John Wallner. New York: Morrow.

■ Poetry:

"Doing a Good Deed" in:
Ciardi, J. (1985). *Doodle Soup*. Boston: Houghton Mifflin. (page 24)

"Ice Cream" by Valerie Worth in:
Moore, L. (1992). *Sunflakes: Poems for Children*. Ill. by Jan Ormerod. New York: Clarion. (page 25)

"On a Trip Through Yellowstone" in:
Kennedy, X. J. (1990). *Fresh Brats*. Ill. by James Watts. New York: McElderry. (page 30)

"Special Flavor" in:
Kennedy, X. J. (1989). *Ghastlies, Goops & Pincushions*. Ill. by Ron Barrett. New York: McElderry. (page 10)

"A Vote for Vanilla" in:
Merriam, E. (1992). *The Singing Green*. Ill. by Kathleen Collins Howell. New York: Morrow. (page 4)

"Bleezer's Ice Cream" in:
Prelutsky, J. (1984). *The New Kid on the Block*. Ill. by James Stevenson. New York: Greenwillow. (pages 48–49)

"Eighteen Flavors" in:
Silverstein, S. (1974). *Where the Sidewalk Ends*. New York: Harper & Row. (page 116)

1. Ask students to vote on their favorite ice-cream. Graph the results.

2. Invite students to make ice-cream using the recipe in *The Scoop on Ice Cream* (Cobb, 1985).

3. Challenge students to invent new flavors of ice cream. Ask them to name and illustrate their "inventions."

4. Plan a field trip to a neighborhood ice-cream parlor. Then ask students to write about the trip. If there isn't a parlor nearby, ask students to imagine a visit instead.

5. Write patterned poetry about ice cream, following this pattern:

I Like Ice Cream
I like ice cream.
Cold ice cream. (adj.)
Sweet ice cream. (adj.)
Chocolate ice cream. (adj.)
Vanilla ice cream. (adj.)
Any kind of ice cream.
I like ice cream.
Ice cream *in a box.* (prep. phrase)
Ice cream *in a cup.* (prep. phrase)
Ice cream *in a cone.* (prep. phrase)
Ice cream *in my mouth.* (prep. phrase)
I like ice cream!
Smooth ice cream (adj.)
Tasty ice cream (adj.)
Creamy ice cream (adj.)
Wonderful ice cream (adj.)
Glorious ice cream (adj.)
Icy ice cream (adj.)
I like ice cream! (adj.)

J·U·L·Y 24

■ Date: July 24

■ This date is special because:
It is Amelia Earhart's birthday (1898).

Books that relate to this date

■ Picture Books:

Bendick, J. (1992). *Eureka! It's an Airplane!* Ill. by Sal Murdocca. Brookfield, CT: Millbrook.

Blau, M. (1983). *Whatever Happened to Amelia Earhart?* New York: Raintree.

Boyne, W. J. (1988). *The Smithsonian Book of Flight for Young People.* New York: Macmillan.

Brown, D. (1993). *Ruth Law Thrills a Nation.* New York: Ticknor & Fields.

Brown, F. G. (1985). *Amelia Earhart Takes Off.* Ill. by Lydia Halverson. New York: Whitman.

Bursik, R. (1992). *Amelia's Fantastic Flight.* New York: Holt.

Chadwick, R. (1987). *Aviation.* Minneapolis: Lerner.

Crews, D. (1986). *Flying.* New York: Greenwillow.

Florian, D. (1984). *Airplane Ride.* New York: Harper.

Hockman, H. (1992). *What's Inside Planes?* New York: Dorling Kindersley.

Hughes, S. (1986). *Up and Up.* New York: Lothrop.

Jeunesse, G. (1989). *Airplanes and Flying Machines.* Ill. by Donald Grant. New York: Scholastic.

Martin, A. M. (1991). *Karen's Plane Trip.* New York: Scholastic.

McPhail, D. (1987). *First Flight.* Boston: Little, Brown.

Quackenbush, R. (1990). *Clear the Cow Pasture, I'm Coming.* New York: Simon & Schuster.

Ross, P. and Ross, J. (1981). *Your First Airplane Trip.* Ill. by Lynn Wheeling. New York: Lothrop.

Stewart, F. T. and Stewart, C. P. (1987). *Flight.* Ill. by George S. Gaadt. New York: Harper.

Wade, M. D. (1992). *Amelia Earhart: Flying for Adventure.* Brookfield, CT: Millbrook.

Woodruff, E. (1991). *The Wing Shop.* Ill. by Stephen Gammell. New York: Holiday House.

■ Novels:

Lauber, P. (1988). *Lost Star: The Story of Amelia Earhart.* New York: Scholastic.

Parlin, J. (1989). *Amelia Earhart.* New York: Bantam.

Randolph, B. (1987). *Amelia Earhart.* New York: Watts.

■ Poetry:

Livingston, M. C. (1989). *Up in the Air.* Ill. by Leonard Everett Fisher. New York: Holiday House.

"Flight Plan" by Jane Merchant in: Prelutsky, J. (1983). *Random House Book of Poetry for Children*. Ill. by Arnold Lobel. New York: Random House. (page 223)

Siebert, D. (1993). *Plane Song*. Ill. by Vincent Nasta. New York: HarperCollins.

"I Can Fly" by Felice Holman and "Up in the Air" by James S. Tippett in: Wolman, B. (1992). *Taking Turns*. Ill. by Catherine Stock. New York: Atheneum. (pages 22, 23)

Activities for Extension:

1. Challenge students to write their own endings to the Amelia Earhart story and tell what they think happened to her.

2. Ask students to plot on a map the course of Amelia Earhart's last flight. How far did she fly?

3. Invite a pilot to talk about flying.

4. Visit a nearby airport or airfield.

5. Contact the Ninety-Nines, an organization of women pilots, and get information about the organization. Write to:

> The Ninety Nines, Inc.
> P.O. Box 59965
> Oklahoma City, OK 73159

J·U·L·Y 30

■ **Date:** July 30

■ **This date is special because:**
It is Henry Ford's birthday.

Books that relate to this date

■ **Picture Books:**

Aird, H. B. and Ruddiman, C. (1986). *Henry Ford: Young Man with Ideas*. Ill. by Wallace Wood. New York: Macmillan.

Bendick, J. (1992). *Eureka: It's an Automobile*. Ill. by Sal Mardocca. Brookfield, CT: Millbrook.

Cole, J. (1983). *Cars and How They Go*. Ill. by Gail Gibbons. New York: Harper.

Demarest, C. L. (1992). *My Little Red Car*. Honesdale, PA: Boyds Mills Press.

Denslow, S. P. (1991). *Riding with Aunt Lucy*. Ill. by Nancy Carpenter. New York: Bradbury.

Kent, Z. (1990). *The Story of Henry Ford and the Automobile*. Chicago: Children's Press.

Mitchell, B. (1986). *We'll Race You Henry: A Story About Henry Ford*. Ill. by Kathy Haubrich. Minneapolis: Carolrhoda.

Newton, L. P. (1987). *William the Vehicle King*. Ill. by Jacqueline Rogers. New York: Bradbury.

Osborne, V. (1988). *Rex, the Most Special Car in the World*. Ill. by Scoular Anderson. Minneapolis: Carolrhoda.

Oxenbury, H. (1983). *The Car Trip*. New York: Dial.

Rockwell, A. (1984). *Cars*. New York: Dutton.

Royston, A. (1993). *The A-To-Z Book of Cars*. Ill. by Terry Pastor. New York: Scholastic.

Sutton, R. (1990). *Eyewitness Books: Cars*. New York: Knopf.

■ **Poetry:**

Livingston, M. C. (1993). *Roll Along: Poems on Wheels*. New York: McElderry. (pages 47-48)

Activities for Extension:

1. Take a class survey of kinds of cars driven by family members. Chart the results in a picture graph.

2. Ask students to make cars out of recycled materials: milk cartons, shoe boxes, paper towel tubes, and so on. Decorate and have a car show.

■ **Date:** Any day in August

■ **This month is special because:** It is National Vacation Month.

Books that relate to this month:

■ Picture Books:

Ahlberg, A. (1992). *Skeleton Crew*. Ill. by Andre Amstutz. New York: Greenwillow.

Baker, L. (1990). *Morning Beach*. Boston: Little, Brown.

Brandenberg, F. (1991). *A Fun Weekend*. Ill. by Alexa Brandenberg. New York: Greenwillow.

Brisson, P. (1990). *Kate Heads West*. Ill. by Rick Brown. New York: Bradbury.

Brisson, P. (1992). *Kate on the Coast*. Ill. by Rick Brown. New York: Bradbury.

Brisson, P. (1989). *Your Best Friend, Kate*. Ill. by Rick Brown. New York: Bradbury.

Brown, M. (1993). *Arthur's Family Vacation*. Boston: Little, Brown.

Brown, M. (1987). *Arthur's Vacation*. Boston: Little, Brown.

Brown, M. (1988). *Dinosaurs Travel*. Boston: Little, Brown.

Brown, R. (1987). *Our Puppy's Vacation*. New York: Potter.

Chall, M. W. (1992). *Up North at the Cabin*. Ill. by Steve Johnson. New York: Lothrop.

DeSaix, D. D. (1993). *In the Back Seat*. New York: Farrar Straus & Giroux.

Hest, A. (1989). *Travel Tips from Harry: A Guide to Family Vacations in the Sun*. Ill. by Sue Truesdell. New York: Morrow.

Khalsa, D. K. (1988). *My Family Vacation*. New York: Potter.

Krupp, R. R. (1992). *Let's Go Traveling*. New York: Morrow.

McPhail, D. (1987). *Emma's Vacation*. New York: Dutton.

Monfried, L. (1990). *The Daddies Boat*. Ill. by Michele Chessare. New York: Dutton.

Reiger, L. (1993). *Tomorrow on Rocky Pond*. New York: Greenwillow.

Rockwell, A. (1989). *On Our Vacation*. New York: Dutton.

Roffey, M. (1988). *I Spy on Vacation*. New York: Four Winds Press.

Rylant, C. (1985). *The Relatives Came*. Ill. by Stephen Gammell. New York: Bradbury.

Selway, M. (1992). *Don't Forget to Write*. Nashville: Ideas Children's Books.

Sheldon, D. (1993). *Harry on Vacation*. Ill. by Sue Heap. New York: Candlewick.

Simont, M. (1989). *The Lovely Summer*. New York: Bantam Doubleday.

Stevenson, J. (1988). *The Worst Person in the World at Crab Beach*. New York: Greenwillow.

Van Allsburg, C. (1991). *The Wretched Stone*. Boston: Houghton Mifflin.

Williams, V. (1988). *Stringbean's Trip to the Shining Sea*. Ill. by Jennifer Williams. New York: Greenwillow.

Yolen, J. (1993). *On Vacation*. Photos by Tana Hoban. New York: Greenwillow.

Zolotow, C. (1993). *The Moon Was the Best*. Photos by Tana Hoban. New York: Greenwillow.

■ **Poetry:**

"Vacation" in:
Hoberman, M. A. (1991) *Fathers, Mothers, Sisters, Brothers: A Collection of Family Poems*. Ill. by Maryln Hafner. Boston: Little, Brown. (pages 28–29)

"Traveling" in:
Merriam, E. (1992). *The Singing Green*. Ill. by Kathleen Collins Howell. New York: Morrow. (pages 30–31)

 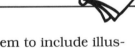

Activities for Extension:

1. Invite students to write about their dream vacations. Ask them to include illustrations and souvenirs they would purchase on this trip.

2. Using travel brochures, plan a trip with a given budget limit.

3. Take a field trip to a travel agency. Ask students to write about it.

4. Ask students to bring postcards from their homes. Mark the different locations on a map. Give out awards for the farthest location, most exotic location, closest to the equator, etc. Encourage students to research their location or design their own postcard.

A·U·G·U·S·T 1

■ **Date:** August 1

■ **This date is special because:**
It is Gail Gibbon's birthday (1944).

Books that relate to this date
■ **Picture Books:**

Gibbons, G. (1990). *Beacons of Light: Lighthouses*. New York: Morrow.

Gibbons, G. (1983). *Boat Book*. New York: Holiday.

Gibbons, G. (1989). *Catch the Wind!: All about Kites*. Boston: Little, Brown.

Gibbons, G. (1985). *Check it Out! The Book about Libraries*. San Diego: Harcourt Brace Jovanovich.

Gibbons, G. (1982). *Christmas Time*. New York: Holiday.

Gibbons, G. (1979). *Clocks and How They Go*. New York: Crowell.

Gibbons, G. (1987). *Deadline! From News to Newspaper*. New York: Crowell.

Gibbons, G. (1984). *Department Store*. New York: Crowell.

Gibbons, G. (1987). *Dinosaurs*. New York: Holiday.

Gibbons, G. (1989). *Easter*. New York: Holiday.

Gibbons, G. (1988). *Farming*. New York: Holiday.

Gibbons, G. (1985). *Fill It Up! All about Service Stations*. New York: Crowell.

Gibbons, G. (1984). *Fire! Fire!* New York: Crowell.

Gibbons, G. (1986). *From Path to Highway: The Story of the Boston Post Road*. New York: Crowell.

Gibbons, G. (1991). *From Seed to Plant*. New York: Holiday.

Gibbons, G. (1992). *The Great St. Lawrence Seaway*. New York: Morrow.

Gibbons, G. (1984). *Halloween*. New York: Holiday.

Gibbons, G. (1986). *Happy Birthday!* New York: Holiday.

Gibbons, G. (1990). *How a House Is Built*. New York: Holiday.

Gibbons, G. (1985). *Lights! Camera! Action! How a Movie Is Made*. New York: Crowell.

Gibbons, G. (1980). *Locks and Keys*. New York: Crowell.

Gibbons, G. (1989). *Marge's Diner*. New York: Crowell.

Gibbons, G. (1985). *The Milk Makers*. New York: Macmillan.

Gibbons, G. (1989). *Monarch Butterfly*. New York: Holiday.

Gibbons, G. (1983). *New Road!* New York: Crowell.

Gibbons, G. (1983). *Paper, Paper Everywhere*. San Diego: Harcourt Brace Jovanovich.

Gibbons, G. (1985). *Playgrounds*. New York: Holiday.

Gibbons, G. (1982). *The Post Office Book: Mail and How It Moves*. New York: Crowell.

Gibbons, G. (1991). *The Puffins Are Back!* New York: HarperCollins.

Gibbons, G. (1984). *The Seasons of Arnold's Apple Tree.* San Diego: Harcourt Brace Jovanovich.

Gibbons, G. (1992). *Sharks!* New York: Holiday.

Gibbons, G. (1983). *Sun Up, Sun Down.* San Diego: Harcourt Brace Jovanovich.

Gibbons, G. (1988). *Sunken Treasure.* New York: Crowell.

Gibbons, G. (1991). *Surrounded by Sea: Life on a New England Fishing Island.* Boston: Little, Brown.

Gibbons, G. (1983). *Thanksgiving Day.* New York: Holiday.

Gibbons, G. (1976). *Things to Make and Do for Halloween.* New York: Watts.

Gibbons, G. (1987). *The Pottery Place.* San Diego: Harcourt Brace Jovanovich.

Gibbons, G. (1982). *Tool Book.* New York: Holiday.

Gibbons, G. (1987). *Trains.* New York: Holiday.

Gibbons, G. (1981). *Trucks.* New York: Crowell.

Gibbons, G. (1984). *Tunnels.* New York: Holiday.

Gibbons, G. (1986). *Up Goes the Skyscraper!* New York: Four Winds.

Gibbons, G. (1986). *Valentine's Day.* New York: Holiday.

Gibbons, G. (1987). *Weather Forecasting.* New York: Four Winds.

Gibbons, G. (1990). *Weather Words and What They Mean.* New York: Holiday.

Gibbons, G. (1991). *Whales.* New York: Holiday.

Gibbons, G. (1987). *Zoo.* New York: Crowell.

Activities for Extension:

1. Challenge students to create informational books of their own. Encourage them to choose topics of interest for other students.

2. Using *Check it Out* (Gibbons, 1985), visit the library and take a tour.

3. Using *Farming* (Gibbons, 1988), visit a local farm.

4. Using *Department Store* (Gibbons, 1984), visit a local store.

5. Ask students to vote on their favorite Gail Gibbon's book. Graph the results.

A·U·G·U·S·T 9

■ Date: August 9

■ This date is special because:
It is Jose Aruego's birthday.

Books that relate to this date
■ Picture Books:

Aruego, J. and Dewey, A. (1988). *Rocka-bye Crocodile*. New York: Greenwillow.

Aruego, J. and Dewey, A. (1981). *Marie Louise and Christophe at the Carnival*. New York: Scribner.

Dragonwagon, C. (1987). *Alligators Arrived with Apples*. Ill. by Jose Aruego and Ariane Dewey. New York: Macmillan.

Ginsburg, M. (1992). *Merry-go-round: Four Stories*. Ill. by Jose Aruego and Ariane Dewey. New York: Greenwillow.

Ginsburg, M. (1981.) *Where Does the Sun Go at Night?* Ill. by Jose Aruego and Ariane Dewey. New York: Greenwillow.

Kraus, R. (1980). *Another Mouse to Feed*. Ill. by Jose Aruego and Ariane Dewey. New York: Windmill/Wanderer Books.

Kraus, R. (1987). *Come Out and Play, Little Mouse*. Ill. by Jose Aruego and Ariane Dewey. New York: Greenwillow.

Kraus, R. (1990). *Musical Max*. Ill. by Jose Aruego and Ariane Dewey. New York: Simon & Schuster.

Pomerantz, C. (1984). *One Duck, Another Duck*. Ill. by Jose Aruego and Ariane Dewey. New York: Greenwillow.

Raffi. (1989). *Five Little Ducks*. Ill. by Jose Aruego and Ariane Dewey. New York: Crown.

Shannon, George. (1982). *Dance Away!* Ill. by Jose Aruego and Ariane Dewey. New York: Greenwillow.

Shannon, George. (1981). *Lizard's Song*. Ill. by Jose Aruego and Ariane Dewey. New York: Greenwillow.

Shannon, G. (1983). *The Surprise*. Ill. by Jose Aruego and Ariane Dewey. New York: Greenwillow.

Sharmat, M. W. (1978). *Mitchell Is Moving*. Ill. by Jose Aruego and Ariane Dewey. New York: Macmillan.

Sharmat, M. (1980). *Gregory, the Terrible Eater*. Ill. by Jose Aruego and Ariane Dewey. New York: Four Winds.

Winter, F. H. (1988). *Filipinos in America*. Minneapolis: Lerner.

 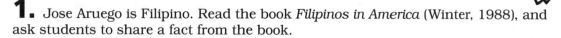

Activities for Extension:

1. Jose Aruego is Filipino. Read the book *Filipinos in America* (Winter, 1988), and ask students to share a fact from the book.

2. Ask children to create their own patterned language books using *Alligators Arrived with Apples* (Dragonwagon, 1987).

A·U·G·U·S·T 13

■ Date: August 13

■ This date is special because:

It is Annie Oakley's birthday (1860).

Books that relate to this date

■ Picture Books:

Gerrard, Roy. (1989). *Rosie and the Rustlers*. New York: Farrar, Straus & Giroux.

Guthrie, M. M. (1992). *Woody's 20 Grow Big Songs*. Ill. by Woody Guthrie. New York: HarperCollins.

Johston, T. (1993). *The Cowboy and the Black-Eyed Pea*. Ill. by Warren Ludwig. New York: Putnam.

Khalsa, D. K. (1990). *Cowboy Dreams*. New York: Potter.

Kimmel, E. A. (1989). *Charlie Drives the Stage*. Ill. by Glen Rounds. New York: Holiday.

Landau, E. (1990). *Cowboys*. New York: Watts.

Nixon, J. L. (1980). *If You Say So, Claude*. Ill. by Lorinda Bryan Cauley. New York: Warne.

McGregor, M. (1992). *Cowgirl*. New York: Walker.

Purdy, C. (1985). *Iva Dunnit and the Big Wind*. Ill. by Steven Kellogg. New York: Dial.

San Souci, R. D. (1993). *Cut from the Same Cloth: American Women of Myth, Legend, and Tall Tale*. Ill. by Brian Pinkney. New York: Philomel.

Scott, A. H. (1993). *A Brand Is Forever*. Ill. by Ronald Himler. New York: Clarion.

Tinkelman, M. (1984). *Cowgirl*. New York: Greenwillow.

Turner, A. (1985). *Dakota Dugout*. Ill. by Ronald Himler. New York: Macmillan.

Quackenbush, R. (1988). *Who's That Girl with the Gun? A Story of Annie Oakley*. Englewood Cliffs, NJ: Prentice-Hall.

Wolf, B. (1985). *Cowboy*. New York: Morrow.

■ Poetry:

Gerrard, R. (1989). *Rosie and the Rustlers*. New York: Sunburst.

Hopkins, L. B. (1972). *Girls Can Too! A Book of Poems*. Ill. by Emily McCully. New York: Watts.

1. Encourage students to read *Who's That Girl with the Gun? A Story of Annie Oakley* and create a time line of Annie Oakley's life.

2. Encourage students to make pretend horses out of wrapping paper tubes. Then ask them to decorate their horses, and have a parade.

3. Using *Iva Dunnit and the Big Wind* (Purdy, 1985), ask students to listen for Old West terms and list them. Chart the Old West terms, contrasting them with modern day usage.

4. Using *Cowboy Dreams* (Khalsa, 1990), share with the class Old West music mentioned in the book.

5. Ask students to illustrate one of the songs from activity 4.

AUGUST 19

■ **Date:** August 19

■ **This date is special because:**
It is National Aviation Day.

Observed annually on Orville Wright's birthday (1871).

Books that relate to this date

■ **Picture Books:**

Berliner, D. (1990). *Before the Wright Brothers*. New York: Lerner.

Boyne, W. J. (1988). *The Smithsonian Book of Flight for Young People*. New York: Macmillan.

Browne, E. (1993). *No Problem*. Ill. by David Parkins. Cambridge, MA: Candlewick.

Burleigh, R. (1991). *Flight*. Ill. by Mike Wimmer. New York: Putnam.

Churchill, E. R. (1988). *Instant Paper Airplanes*. Ill. by James Michaels. New York: Sterling.

Freedman, R. (1991). *The Wright Brothers: How They Invented the Airplane*. Photos by Wilbur & Orville Wright. New York: Scholastic.

Hook, J. (1989). *The Wright Brothers*. Ill. by Peter Lowe. New York: Bookwright.

Jaspersohn, W. (1991). *A Week in the Life of an Airline Pilot*. Boston: Little, Brown.

Jefferis, D. (1987). *Epic Flights*. Ill. by Ron Jobson and Michael Roffe. New York: Watts.

Jefferis, D. (1988). *The First Flyers*. Ill. by Ron Jobson and Michael Roffe. New York: Watts.

Jeunesse, G. (1992). *Airplanes and Flying Machines*. Ill. by Donald Grant. New York: Cartwheel.

Magee, D. and Newman, R. (1992). *Let's Fly from A to Z*. New York: Cobblehill.

Marquardt, M. (1989). *Wilbur and Orville and the Flying Machine*. Ill. by Mike Eagle. Milwaukee: Raintree.

Maurer, R. (1990). *Airborne, the Search for the Secret of Flight*. New York: Simon & Schuster with WGBH.

Nahum, A. (1990). *Flying Machine*. New York: Knopf.

Parlin, J. (1989). *Amelia Earhart*. New York: Bantam Doubleday Dell.

Paulsen, G. (1988). *Full of Hot Air*. New York: Bantam Doubleday Dell.

Radford, D. (1991). *Harry at the Airport*. New York: Macmillan.

Taylor, R. L. (1990). *The First Flight: The Story of the Wright Brothers*. New York: Watts.

Yang, T. (1992). *Exotic Paper Airplanes*. Fort Bragg, CA: Cypress House.

Zisfein, M. B. (1981). *Flight: A Panorama of Aviation*. Ill. by Robert A. Parker. New York: Pantheon.

■ **Novels:**

Byars, B. (1987). *Coast to Coast*. New York: Bantam Doubleday Dell.

■ Poetry:

"Jet Planes at Night" in:
Morrison, L. (1992). *Whistling the Morning In*. Ill. by Joel Cook. Honesdale, PA: Wordsong. (page 31)

Aviation poems in:
Prelutsky, J. (1983). *The Random House Book of Poetry for Children*. Ill. by Arnold Lobel. New York: Random House. (pages 223–224)

Siebert, D. (1993). *Plane Song*. Ill. by Vincent Nasta. New York: HarperCollins.

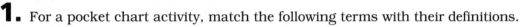

Activities for Extension:

1. For a pocket chart activity, match the following terms with their definitions.

Cabin—has seats for the passengers

Elevators—on the tail; pilot moves them up or down to make the plane go up or down.

Fuselage—central body of the plane.

Flaps (on the wing)—give the plane lift, used on take-off and landing

Galley—place where meals are prepared on the plane

Hold—the baggage and cargo compartment under the passenger cabin

Hangar—garage for airplanes

Kerosene—fuel for jet plane

Nose—front of the airplane

2. Ask students to brainstorm famous brothers in history.

3. Help students find Kitty Hawk, N. C. on the map. You might want to share a picture of this location with the class.

4. Using the book *Instant Paper Airplanes* (Churchill, 1988), students can create their own paper airplanes, decorate the planes, and have a distance fair.

5. Invite students to create flying machines from scrap materials in the classroom or at home. Do they fly? Why or why not? Discuss.

A·U·G·U·S·T 29

■ **Date:** August 29

■ **This date is special because:**
Chop Suey was invented on this day.

Books that relate to this date
■ **Picture Books:**

Hassall, N. (1992). *The Heavenly Horse.* Ill. by Maureen Hyde. New York: Green Tiger.

Louie, Ai-Ling. (1982). *Yeh Shen: A Cinderella Story from China.* Ill. by Ed Young. New York: Philomel.

Tan, A. (1992). *The Moon Lady.* Ill. by Gretchen Schields. New York: Macmillan.

Waters, K. and Slovenz-Low, M. (1990). *Lion Dancer: Ernie Wan's Chinese New Year.* Photos by Martha Cooper. New York: Scholastic.

Winget, M., (Ed.). (1992). *Vegetarian Cooking Around the World.* Photos by Robert L. Wolfe and Diane Wolfe. Minneapolis: Lerner .

Wyndham, R. (1968). *Chinese Mother Goose Rhymes.* Ill. by Ed Young. New York: World Pub. Co.

Young, E. (1980). *High on a Hill: A Book of Chinese Riddles.* New York: Collins.

Young, E. (1989). *Lon Po Po: A Red Riding Hood Story from China.* New York: Philomel.

Young, E. (1978). *The Terrible Nung Gwama: A Chinese Folktale.* New York: Collins & World.

■ **Novel:**

Kline, S. (1990). *Orp and the Chop Suey Burgers.* New York: Putnam.

 **Activities for Extension:**

1. Visit a Chinese restaurant. Ask students to pay close attention to eating utensils, decor, etc.

2. Make Chop Suey in the classroom. Have a taste test.

3. Invite students to create their own recipe for Chop Suey as Orp does in the novel, *Orp and the Chop Suey Burgers* (Kline, 1990).

4. Bring in other Chinese vegetables (water chestnuts, bamboo shoots, corn spears, bean sprouts, etc.). Invite students to taste and write about them.

A·U·G·U·S·T 30

■ Date: August 30

■ This date is special because:
It is Donald Crews' birthday (1938).

Books that relate to this date

■ Picture Books:

Branley, F. M. (1988) *Eclipse: Darkness in Daytime*. Ill. by Donald Crews. New York: Crowell.

Crews, D. (1985). *Bicycle Race*. New York: Greenwillow.

Crews, D. (1991). *Big Mama's*. New York: Greenwillow.

Crews, D. (1982). *Carousel*. New York: Greenwillow.

Crews, D. (1986). *Flying*. New York: Greenwillow.

Crews, D. (1978). *Freight Train*. New York: Greenwillow.

Crews, D. (1982). *Harbor*. New York: Greenwillow.

Crews, D. (1981). *Light*. New York: Greenwillow.

Crews, D. (1983). *Parade*. New York: Greenwillow.

Crews, D. (1984). *School Bus*. New York: Greenwillow.

Crews, D. (1992). *Shortcut*. New York: Greenwillow.

Crews, D. (1986). *Ten Black Dots*. New York: Greenwillow.

Crews, D. (1980). *Truck*. New York: Greenwillow.

Crews, D. (1967). *We Read: A to Z*. New York: Harper & Row/Greenwillow.

Dennis, J. R. (1971). *Fractions Are Parts of Things*. Ill. by Donald Crews. New York: Crowell.

Giganti, P. (1992). *Each Orange Had Eight Slices: A Counting Book*. Ill. by Donald Crews. New York: Greenwillow.

Giganti, P. (1988). *How Many Snails? A Counting Book*. Ill. by Donald Crews. New York: Greenwillow.

Jonas, A. (1983). *Round Trip*. New York: Greenwillow.

Jonas, A. (1987). *Reflections*. New York: Greenwillow.

Jonas, A. (1985). *The Trek*. New York: Greenwillow.

Kalan, R. (1979). *Blue Sea*. Ill. by Donald Crews. New York: Greenwillow.

Kalan, R. (1978). *Rain*. Ill. by Donald Crews. New York: Greenwillow.

■ Resource Book:

Kovacs, D. and Preller, J. (1991). *Meet The Authors and Illustrators: 60 Creators of Favorite Children's Books Talk about Their Work*. New York: Scholastic. (pages 24–25).(Includes an interview with Donald Crews.)

1. Ask students to make a concept book using Donald Crews' books as examples.

2. Donald Crews is married to Ann Jonas. Read some of her books (which are included in the book list) and look for Donald in the illustrations. (You'll find him in *The Trek*.)

3. Help students find Donald Crews in his own illustrations.

4. Donald Crews hides the date that he wrote the book in his illustrations. Find this date in each of his books.

5. Ask students to illustrate a new book, "Car," using the format Crews uses in his other transportation books.

■ **Date:** Any day in September

■ **This month is special because:** It is Back to School Month.

Books that relate to this month
■ **Picture Books:**

Adler, D. A. (1989). *A Teacher on Roller Skates and Other School Riddles*. Ill. by John Wallner. New York: Holiday House.

Ahlberg, A. (1987). *The Cinderella Show*. Ill. by Janet Ahlberg. New York: Viking.

Ahlberg, A. (1988). *Starting School*. Ill. by Janet Ahlberg. New York: Viking.

Alexander, M. (1989). *Move Over, Twerp*. New York: Dial.

Bellow, C. (1990). *Toad School*. New York: Macmillan.

Brown, M. (1989). *Arthur's Teacher Trouble*. Boston: Little, Brown.

Bourgeois, P. (1990). *Too Many Chickens*. Ill. by Bill Slavin. Boston: Little, Brown.

Calmenson, S. (1989). *The Principal's New Clothes*. Ill. by Denise Brunkus. New York: Scholastic.

Carlson, N. (1992). *Arnie and the New Kid*. New York: Puffin.

Cazet, D. (1992). *Are There Any Questions?* New York: Orchard.

Cazet, D. (1990). *Never Spit on Your Shoes*. New York: Orchard.

Cohen, M. (1980). *First Grade Takes a Test*. Ill. by Lillian Hoban. New York: Greenwillow.

Cohen, M. (1980). *No Good in Art*. Ill. by Lillian Hoban. New York: Greenwillow.

Cohen, M. (1989). *See You in Second Grade*. Ill. by Lillian Hoban. New York: Greenwillow.

Delacre, L. (1989). *Time for School, Nathan*. New York: Scholastic.

Denton, T. (1990). *The School for Laughter*. Boston: Houghton Mifflin.

Hatchett, R. (1988). *The One-Room School at Squabble Hollow*. New York: Four Winds.

Hoffman, P. (1991). *Meatball*. Ill. by Emily Arnold McCully. New York: HarperCollins.

Keller, H. (1991). *The New Boy*. New York: Greenwillow.

Kuklin, S. (1990). *Going to My Nursery School*. New York: Macmillan.

MacLachlan, P. (1991). *Three Names*. Ill. by Alexander Pertzoff. New York: Harper.

Martin, A. (1992). Rachel Parker, *Kindergarten Show-Off*. Ill. by Nancy Poydar. New York: Holiday House.

McMillan, B. (1993). *Mouse Views: What the Class Pet Saw*. New York: Holiday House.

McMillan, B. (1991). *Play Day*. New York: Holiday House.

Miller, M. B. and Ancona, G. (1991). *Handtalk School*. New York: Four Winds.

O'Donnell, P. (1993). *Carnegie's Excuse*. New York: Scholastic.

Oppenheim, J. (1983). *Mrs. Peloki's Class Play*. New York: Putnam.

Pinkwater, D. (1993). *Author's Day*. New York: Macmillan.

Pulver, R. (1991). *Mrs. Toggle and the Dinosaur*. Ill. by R. W. Alley. New York: Macmillan.

Pulver, R. (1990). *Mrs. Toggle's Zipper*. Ill. by R. W. Alley. New York: Macmillan.

Pulver, R. (1992). *Nobody's Mother Is in the 2nd Grade*. Ill. by G. Brian. New York: Dial.

Schwartz, A. (1988). *Annabelle Swift, Kindergartner*. New York: Orchard.

Van Leeuwen, J. (1990). *Oliver Pig at School*. New York: Dial.

Wells, R. (1983). *Timothy Goes to School*. New York: Puffin.

Zimelman, N. (1987). *Please Excuse Jaspar*. Nashville: Abingdon.

Novels:

Gilson, J. (1991). *Itchy Richard*. Ill. by Diane DeGroat. Boston: Houghton Mifflin.

Greenwald, S. (1988). *Write On, Roxy!* Boston: Little, Brown.

Kline, S. (1990). *Horrible Harry in Room 2B*. Ill. by Frank Remkiewicz. New York: Puffin.

Kline, S. (1992). *Horrible Harry's Secret*. Ill. by Frank Remkiewicz. New York: Puffin.

Lawlor, L. (1988). *How to Survive 3rd Grade*. Ill. by Abby Levine. New York: Whitman.

Shreve, S. (1984). *The Flunking of Joshua T. Bates*. Ill. by Diane DeGroat. New York: Knopf.

Poetry:

Baer, E. (1990). *This Is the Way We Go to School*. Ill. by Steve Bjorkman. New York: Scholastic.

Dakos, K. (1990). *If You're Not Here, Please Raise Your Hand: Poems About School*. Ill. by G. Brian Karas. New York: Macmillan.

Dakos, K. (1993). *Don't Read This Book, Whatever You Do! More Poems about School*. Ill. by G. Brian Karas. New York: Macmillan.

Hennessy, B. G. (1990). *School Days*. Ill. by Tracey Campbell Pearson. New York: Viking.

"Last Day of School" in Hubbel, P. (1988). *The Tigers Brought Pink Lemonade*. Ill. by Ju-Hong Chen. New York: Atheneum. (page 5)

"September Is" by Bobbi Katz and "Lunchbox" by Valerie Worth in: Moore, L. (1992). *Sunflakes: Poems for Children*. Ill. by Jan Ormerod. New York: Clarion (page 74)

"Homework! Oh, Homework!" in: Prelutsky, J. (1984). *The New Kid on the Block*. Ill. by James Stevenson. New York: Greenwillow. (pages 54–55)

"Homework" by Russell Hoban and "Homework" by Jane Yolen in: Prelutsky, J. (1983). *Random House Book of Poetry for Children*. Ill. by Arnold Lobel. New York: Random House. (page 141)

"School Days" in: Zolotow, C. (1987). *Everything Glistens and Everything Sings*. Ill. by Margot Tomes. San Diego: Harcourt Brace Jovanovich. (page 9)

Activities for Extension:

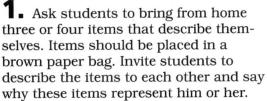

1. Ask students to bring from home three or four items that describe themselves. Items should be placed in a brown paper bag. Invite students to describe the items to each other and say why these items represent him or her.

2. Students can write and share three things about themselves. For example: I have a rock collection, I write plays in my spare time, I don't like chocolate. Who am I? Students might want to make a riddle game of this.

3. Ask students to make a collage describing themselves using pictures from magazines.

4. Encourage students to write bio poems, following this format:

Line 1: First name
Line 2: Son/Daughter of..., or Brother/Sister of...
Line 3: Who likes (*3 things they like*)
Line 4: Who fears (*3 things they fear*)
Line 5: Who would like to see (*3 things*)
Line 6: Resident of state, city, street
Line 7: Last name

For example:
    Jenny
    Sister of *Annie*
    Who likes *her family, brownies, and vacations*
    Who fears *spiders, small places, and big dogs*
    Who would like to see the *moon, Hawaii, and more of her grandparents*
    Resident of *Nebraska, Omaha, Pacific Street*
    Jones

L·A·B·O·R D·A·Y

Date: The first Monday in September

This date is special because:
It is Labor Day.

Books that relate to this date

Picture Books:

Carlson, N. (1991). *Take Time to Relax.* New York: Viking.

Edwards, M. (1991). *Chicken Man.* New York: Lothrop.

Grossman, P. (1991). *The Night Ones.* Ill. by Lydia Dabcovich. San Diego: Harcourt Brace Jovanovich.

Johnson, J. (1985). *Fire Fighters A to Z.* New York: Walker.

Johnson, J. (1988). *Librarians A to Z.* New York: Walker.

Johnson, J. (1988). *Police Officers A to Z.* New York: Walker.

Johnson, J. (1988). *Sanitation Workers A to Z.* New York: Walker.

Johnson, J. (1987). *Teachers A to Z.* New York: Walker.

Klein, N. (1973). *Girls Can Be Anything.* Ill. by Roy Doty. New York: Dutton.

Kunnas, M. (1985). *The Nighttime Book.* New York: Crown.

Merriam, E. (1991). *Daddies at Work.* New York: Simon & Schuster.

Merriam, E. (1991). *Mommies at Work.* New York: Simon & Schuster.

Rylant, C. (1989). *Mr. Griggs' Work.* Ill. by Julie Downing. New York: Orchard.

Schwartz, A. (1982). *Bea and Mr. Jones.* New York: Bradbury.

Shanahan, D. (1993). *Buckledown the Workhound.* Boston: Little, Brown.

Sharmat, M. W. (1990). *I'm Santa Claus and I'm Famous.* Ill. by Marylin Hafner. New York: Holiday House.

Shepard, S. (1991). *Elvis Hornbill, International Business Bird.* New York: Holt.

Simon, N. (1980). *I'm Busy Too.* Ill. by Dora Leder. Chicago: Whitman.

Singer, M. (1992). *Chester, the Out-Of-Work Dog.* Ill. by Cat Bowman Smith. New York: Holt.

Novels:

Goldreich, G. (1974). *What Can She Be? An Architect.* New York: Lothrop.

Goldreich, G. (1976). *What Can She Be? A Farmer.* New York: Lothrop.

Goldreich, G. (1977). *What Can She Be? A Film Producer.* New York: Lothrop.

Goldreich, G. (1973). *What Can She Be? A Lawyer.* New York: Lothrop.

Goldreich, G. (1975). *What Can She Be? A Musician.* New York: Lothrop.

Goldreich, G. (1981). *What Can She Be? A Scientist.* New York: Lothrop.

Goldreich, G. (1974). *What Can She Be? A Veterinarian.* New York: Lothrop.

Hoban, J. (1990). *Buzby.* Ill. by John Himmelman. New York: Harper & Row.

Kessler, E. (1990). *Stan and the Hot Dog Man*. New York: Harper & Row.

■ Poetry:

"A Young Farmer of Leeds" in: deRegniers, B. S., and others. (1988). *Sing a Song of Popcorn*. New York: Scholastic. (page 111)

Field, R. (1988). *General Store*. Ill. by Giles Laroche. Boston: Little, Brown.

"The Contrary Waiter" by Edgar Parker, "Waiters" by Mary Ann Hoberman, and "The Riveter" by Mabel Watts in: Prelutsky, J. (1983). *The Random House Book of Poetry for Children*. Ill. by Arnold Lobel. New York: Random House. (pages 90, 173, 195)

"The Barber of Shrubbery Hollow" in: Prelutsky, J. (1990). *Something BIG Has Been Here*. Ill. by James Stevenson. New York: Greenwillow. (page 128)

Activities for Extension:

1. Ask students to create alphabet books of careers of their choice. Use the Johnson books on page 130 as guides.

2. Invite adults to talk about their different occupations and educations.

3. Ask students to interview their parents or caregivers about their jobs. Share the report back with the class.

4. Encourage students to make a collage from magazine pictures depicting many occupations.

5. Challenge students to match the object to the career in a pocket chart activity.

Example:
Firefighter—Water hose
Chefs—Oven
Carpenter—Hammer
Barber—Scissors
Students can add others.

GRANDPARENT'S DAY

- **Date:** Sunday following Labor Day

- **This date is special because:**
It is Grandparent's Day.

Books that relate to this date

- **Picture Books:**

Ackerman, K. (1988). *Song and Dance Man*. Ill. by Stephen Gammell. New York: Knopf.

Blos, J. W. (1989). *The Grandpa Days*. Ill. by Emily Arnold McCully. New York: Simon & Schuster.

Bunting, E. (1989). *The Wednesday Surprise*. Ill. by Donald Carrick. New York: Clarion.

Butterworth, N. (1992). *My Grandma Is Wonderful*. New York: Candlewick.

Butterworth, N. (1992). *My Grandpa Is Amazing*. New York: Candlewick.

Carlson, N. (1993). *A Vist to Grandma's*. New York: Puffin.

Carlstrom, N. (1990). *Grandpappy*. Ill. by Laurel Molk. Boston: Little, Brown.

Caseley, J. (1991). *Dear Annie*. New York: Greenwillow.

Caseley, J. (1990). *Grandpa's Garden Lunch*. New York: Greenwillow.

Caseley, J. (1986). *When Grandpa Came to Stay*. New York: Greenwillow.

Crews, D. (1991). *Big Mama's*. New York: Greenwillow. (African American)

Daly, N. (1992). *Papa Lucky's Shadow*. New York: Macmillan. (African American)

DeFelice, C. (1992). *When Grampa Kissed His Elbow*. Ill. by Karl Swanson. New York: Macmillan.

de Paola, T. (1981). *Now One Foot, Now the Other*. New York: Putnam.

de Paola, T. (1993). *Tom*. New York: Putnam.

Greenfield, E. (1980). *Grandmama's Joy*. Ill. by Carole Byard. New York: Putnam. (African American)

Greenfield, E. (1988). *Grandpa's Face*. Ill. by Floyd Cooper. New York: Philomel.

Griffith, J. V. (1987). *Grandaddy's Place*. Ill. by James Stevenson. New York: Greenwillow.

Hest, A. (1992). *The Go-Between*. Ill. by DyAnne DiSalvo-Ryan. New York: Macmillan.

Hest, A. (1989). *The Midnight Eaters*. Ill. by Karen Gundersheimer. New York: Four Winds.

Hest, A. (1986). *The Purple Coat*. Ill. by Amy Schwartz. New York: Macmillan.

Johnston, T. (1991). *Grandpa's Song*. Ill. by Brad Sneed. New York: Dial.

Keller, H. (1989). *The Best Present*. New York: Greenwillow.

Konigsburg, E. L. (1992). *Amy Elizabeth Explores Bloomingdale's*. New York: Macmillan.

Lasky, K. (1993). *My Island Grandma*. Ill. by Amy Schwartz. New York: Morrow.

Lasky, K. (1988). *Sea Swan*. Ill. by Catherine Sto New York: Macmillan.

McCully, E. A. (1993). *Grandmas at Bat*. New York: Harper.

McCully, E. A. (1990). *Grandmas at the Lake*. New York: Harper.

McCully, E. A. (1988). *The Grandma Mix-Up*. New York: Harper.

Roe, E. (1989). *Staying with Grandma*. Ill. by Jacqueline Rogers. New York: Bradbury.

Russo, M. (1991). *A Visit to Oma*. New York: Greenwillow.

Stevenson, J. (1991). *Brrr!* New York: Greenwillow.

Stevenson, J. (1977). *Could Be Worse*. New York: Greenwillow.

Stevenson, J. (1991). *That's Exactly the Way it Wasn't*. New York: Greenwillow.

Stevenson, J. (1986). *There's Nothing to Do*. New York: Greenwillow.

Stevenson, J. (1983). *What's under My Bed?* New York: Greenwillow.

Wild, M. (1994). *Our Granny*. Ill. by Julie Vivas. New York: Ticknor & Fields.

■ Poetry:

Stolz, M. (1991). *Go Fish*. Ill. by Pat Cummings. New York: Harper. (African American)

Vigna, J. (1984). *Grandma Without Me*. Ill. by Kathleen Tucker. New York: Whitman.

Waddell, M. (1991). *Grandma's Bill*. Ill. by Jane Johnson. New York: Orchard.

Waddell, M. (1990). *My Great Grandpa*. Ill. by Dom Mansell. New York: Putnam.

Williams, B. (1991). *Kevin's Grandma*. New York: Puffin.

"The Visit" in:
Esbensen, B. (1992). *Who Shrank My Grandmother's House? Poems of Discovery*. Ill. by Eric Beddows. New York: HarperCollins. (page 47)

"Grandmas and Grandpas" in:
Hoberman, M. A. (1991). *Fathers, Mothers, Sisters, Brothers: A Collection of Family Poems*. Ill. by Marylin Hafner. Boston: Little, Brown.(pages 8-9)

Livingston, M. C. (1990). *Poems for Grandmothers*. Ill. by Patricia Cullen-Clark. New York: Holiday House.

"The Grandfather I Never Knew," "Nanny," "Grandfather" in:
Livingston, M. C. (1985). *Worlds I Know and Other Poems*. Ill. by Tim Arnold. (page 29,30, 31, 44, 45).

"Some Things about Grandpas" by Alice Low in:
Low, A. (1991). *The Family Read-aloud Holiday Treasury*. Ill. by Marc Brown. Boston: Little, Brown. (page 110)

"Grandpa in March" by Arnold Adoff in:
Moore, L. (1992). *Sunflakes: Poems for Children*. Ill. by Jan Ormerod. New York: Clarion (page 68)

1. Ask students to make cards for their grandparents. Students who do not have grandparents can make cards for other relatives.

2. Encourage students to interview their grandparents or other older relatives. Students might want to use the following questions:

       What was school like?

       What was your favorite subject?

       How has the world changed since you were a child?

       How much did coffee, candy, a movie ticket, etc., cost when you
         were a child?

       What is your favorite memory of childhood?

3. Invite grandparents or older relatives into classroom for a class party.

4. Invite interested grandparents or older relatives to talk about hobbies they have, their school memories, and so on.

S·E·P·T·E·M·B·E·R 8

■ **Date:** September 8

■ **This date is special because:**
It is Jack Prelutsky's birthday (1940).

Books that relate to this date

■ **Picture Books:**

Prelutsky, J. (1982). *The Baby Eggs Are Hatching*. Ill. by James Stevenson. New York: Greenwillow.

Prelutsky, J. (1990). *Beneath a Blue Umbrella*. Ill. by Garth Williams. New York: Greenwillow.

Prelutsky, J. (1991). *For Laughing Out Loud: Poems to Tickle Your Funnybone*. Ill. by Marjorie Priceman. New York: Knopf.

Prelutsky, J. (1980). *The Headless Horseman Rides Tonight: More Poems to Trouble Your Sleep*. Ill. by Arnold Lobel. New York: Greenwillow.

Prelutsky, J. (1981). *It's Christmas*. Ill. by Marylin Hafner. New York: Greenwillow.

Prelutsky, J. (1977). *It's Halloween*. Ill. by Marylin Hafner. New York: Greenwillow.

Prelutsky, J. (1984). *It's Snowing! It's Snowing!* Ill. by Jeanne Titherington. New York: Greenwillow.

Prelutsky, J. (1982). *It's Thanksgiving*. Ill. by Marylin Hafner. New York: Greenwillow.

Prelutsky, J. (1983). *It's Valentine's Day*. Ill. by Yossi Abolafia. New York: Greenwillow.

Prelutsky, J. (1982). *Kermit's Garden of Verses*. Ill. by Bruce McNally. New York: Random House.

Prelutsky, J. (1985). *My Parents Think I'm Sleeping*. Ill. by Yossi Abolafia. New York: Greenwillow.

Prelutsky, J. (1984). *The New Kid on the Block*. Ill. by James Stevenson. New York: Greenwillow.

Prelutsky, J. (1989). *Poems of A. Nonny Mouse*. Ill. by Herik Drescher. New York: Knopf.

Prelutsky, J. (1980). *Rainy Rainy Saturday*. Ill. by Marylin Hafner. New York: Greenwillow.

Prelutsky, J. (1983). *The Random House Book of Poetry*. Ill. by Arnold Lobel. New York: Random House.

Prelutsky, J. (1986). *Read-Aloud Rhymes for the Very Young*. Ill. by Marc Brown. New York: Knopf.

Prelutsky, J. (1986). *Ride a Purple Pelican*. Ill. by Garth Williams. New York: Greenwillow.

Prelutsky, J. (1980). *Rolling Harvey down the Hill*. Ill. by Victoria Chess. New York: Greenwillow.

Prelutsky, J. (1982). *The Sheriff of Rottenshot: Poems*. Ill. by Victoria Chess. New York: Greenwillow.

Prelutsky, J. (1990). *Something BIG Has Been Here*. Ill. by James Stevenson. New York: Greenwillow.

Prelutsky, J. (1988). *Tyrannosaurus Was a Beast*. Ill. by Arnold Lobel. New York: Greenwillow.

Prelutsky, J. (1984). *What I Did Last Summer*. Ill. by Yossi Abolafia. New York: Greenwillow.

Prelutsky, J. (1983). *Zoo Doings*. Ill. by Paul O. Zelinsky. New York: Greenwillow.

■ **Resource Book:**

Zinsser, W. (1990). *Worlds of Childhood: The Art and Craft of Writing for Children*. Boston: Houghton Mifflin. (pages 97–120) (additional information on Jack Prelutsky)

Activities for Extension:

1. Read some of the above poems and vote on a class favorite.

2. Ask students to write their own humorous poems.

3. Listen to Jack Prelutsky perform his books *Something BIG Has Been Here* and *The New Kid on the Block* on audio tape. Ask students to illustrate their favorite poems while listening to them.

4. Allow students to make audiocassette tape recordings of themselves reading poems written by Jack Prelutsky or fellow classmates.

5. Encourage students to do a creative drama presentation of one of the above poems.

6. Read *Poems of A. Nonny Mouse* (Prelutsky, 1983). Ask students to determine which poems were written by Jack Prelutsky. Vote and chart the results.

S·E·P·T·E·M·B·E·R 13

■ **Date:** September 13

■ **This date is special because:**
It is Milton Hershey's birthday.

Books that relate to this date

■ Picture Books:

Ammon, R. (1987). *The Kids' Book of Chocolate*. New York: Atheneum.

Chocolate! Chocolate! Chocolate! The Complete Book of Chocolate. (1989). New York: Scholastic.

Dineen, J. (1991). *Chocolate*. Ill. by John Yates. Minneapolis: Carolrhoda.

Hearn, M. P. (1983). *The Chocolate Book*. New York: Caedmon.

Howe, J. (1990). *Harold and Chester in Hot Fudge*. Ill. by Lesle Morrill. New York: Morrow.

Inkpen, M. (1987). *Gumboot's Chocolatey Day*. New York: Dell.

Mitgutsch, A. (1975). *From Cacao Bean to Chocolate*. Minneapolis: Carolrhoda.

Pelham, D. (1992). *Sam's Surprise*. New York: Dutton.

Wells, R. (1989). *Max's Chocolate Chicken*. New York: Dial.

■ Novels:

Catling, P. S. (1979). *Chocolate Touch*. New York: Morrow.

Dahl, R. (1964). *Charlie and the Chocolate Factory*. Ill. by Joseph Schindelman. New York: Knopf.

Smith, R. K. (1989). *Chocolate Fever*. New York: Putnam.

■ Poetry:

"Lament, for Cocoa" by John Updike in: Cole, W. (1981). *Poem Stew*. Ill. by Karen Ann Weinhaus. New York: Harper & Row. (page 54)

1. Brainstorm words associated with chocolate or products made from chocolate.

2. Create a sensory chart of chocolate.

smells like:	
sounds like:	
tastes like:	
looks like:	
feels like:	

3. Ask students to write two-word poems about chocolate. Two-word poems are a collection of phrases with two words. For example, the following is a two-word poem for a Hershey's Kiss:

Sweet mountain
Mouthwatering mass
Melting teardrop
Crunchy sweet
Pointy smooth
Yummy brown
Slurpy thud
Hershey's Kiss.

Collect the poems in a class book.

4. Ask students to take a class survey on the favorite types of chocolate or candy bars. Chart results with illustrations.

5. Encourage students to ask their parents and other older relatives which candy they like or liked. Chart the results. How do they compare with the results gathered for Activity 4 above? Discuss.

6. Offer the following candy bar quiz to students. Have students make up others. (Thanks to Gordon Greene from the University of Nebraska for this quiz.)
1. A constellation of stars (Milky Way)
2. A giggle or a short laugh (Snickers or Chuckles)
3. A clumsy person (Butterfinger)
4. Small hills (Mounds)
5. A long run (Marathon)
6. A planet (Mars)
7. What a worker looks forward to (Payday)
8. Equals 10 million pennies ($100,000 bar)
9. Comes before one (Zero)
10. Led an expedition with Lewis (Clark)
11. Were sword fighters (Three Musketeers)
12. Two pronouns for girl (Hershey)
13. One of Charlie Brown's friends (Peppermint Patty)

SEPTEMBER 14

■ **Date:** September 14

■ **This date is special because:**
It is National Anthem Day.

Books that relate to this date

■ Picture Books:

Beall, P. C. (1987). *Wee Sing America: Songs of Patriots and Pioneers*. Los Angeles: Price, Stern & Sloan.

Glazer, T. (1987). *America the Beautiful: A Collection of Best-Loved Patriotic Songs*. Ill. by Barbar Corrigan. Garden City, NY: Doubleday.

Patterson, L. (1991). *Francis Scott Key: Poet and Patriot*. New York: Chelsea House.

Spier, P. (1973). *The Star-Spangled Banner*. Garden City, NY: Doubleday.

Young, W. (1986). *Song Wise, Volume One: The Star-Spangled Banner*. Ill. by Craig White. San Juan Capistrano, CA: Joy Publications.

■ Poetry:

"Fireworks" in:
Chandra, D. (1990). *Balloons and Other Poems*. Ill. by Leslie Bowman. New York: Farrar, Straus, & Giroux. (page 4)

"Fourth of July" in:
Livingston, M. C. (1985). *Celebrations*. Ill. by Leonard Everett Fisher. New York: Holiday House. (page 20)

"Fireworks" in:
Livingston, M. C. (1989). *Remembering and Other Poems*. New York: McElderry (page 5)

"And My Heart Soars" by Chief Dan George in:
Low, A. (1991). *The Family Read-Aloud Holiday Treasury*. Ill. by Marc Brown. Boston: Little, Brown. (page 75)

"The Fourth" in:
Silverstein, S. (1974). *Where the Sidewalk Ends*. New York: Harper & Row. (page 116)

1. Write the words to the "Star Spangled Banner" on a chart and discuss.

2. Ask students to illustrate the "Star Spangled Banner."

3. Sing the national anthem around the flag.

4. Challenge students to write their own patriotic songs.

5. List the places that the "Star-Spangled Banner" is generally sung.

6. Students can send for a copy of the original "Star-Spangled Banner." Send $1.00 and mail to:

> The Star-Spangled Banner Flag House,
> 844 East Pratt Street,
> Baltimore, MD 21202

Ask for the Flag House Materials for kids. (from *Free Stuff for Kids*, Meadowbrook Press, 1993, page 67)

S·E·P·T·E·M·B·E·R 15

■ **Date:** September 15

■ **This date is special because:**
It is Tomie de Paola's birthday (1934).

Books that relate to this date
■ **Picture Books:**

de Paola, T. (1989). *Art Lesson*. New York: Putnam.

de Paola, T. (1979). *Big Anthony and the Magic Ring*. San Diego: Harcourt Brace Jovanovich.

de Paola, T. (1978). *Bill and Pete*. New York: Putnam.

de Paola, T. (1987). *Bill and Pete Go down the Nile*. New York: Putnam.

de Paola, T. (1991). *Bonjour, Mr. Satie*. New York: Putnam.

de Paola, T. (1987). *Book of Christmas Carols*. New York: Putnam.

de Paola, T. (1988). *Book of Poems*. New York: Putnam.

de Paola, T. (1984). *Charlie Needs a Cloak*. New York: Simon & Schuster.

de Paola, T. (1981). *The Comic Adventures of Old Mother Hubbard*. New York: Harcourt Brace Jovanovich.

de Paola, T. (1984). *David and Goliath*. New York: Putnam.

de Paola, T. (1980). *The Christmas Tree Book*. New York: Holiday House.

de Paola, T. (1986). *Favorite Nursery Tales*. New York: Putnam.

de Paola, T. (1982). *Francis: The Poor Man of Assisi*. New York: Holiday House.

de Paola, T. (1981). *Friendly Beasts: An Old English Christmas*. New York: Putnam.

de Paola, T. (1989). *Haircuts for the Wooleys*. New York: Putnam.

de Paola, T. (1992). *Jingle, the Christmas Clown*. New York: Putnam.

de Paola, T. (1983). *The Legend of Bluebonnet: An Old Tale of Texas*. New York: Putnam.

de Paola, T. (1988). *The Legend of the Indian Paint Brush*. New York: Putnam.

de Paola, T. (1990). *Little Grunt and the Big Egg: A Prehistoric Fairy Tale*. New York: Holiday House.

de Paola, T. (1986). *Merry Christmas, Strega Nona*. San Diego: Harcourt Brace Jovanovich.

de Paola, T. (1987). *The Miracles of Jesus*. New York: Holiday House.

de Paola, T. (1989). *My First Chanukah*. New York: Putnam.

de Paola, T. (1984). *The Mysterious Grant of Barletta: An Italian Tale*. San Diego: Harcourt Brace Jovanovich.

de Paola, T. (1981). *Now One Foot, Now the Other*. New York: Putnam.

de Paola, T. (1992). *Patrick: A Patron Saint of Ireland*. New York: Holiday House.

de Paola, T. (1983). *Sing, Pierrot, Sing: A Picture Book in Mime*. San Diego: Harcourt Brace Jovanovich.

de Paola, T. (1983). *The Story of Three Wise Kings*. New York: Putnam.

de Paola, T. (1975). *Strega Nona*. Englewood Cliffs, NJ: Prentice-Hall.

de Paola, T. (1982). *Strega Nona's Magic Lesson*. San Diego: Harcourt Brace Jovanovich.

de Paola, T. (1993). *Tom*. New York: Putnam.

de Paola, T. (1989). *Tony's Bread: An Italian Folktale*. New York: Putnam.

de Paola, T. (1989). *Too Many Hopkins*. New York: Putnam.

■ Resource Books:

Kovacs, D. and Preller, J. (1991). *Meet the Authors and Illustrators: 60 Creators of Favorite Children's Books Talk about Their Work*. New York: Scholastic. (pages 28–29) (an interview with Tomie de Paola)

Activities for Extension:

1. Read de Paola's legend books and ask students to write their own.

2. Tomie is an unusual spelling of Tommy. Brainstorm other unusual spellings of names.

3. Tomie de Paola has a very distinctive illustrative style. Challenge students to draw a de Paola person or animal.

4. Students can choose their favorite Tomie de Paola book and perform the story with puppets.

5. Ask students to write another Strega Nona story.

S·E·P·T·E·M·B·E·R 19

■ **Date:** September 19

■ **This date is special because:**
It is International Day of Peace.

Books that relate to this date

■ Picture Books:

Auer, M. (1992). *The Blue Boy*. New York: Macmillan.

Durrell, A. (1990). *The Big Book for Peace*. New York: Dutton.

Geisel, T. S. (1984). *The Butter Battle Book*. New York: Random House.

Lattimore, D. N. (1987). *The Flame of Peace*. New York: Harper & Row.

Merriam, E. (1992). *Fighting Words*. Ill. by David Small. New York: Morrow.

Scholes, K. (1990). *Peace Begins with You*. Ill. by Robert Ingpen. San Francisco: Sierra.

Small, D. (1992). *Ruby Mae Has Something to Say*. New York: Crown.

Spier, P. (1980). *People*. New York: Doubleday.

Trundle, R. (1990). *The Usborne Book of Peoples of the World*. London: Usborne.

Wild, M. (1991). *Let the Celebrations Begin*. Ill. by Julie Vivas. New York: Orchard.

■ Poetry:

Baer, E. (1992). *The Wonder of Hands*. Photos by Tana Hoban. New York: Macmillan. (many cultures represented)

"O Say" in:
Livingston, M. C. (1989). *Remembering and Other Poems*. New York: McElderry. (page 21)

"Hug O'War" and "The Generals" in:
Silverstein, S. (1974). *Where the Sidewalk Ends*. New York: Harper & Row. (pages 19, 150–151)

Yolen, J. (1992). *Street Rhymes Around the World*. Honesdale, PA: Wordsong.

  ## Activities for Extension:

1. Ask students to write their own definitions of peace.

2. Encourage students to make a list of words associated with peace..

3. Students can write to the United Nations for information. Write to: United Nations, New York, NY 10017. Phone: 212-963-1234.

4. Ask students to write their own peace treaty for the classroom.

SEPTEMBER 26

■ Date: September 26

■ This date is special because:
It is Johnny Appleseed's birthday (1774).

Books that relate to this date

■ Picture Books:

Bourgeois, P. (1987). *The Amazing Apple Book*. Ill. by Linda Hendry. Reading, MA: Addison-Wesley.

Burns, D. L. (1989). *Arbor Day*. Ill. by Kathy Rogers. Minneapolis: Carolrhoda.

Gibbons, G. (1984). *The Seasons of Arnold's Apple Tree*. San Diego: Harcourt Brace Jovanovich.

Johnson, S. A. (1983). *Apple Trees*. Photos by Hiroo Koike. Minneapolis: Lerner.

Jeunesse, G. and de Bourgoing, P. (1991). *Fruit*. Ill. by P. M. Valet. New York: Scholastic.

Kellogg, S. (1988). *Johnny Appleseed*. New York: Morrow.

Micucci, C. (1992). *The Life and Times of the Apple*. New York: Orchard.

Nottridge, R. (1990). *Apples*. Ill. by John Yates. Minneapolis: Carolrhoda.

Parnall, P. (1988). *Apple Tree*. New York: Macmillan.

Patent, D. H. (1990). *An Apple a Day: From Orchard to You*. Ill. by William Munoz. New York: Dutton.

Rockwell, A. (1989). *Apples and Pumpkins*. Ill. by Lizzy Rockwell. New York: Macmillan.

Schnieper, C. (1982). *An Apple Tree Through the Year*. Photos by Othmar Baumi. Minneapolis: Carolrhoda.

■ Poetry:

"The Apple," "Take One Apple," "At the End of the Summer," and "Grandma Ida's Cookie Dough for Apple Pie Crust" in:
Adoff, A. (1979). *Eats Poems*. Ill. by Susan Russo. New York: Morrow.

Lindbergh, R. (1990). *Johnny Appleseed: A Poem* Ill. by Kathy Jakoben. Boston: Little, Brown.

1. Ask each student to bring an apple to school and measure its weight or dimension. Whose is the heaviest? The biggest? Chart the results.

2. Ask students to bring in a recipe using apples. With the class, brainstorm all the uses of apples in recipes: pies, turnovers, cakes, butter, caramel apples, apple bread, vinegar, juice and cider, applesauce.

3. You might want to make a pocket chart activity with different types of apples and the matching descriptions:

Golden Delicious: Popular yellow apple

Winesap: Grown by pioneers for apple cider

Gravenstein: Originated in Germany in the 1600's

Granny Smith: Tart taste, green

Rome Beauty: Large apples

Cox's Orange Pippins: Orange color, grown in England

Cortland: Often used in salads because they don't turn brown as quickly as other types

York Imperial: Odd, lopsided shape

Rhode Island Greening: Green, good for baking in pies

4. Put the following facts about apples on a bulletin board:

Did you know?
- One of George Washington's hobbies was pruning his apple trees.
- In early America, apple cider was a popular drink before there was running water.
- Cowboys fed apples to their horses as a special treat.

Add more fun facts about apples from *The Life and Times of the Apple* (Micucci, 1992).

5. Ask students to survey friends and family about their favorite kinds of apples. Chart the results.

6. Ask students to divide a piece of paper into four equal parts. Label each part with the seasons of the year. Then invite students to draw or describe how an apple tree would look in each of the seasons. Use *The Seasons of Arnold's Apple Tree* (Gibbons, 1984) as a resource.

7. Illustrate fractions by slicing an apple in equal parts.

8. Tell the following story of the little red house with no windows and no doors, with a star inside. You will need an apple and a sharp knife.

Once upon a time a boy named Jacob was very bored. His mother told him that he could spend his time looking for one of nature's secrets. She told him to search for a little red house with no windows and no doors with a star inside.

Jacob began his search for a little red house with no windows and no doors with a star inside. He looked all over his front porch and down the street, but couldn't find this little red house. When the mail carrier arrived, Jacob asked her whether she had seen a little red house with no windows and no doors with a star inside. The mail carrier said she hadn't seen such a house. She encouraged Jacob to ask his grandmother about it.

So Jacob went to ask his grandmother whether she had seen a little red house with no windows and no doors with a star inside. His grandmother told him that the wind had the answer.

Jacob was very confused by now. He just couldn't figure out what a little red house with no windows and no doors with a star inside might be. He walked home and asked the wind about it. The wind blew Jacob along home until he was standing under the apple tree in his backyard. An apple fell on his head and Jacob examined it. It was red. It had no windows. It had no doors. Did it have a star inside?

Jacob asked his mother to cut the apple. His mother cut the apple in half, and sure enough, there was a star inside. Jacob found nature's secret!

Note: The apple must be cut in half horizontally to show the seeds in the shape of a star.

S·E·P·T·E·M·B·E·R 27

■ Date: September 27

■ This date is special because:
It is Paul Goble's birthday (1933).

Books that relate to this date

■ Picture Books:

Goble, P. (1989). *Beyond the Ridge*. New York: Bradbury.

Goble, P. (1984). *Buffalo Woman*. New York: Bradbury.

Goble, P. (1992). *Crow Chief: A Plains Indian Story*. New York: Bradbury.

Goble, P. (1987). *Death of the Iron Horse*. New York: Bradbury.

Goble, P. (1990). *Dream Wolf*. New York: Bradbury.

Goble, P. (1980). *The Gift of the Sacred Dog*. New York: Bradbury.

Goble, P. (1978). *The Girl Who Loved Wild Horses*. New York: Bradbury.

Goble, P. (1985). *The Great Race of the Birds and Animals*. New York: Bradbury.

Goble, P. (1988). *Her Seven Brothers*. New York: Bradbury.

Goble, P. (1989). *Iktomi and the Berries: A Plains Indian Story*. New York: Orchard.

Goble, P. (1988). *Iktomi and the Boulder: A Plains Indian Story*. New York: Orchard.

Goble, P. (1991). *Iktomi and the Buffalo Skull*. New York: Orchard.

Goble, P. (1990). *Iktomi and the Ducks*. New York: Orchard.

Goble, P. (1992). *Love Flute*. New York: Bradbury.

Goble, P. (1983). *Star Boy*. New York: Bradbury.

Activities for Extension:

1. Do a chart of the different Native American tribes discussed in Goble's books.

2. Find the locations of the various Plains tribes on a map of the United States.

3. Ask students to write their own Iktomi books.

4. Students can write to the closest Native American reservation for information on their cultural history and activities open to the general public.

■ **Date:** Any day in October

■ **This month is special because:** It is National Pasta Month.

Books that relate to this month

■ Picture Books:

de Paola, T. (1975). *Strega Nona*. Englewood Cliffs, NJ: Prentice-Hall.

Dooley, N. (1991). *Everybody Cooks Rice*. Ill. by Peter J. Thorton. Minneapolis: Carolrhoda.

Engel, D. (1991). *Gino Badino*. New York: Morrow.

Gelman, R. G. (1992). *More Spaghetti, I Say!* Ill. by Mort Gerberg. New York: Scholastic.

Haycock, K. (1990). *Pasta*. Minneapolis: Carolrhoda.

Hines, A. G. (1986). *Daddy Makes the Best Spaghetti*. New York: Clarion.

Leffler-Cocca, M. (1995). *Wednesday Is Spaghetti Day*. New York: Grossett & Dunlap.

Machotka, H. (1992). *Pasta Factory*. Boston: Houghton Mifflin.

Thomson, P. (1993). *Siggy's Spaghetti* Works. Ill. by Gloria Kamen. New York: Tambourine.

■ Poetry:

"Dinner Tonight" in:
Adoff, A. (1979). *Eats: Poems*. Ill. by Susan Russo. New York: Mulberry.

"The Spaghetti Nut" by Jack Prelutsky in:
de Regniers, B. S., and others. (1988). *Sing a Song of Popcorn*. Ill. by nine Caldecott artists. New York: Scholastic. (page 109)

"Italian Noodles" in:
Kennedy, X. J. (1989). *Ghastlies, Goops and Pincushions*. Ill. by Ron Barrett. New York: McElderry. (page 43)

"Spaghetti! Spaghetti!" in:
Moore, L. (1982) S*unflakes: Poems for Children*. Ill. by Jan Ormerod. New York: Clarion. (page 28)

"Spaghetti" in:
Silverstein, S. (1974). *Where the Sidewalk Ends*. New York: Harper & Row. (page 100)

1. Ask students to bring their favorite pasta recipes from home. Create a classroom cookbook.

2. Do a pocket chart activity for different pasta shapes and their names.

3. Prepare some of the recipes from *Everybody Cooks Rice* (Dooley, 1991). Students can vote on their favorite.

4. Have a spaghetti sauce tasting party with different brands from the grocery store.

5. Ask students to create advertisements for their favorite pasta from the list above.

6. Invite students to create artwork from pasta.

O·CTO·B·E·R 10

■ **Date:** October 10

■ **This date is special because:**
It is James Marshall's birthday (1942).

Books that relate to this date

■ **Picture Books:**

Allard, H. (1985). *Miss Nelson Has a Field Day.* Ill. by James Marshall. Boston: Houghton Mifflin.

Allard, H. (1982). *Miss Nelson Is Back.* Ill. by James Marshall. Boston: Houghton Mifflin.

Allard, H. (1977). *Miss Nelson Is Missing!* Ill. by James Marshall. Boston: Houghton Mifflin.

Allard, H. (1981). *The Stupids Die.* Ill. by James Marshall. Boston: Houghton Mifflin.

Allard, H. (1978). *The Stupids Have a Ball.* Ill. by James Marshall. Boston: Houghton Mifflin.

Allard, H. (1974). *The Stupids Step Out.* Ill. by James Marshall. Boston: Houghton Mifflin.

Allard, H. (1989). *The Stupids Take Off.* Ill. by James Marshall. Boston: Houghton Mifflin.

Allen, J. (1985). *Nosey Mrs. Rat.* Ill. by James Marshall. New York: Viking Kestrel.

Marshall, E. (1985). *Four on the Shore.* Ill. by James Marshall. New York: Dial/Dutton.

Marshall, E. (1984). *Fox All Week.* Ill. by James Marshall. New York: Dial/Dutton.

Marshall, E. (1982). *Fox and His Friends.* Ill. by James Marshall. New York: Dial.

Marshall, E. (1983). *Fox at School.* Ill. by James Marshall. New York: Dial.

Marshall, E. (1982). *Fox in Love.* Ill. by James Marshall. New York: Dial.

Marshall, E. (1983). *Fox on Wheels.* Ill. by James Marshall. New York: Dial/Dutton.

Marshall, E. (1980). *Space Case.* Ill. by James Marshall. New York: Dial.

Marshall, E. (1981). *Three by the Sea.* Ill. by James Marshall. New York: Dial.

Marshall, E. (1980). *Troll Country.* Ill. by James Marshall. New York: Dial.

Marshall, J. (1989). *Cinderella.* Boston: Little, Brown.

Marshall, J. (1991). *Old Mother Hubbard and Her Wonderful Dog.* New York: Straus & Giroux.

Marshall, J. (1989). *The Three Little Pigs.* New York: Dial.

Marshall, J. (1990). *Hansel and Gretel.* New York: Dial.

Marshall, J. (1987). *Red Riding Hood.* New York: Dial.

Marshall, J. (1984). *The Cut-Ups.* New York: Viking Kestrel.

Marshall, J. (1989). *The Cut-Ups at Camp Custer.* New York: Viking Kestrel.

Marshall, J. (1990). *The Cut-Ups Carry On*. New York: Viking.

Marshall, J. (1987). *The Cut-Ups Cut Loose*. New York: Viking Kestrel.

Marshall, J. (1990). *Fox Be Nimble*. New York: Dial.

Marshall, J. (1988). *Fox on the Job*. New York: Dial.

Marshall, J. (1992). *Fox Outfoxed*. New York: Dial.

Marshall, J. (1992). *George and Martha*. Boston: Houghton Mifflin.

Marshall, J. (1984). *George and Martha Back in Town*. Boston: Houghton Mifflin.

Marshall, J. (1973). *George and Martha Encore*. Boston: Houghton Mifflin.

Marshall, J. (1978). *George and Martha, One Fine Day*. Boston: Houghton Mifflin.

Marshall, J. (1976). *George and Martha Rise And Shine*. Boston: Houghton Mifflin.

Marshall, J. (1988). *George and Martha `Round and `Round*. Boston: Houghton Mifflin.

Marshall, J. (1980). *George and Martha, Tons of Fun*. Boston: Houghton Mifflin.

Marshall, J. (1988). *Goldilocks and the Three Bears*. New York: Dial.

Marshall, J. (1986). *Merry Christmas, Space Case*. New York: Dial.

Marshall, J. (1991). *Rats on the Roof and Other Stories*. New York: Dial.

Marshall, J. (1981). *Taking Care of Carruthers*. Boston: Houghton Mifflin.

Marshall, J. (1986). *Three up on a Tree*. New York: Dial.

Marshall, J. (1986). *Wings: A Tale of Two Chickens*. New York: Viking Kestrel.

Marshall, J. (1973). *Yummers!* Boston: Houghton Mifflin.

Marshall, J. (1986). *Yummers Too: The Second Course*. Boston: Houghton Mifflin.

McFarland, J. (1981). *The Exploding Frog and Other Fables from Aesop*. Ill. by James Marshall. Boston: Little, Brown.

Moore, C. C. (1985). *The Night Before Christmas*. Ill. by James Marshall. New York: Scholastic.

Nash, O. (1991). *The Adventures of Isavel*. Ill. by James Marshall. Boston: Little, Brown.

Pinkwater, D. (1982). *Roger's Umbrella*. Ill. by James Marshall. New York: Dutton.

Pomerantz, C. (1974). *The Piggy in the Puddle*. Ill. by James Marshall. New York: Macmillan.

Wahl, J. (1978). *Carrot Nose*. Ill. by James Marshall. New York: Farrar, Straus & Giroux.

Yolen, J. (1980). *How Beastly! A Menagerie of Nonsense Poems*. Ill. by James Marshall. New York: Collins.

■ Resource Book:

Kovacs, D. & Preller, J. (1991). *Meet the Authors and Illustrators: 60 Creators of Favorite Children's Books Talk about Their Work*. New York: Scholastic. (pages 46–57) (an interview with James Marshall)

1. Make paper sack puppets of George and Martha and put on a play.

2. Invite students to write their own George and Martha stories.

3. Ask students to illustrate a typical scene from the Stupids.

4. Challenge students to write *Yummers 3*.

5. Start a class collection of stamps, buttons, rocks, or some other area of interest.

6. Invite children to illustrate their own versions of a fairy tale.

OCTOBER 11

- **Date:** October 11

- **This date is special because:**
It is Eleanor Roosevelt's birthday (1884).

Books that relate to this date

- **Picture Books:**

Adler, D. A. (1991). *A Picture Book of Eleanor Roosevelt.* Ill. by Robert Casilla. New York: Holiday.

Blumberg, R. (1981). *First Ladies.* New York: Watts.

Faber, D. (1985). *Eleanor Roosevelt: First Lady of the World.* Ill. by Donna Ruff. New York: Viking Kestrel.

Jacobs, W. J. (1983). *Eleanor Roosevelt: A Life of Happiness and Tears.* New York: Coward-McCann.

McAuley, K. (1987). *Eleanor Roosevelt.* New York: Chelsea.

Toor, R. (1989). *Eleanor Roosevelt.* New York: Chelsea.

Whitney, S. (1982). *Eleanor Roosevelt.* New York: Watts.

- **Novel:**

Freedman, R. (1993). *Eleanor Roosevelt: A Life of Discovery.* New York: Clarion.

Weidt, M. N. (1991). *Stateswomen to the World: A Story about Eleanor Roosevelt.* Ill. by Lydia M. Anderson. Minneapolis: Carolrhoda.

- **Poetry:**

Hopkins, L. B. (1972). *Girls Can Too! A Book of Poems.* Ill. by Emily McCully. New York: Watts.

  Activities for Extension:

1. Brainstorm characteristics of Eleanor Roosevelt which have contributed to her remaining as one of the most famous and popular first ladies.

2. Make a list of living first ladies and the years they were in the White House.

3. Name the important projects each of the living first ladies has been associated with.

4. Ask students to research who the current first lady is. Find articles from the newspaper about her. Or is it a him? If the president is a woman, what should you call her spouse? First man? Discuss these questions.

O·CTO·B·E·R 12

■ Date: October 12

■ This date is special because:
It is Columbus Day.

Books that relate to this date
■ Picture Books:

Adler, D. A. (1991). *A Picture Book of Christopher Columbus*. Ill. by John Wallner & Alexandra Wallner. New York: Holiday House.

Adler, D. A. (1991). *Christopher Columbus: Great Explorer*. Ill. by Lyle Miller. New York: Holiday House.

Anderson, J. (1991). *Christopher Columbus: From Vision to Voyage*. Ill. by George Ancona. New York: Dial.

Baker, L. (1990). *Life in the Deserts: Animals, People, Plants*. New York: Scholastic.

Baker, L. (1990). *Life in the Oceans: Animals, People, Plants*. New York: Scholastic.

Baker, L. (1990). *Life in the Rainforets: Animals, People, Plants*. New York: Scholastic.

Ballard, R. B. (1991). *Exploring the Bismarck*. Ill. by Wesley Lowe, Ken Marschall, Jack McMaster, & Margo Stahl. New York: Scholastic.

Byles, M. (1990). *Life in the Polar Lands: Animals, People, Plants*. New York: Scholastic.

Fritz, J. and others. (1992). *The World in 1492*. Ill. by Stefano Vitale. New York: Holt.

Liestman, V. (1991). *Columbus Day*. Ill. by Rick Hanson. Minneapolis: Carolrhoda.

Living History. (1992). *The Voyages of Christopher Columbus*. Orlando, FL: Harcourt Brace Jovanovich.

Maestro, B. and Maestro, G. (1991). *The Discovery of the Americas*. New York: Scholastic.

Marzollo, J. (1991). *In 1492*. Ill. by Steve Bjorkman*. New York: Scholastic.

McGovern, A. (1991). *. . . . If You Sailed on The Mayflower in 1620*. Ill. by Anna DiVito. New York: Scholastic.

Monchieri, L. (1985). *Christopher Columbus*. New York: Silver Burdett.

Sis, P. (1991). *Follow the Dream*. New York: Knopf.

■ Novels:

Brenner, B. (1991). *If You Were There in 1492*. New York: Scholastic.

Conrad, P. (1992). *Pedro's Journal*. New York: Harper.

Liestman, V. (1991). *Columbus Day*. Ill. by Rick Hanson. Minneapolis: Carolrhoda.

Schlein, M. (1992). *I Sailed with Columbus*. Ill. by Tom Newsom. New York: Crowell.

Yue, C. and Yue, D. (1992). *Christopher Columbus: How He Did It*. Boston: Houghton Mifflin.

■ **Poetry:**

"Columbus Day" in:
Livingston, M. C. (1985). *Celebrations*. Ill. by Leonard Everett Fisher. New York: Holiday House. (page 24)

"Columbus Day" by Rosemary Carr & S. Vincent Benet in:
Low, A. (1991). *The Family Read-Aloud Holiday Treasury*. Boston: Little, Brown. (page 112)

Activities for Extension:

1. Using the book *In 1492* (Marzollo, 1991) as a model, ask students to write a poetry book about the current year.

2. Teach children the rhyme "In 1492, Columbus sailed the ocean blue."

3. Ask children to draw an illustration of what Columbus saw upon landing.

4. Encourage students to write a journal entry for one of the shipmates aboard Columbus' ships. Use *Pedro's Journal* (Conrad, 1992) as a pattern.

5. Students can role play the dialog exchange between Queen Isabella and Columbus.

6. Invite students to discover additional books about explorers in the library. Share with the class.

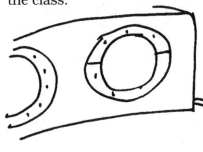

O·C·T·O·B·E·R 15

■ **Date:** October 15

■ **This date is special because:**
It is National Poetry Day.

Books that relate to this date

■ Picture Books:

Adoff, A. (1988). *Chocolate Dreams*. Ill. by Tori MacCombie. New York: Lothrop.

Adoff, A. (1991) *In for Winter, Out for Spring*. Ill. by Jerry Pinkney. San Diego: Harcourt Brace Jovanovich.

Bedard, Michael. (1992). *Emily*. Ill. by Barbar Cooney. New York: Doubleday.

Bennett, J. (1988). *The Writing Book*. New York: Scholastic.

Charles, D. (1989). *Paddy Pig's Poem*. New York: Simon & Schuster.

De Regniers, B. S. (1988). *Sing a Song of Popcorn: Every Child's Book of Poems*. Ill. by Marcia Brown and others. New York: Scholastic.

Disney. (1991). *For Our Children*. Burbank, CA: Walt Disney Pub.

Froman, R. (1974). *Seeing Things*. Ill. by Ray Barber. New York: Crowell.

Froman, R. (1971). *Street Poems*. New York: McCall.

Little, J. (1986). *Hey World, Here I Am!* Ill. by Sue Truesdell. New York: Harper & Row.

■ Novels:

Burch, R. (1986). *King Kong and Other Poets*. New York: Viking.

Byars, B. (1988). *Beans on the Roof*. Ill. by Melodye Rosales. New York: Delacorte.

■ Poetry:

"Poems Can Give You" by Sandra Bogart in:
Booth, D. (1989). *'Til All the Stars Have Fallen*. Ill. by Kady MacDonald Denton. New York: Viking. (page 33)

"Why Pigs Cannot Write Poems" in:
Ciardi, J. (1985). *Doodlesoup*. Ill. by Merle Nacht. Boston: Houghton Mifflin. (page 20)

"Pencils" in:
Esbensen, B. (1992). *Who Shrank My Grandmother's House?* Ill. by Eric Beddows. New York: HarperCollins. (page 9)

Goldstein, B. S. (1992). *Inner Chimes: Poems on Poetry*. Ill. by Jane Breskin Zalbin. Honesdale, PA.: Wordsong.

Higginson, W. J. (1991). *Wind in the Long Grass*. Ill. by Sandra Speidel. New York: Simon & Schuster.

"After English Class" in:
Little, J. (1986). *Hey World, Here I Am!* Ill. by Sue Truesdell. New York: Harper & Row. (page 28)

"Keep a Poem in Your Pocket" by Beatrice Schenk de Regniers in: Low, A. (1991). *The Family Read-Aloud Holiday Treasury*. Ill. by Marc Brown. Boston: Little, Brown. (page 123)

"The Poet" in: Simmie, L. (1984). *Auntie's Knitting a Baby*. Ill. by Anne Simmie. New York: Orchard. (page 25)

"Sometimes Poems" in: Viorst, J. (1981). *If I Were in Charge of the World & Other Worries*. Ill. by Lynne Cherry. New York: Atheneum. (pages 36–37)

Yolen, J. (1992). *Street Rhymes Around the World*. Ill. by 17 International Artists. Honesdale, PA: Wordsong.

Activities for Extension:

1. Ask students to select and perform their favorite poems.

2. Invite children to write and illustrate a poem about their lives.

3. Invite the principal and other support staff to read their favorite poem to the class.

4. Have a poetry reading assembly. Invite the whole school and share poetry from classrooms and from the community outside the school.

5. Encourage students to illustrate their favorite poem.

O·CTO·B·E·R 20

■ Date: October 20

■ This date is special because:
It is Circus Day.

Books that relate to this date

■ Picture Books:

Adler, D. A. (1983). *Cam Jansen and the Mystery of the Circus Clown*. Ill. by Susanna Natti. New York: Viking.

Corcoran, M. (1990). *Night Circus*. New York: Contemp. Bks.

de Paola, T. (1992). *Jingle the Christmas Clown*. New York: Putnam.

Doty, R. (1991). *Wonderful Circus Parade*. New York: Simon & Schuster.

Ehlert, L. (1992). *Circus*. New York: HarperCollins.

Ernst, L. C. (1990). *Ginger Jumps*. New York: Macmillan.

Fitzgerald, F. (1989). *Inside the Circus*. New York: Contemp. Bks.

Garland, M. (1993). *Circus Girl*. New York: Dutton.

Goennel, H. (1992). *The Circus*. New York: Morrow.

Harmer, M. (1981). *Circus*. New York: Childrens.

Hoban, T. (1984). *Round, and Round and Round*. New York: Greenwillow.

Johnson, J. E. (1985). *Here Comes the Circus*. New York: Random House.

Kalman, M. (1991). *Roarr Calder's Circus*. Photos by Donatella Brun. New York: Dell.

Klutz Press. (1990). *Face Painting*. Photos by Thomas Heinser and others. Pala Alto, CA: Klutz Press.

McCully, E. A. (1992). *Mirette on the Highwire*. New York: Putnam.

Moss, M. (1987). *Fairs and Circuses*. New York: Watts.

Spier, P. (1992). *Circus!* New York: Doubleday.

Sullivan, C. (1993). *Circus*. New York: Rizzoli.

Vincent, G. (1989). *Ernest and Celestine at the Circus*. New York: Greenwillow.

Weil, L. (1988). *Let's Go to the Circus*. New York: Holiday.

Wiseman, B. (1988). *Morris and Boris at the Circus*. New York: HarperCollins.

■ Poetry:

"Said the Clown" in:
Causley, C. (1986). *Early in the Morning*. Ill. by Michael Foreman. New York: Viking Kestrel. (page 27)

"Circus Time" in:
Merriam, E. (1992). *The Singing Green*. Ill. by Kathleen Collins Howell. New York: Morrow. (pages 12–13)

Sullivan, C. (1992). *Circus*. Ill. by famous artists. New York: Rizzoli.

Activities for Extension:

1. Put on a circus in your classroom or playground.

2. Brainstorm circus food and other items you see at the circus. Create a collage, or illustrate.

3. Invite a clown into your classroom and have him or her explain clown makeup.

4. Ask students to draw different clown faces.

5. Have a face-painting day, using *Face Painting* (Klutz Press, 1990) as a guide.

O·CTO·B·E·R 26

■ **Date:** October 26

■ **This date is special because:**
It is Steven Kellogg's birthday (1941).

Books that relate to this date

■ Picture Books:

Cummings, P., (Ed. and comp.) (1992). *Talking with Artists*. Ill. by Steven Kellogg. New York: Macmillan.

Guarino, D. (1989). *Is Your Mama a Llama?*. Ill. by Steven Kellogg. New York: Scholastic.

Kellogg, S. (1985). *Chicken Little*. New York: Morrow.

Kellogg, S. (1991). *Jack and the Beanstalk*. New York: Morrow.

Kellogg, S. (1987). *Aster Aardvark's Alphabet Adventures*. New York: Morrow.

Kellogg, S. (1986). *Best Friends*. New York: Dial.

Kellogg, S. (1992). *The Christmas Witch*. New York: Dial.

Kellogg, S. (1988). *Johnny Appleseed*. New York: Morrow.

Kellogg, S. (1992). *Mike Fink: A Tall Tale*. New York: Morrow.

Kellogg, S. (1992). *Mysterious Tadpole*. New York: Dial.

Kellogg, S. (1982). *The Mystery of the Stolen Blue Paint*. New York: Dial.

Kellogg, S. (1993). *Paul Bunyan*. New York: Mulberry.

Kellogg, S. (1986). *Pecos Bill*. New York: Morrow.

Kellogg, S. (1987). *Prehistoric Pinkerton*. New York: Dial.

Kellogg, S. (1983). *Ralph's Secret Weapon*. New York: Dial.

Kellogg, S. (1981). *A Rose for Pinkerton*. New York: Dial.

Kellogg, S. (1982). *Tallyho, Pinkerton!* New York: Dial.

Lindbergh, R. (1990). *The Day the Goose Got Loose*. Ill. by Steven Kellogg. New York: Dial.

Noble, T. H. (1980). *The Day Jimmy's Boa Ate the Wash*. Ill. by Steven Kellogg. New York: Dial.

Noble, T. H. (1989). *Jimmy's Boa and the Big Birthday Bash*. Ill. by Steven Kellogg. New York: Dial.

Paxton, T. (1990). *Engelbert the Elephant*. Ill. by Steven Kellogg. New York: Morrow.

Purdy, C. (1985). *Iva Dunnit and the Big Wind*. Ill. by Steven Kellogg. New York: Dial.

Warren, C. (1983). *The Ten-Alarm Camp-Out*. Ill. by Steven Kellogg. New York: Lothrop.

■ Resource Book:

Kovacs, D. and Preller, J. (1991). *Meet the Authors and Illustrators: 60 Creators of Favorite Children's Books Talk about Their Work*. New York: Scholastic. (an interview with Steven Kellogg) (pages 40–41)

Activities for Extension:

1. Challenge students to write another Pinkerton adventure.

2. Challenge students to write the sequel to *Best Friends* (Kellog, 1986).

3. Invite children to write their own tall tale.

4. Ask students to perform one of the tall tale books that Kellogg has retold and illustrated.

5. Students can make an alphabet book using *Aster Aardvark's Alphabet Adventure* (Kellog, 1987) as a model.

O·CTO·B·E·R 31

■ Date: October 31

■ This date is special because:
It is Halloween.

Books that relate to this date

■ Picture Books:

Adler, D. A. (1988). *I Know I'm a Witch*. Ill. by Sucie Stevenson. New York: Holt.

Adler, D. A. (1985). *The Twisted Witch and Other Spooky Riddles*. Ill. by Victoria Chess. New York: Holiday House.

Alexander, S. (1989). *Who Goes Out on Halloween?*. New York: Bantam Doubleday Dell.

Ancona, G. (1993). *Pablo Remembers: The Fiesta of the Day of the Dead*. New York: Lothrop.

Bond, F. (1983). *The Halloween Performance*. New York: Crowell.

Brown, M. (1983). *Arthur's Halloween*. Boston: Little, Brown.

Bunting, E. (1986). *Scary, Scary Halloween*. Ill. by Jan Brett. Boston: Houghton Mifflin.

Carlson, N. (1982). *Harriet's Halloween Candy.*. New York: Puffin.

Cassedy, S. (1991). *The Best Cat Suit of All*. New York: Dial.

Christelow, E. (1988). *Jerome and the Witchcraft Kids*. New York: Clarion.

Cole, J. and Calmenson, S. (1991). *The Scary Book*. Ill. by Chris Demarest, Marilyn Hirsch, Arnold Lobel, and Dirk Zimmer. New York: Morrow.

Coombs, P. (1992). *Dorrie and the Haunted Schoolhouse*. New York: Clarion.

Devlin, W. and Devlin, H. (1982). *Cranberry Halloween*. New York: Macmillan.

Dillon, J. (1992). *Jeb Scarecrow's Pumpkin Patch*. Boston: Houghton Mifflin.

Faulkner, K. (1990). *Vampire, Werewolf, Witch, Monster*. Ill. by Jonathan Lambert. New York: Smithmark.

Gibbons, G. (1984). *Halloween*. New York: Holiday.

Guthrie, D. (1990). *The Witch Has an Itch*. Ill. by Katy Keck Arnsteen. New York: Simon & Schuster.

Howe, James. (1989). *Scared Silly: A Halloween Treat*. Ill. by Leslie Morrill. New York: Morrow.

Johnston, Tony. (1990). *Soup Bone*. San Diego: Harcourt Brace Jovanovich.

Kraus, R. (1986). *How Spider Saved Halloween*. New York: Scholastic.

Leiner, K. (1992). *Halloween Book*. New York: Macmillan.

Maestro, G. (1992). *More Halloween Howls: Riddles That Come Back to Haunt You*. New York: Dutton.

Martin, B. and Archambault, J. (1985). *The Ghost-Eye Tree*. Ill. by Ted Rand. New York: Holt.

162

Meddaugh, S. (1991). *The Witches' Supermarket*. Boston: Houghton Mifflin.

Peterson, J. (1988). *Tom Little's Great Halloween Scare*. New York: Scholastic.

Polacco, P. (1992). *Picnic at Mudsock Meadow*. New York: Putnam.

Rockwell, A. (1989). *Apples and Pumpkins*. Ill. by Lizzy Rockwell. New York: Macmillan.

Schwartz, A. (1984). *In A Dark, Dark Room and Other Scary Stories*. Ill. by Dirl Zimmer. New York: Scholastic.

Sharmat, M. W. (1990). *Nate the Great and the Halloween Hunt*. New York: Dell.

Silverman, E. (1992). *Big Pumpkin*. Ill. by S. D. Schindler. New York: Macmillan.

Titherington, J. (1989). *Pumpkin, Pumpkin*. New York: Scholastic.

Williams, L. (1986). *The Little Old Lady Who Wasn't Afraid of Anything*. New York: Harper & Row.

Wyllie, S. (1992). *Ghost Train: A Spooky Hologram Book*. Ill. by Brian Lee. New York: Dial.

Ziefert, H. (1992). *Halloween Parade*. Ill. by Lillie James. New York: Viking.

■ Poetry:

Bennett, J. (1989). *Spooky Poems*. Ill. by Mary Rees. Boston: Little, Brown.

Heide, F. P. (1992). *Grim and Ghastly Goings-on*. Ill. by Victoria Chess. New York: Lothrop.

"Halloween" in:
Livingston, M. C. (1985). *Celebrations*. Ill. by Leonard Everett Fisher. New York: Holiday House. (page 26)

Livingston, M. C. (1989). *Halloween Poems*. Ill. by Stephen Gammell. New York: Holiday House.

Merriam, E. (1987). *Halloween A B C*. Ill. by Lane Smith. New York: Collier Macmillan.

Activities for Extension:

1. Brainstorm characters from books that would serve as models for wonderful and easy costumes to create.

2. Have a costume party depicting book characters. Challenge the class to a guessing game. Can they guess who their classmates are depicting?

3. Encourage students to dress as characters from their favorite books and arrange for them to go "trick or treating" to other classes. Instead of distributing candies, costumed students can challenge other classes to guess the books they represent, act out scenes, or read the books themselves as a "treat" for younger students.

4. Have a book-character parade at a local senior center.

Date: Any day in November

This month is special because: It is Harvest Month.

Books that relate to this month
Picture Books:

Allen, T. B. (1989). *On Grandaddy's Farm*. New York: Knopf.

Andrews, J. (1991). *The Auction*. Ill. by Karen Reczuch. New York: Macmillan.

Aylesworth, J. (1991). *Country Crossing*. Ill. by Ted Rand. New York: Atheneum.

Bax, M. (1989). *Edmond Went Far Away*. Ill. by Michael Foreman. San Diego: Harcourt Brace Jovanovich.

Brown, C. (1991) *My Barn*. New York: Greenwillow.

Brown, C. (1989). *Patchwork Farmer*. New York: Greenwillow.

Carrick, C. (1990). *In The Moonlight, Waiting*. Ill. by Donald Carrick. New York: Clarion.

Cross, V. (1992). *Great-Grandma Tells of Threshing Day*. Ill. by Gail Owens. New York: Whitman.

Dunrea, O. (1990). *Eppie M. Says....* New York: Macmillan.

Ehlert, L. (1990). *Color Farm*. New York: Lippincott.

Emberely, R. (1989). *City Sounds*. Boston: Little, Brown.

Florian, D. (1989). *A Year in the Country*. New York: Greenwillow.

Gammell, S. (1990). *Once upon McDonald's Farm*. New York: Macmillan.

Good, E. (1990). *Fall Is Here: I Love it!* Intercourse, PA: Good Books.

Henderson, K. (1989). *I Can Be a Farmer*. New York: Childrens.

Lenski, L. (1980). *Little Farm*. New York: McKay.

Leslie, C. W. (1991). *Nature All Year Long*. New York: Greenwillow.

Levinson, R. (1992). *Country Dawn to Dusk*. Ill. by Kay Chorao. New York: Dutton.

Lewison, W. C. (1992). *Going to Sleep on the Farm*. Ill. by Juan Wijngaard. New York: Dial.

Lindbergh, R. (1990). *Benjamin's Barn*. Ill. by Susan Jeffers. New York: Dial.

Lindbergh, R. (1987). *The Midnight Farm*. Ill. by Susan Jeffers. New York: Dial.

Maas, R. (1990). *When Autumn Comes*. New York: Holt.

McPhail, D. (1991). *Farm Morning*. San Diego: Harcourt Brace Jovanovich.

Merriam, E. (1992). *Fighting Words*. Ill. by David Small. New York: Morrow.

Miller, J. (1989). *Farm Noises*. New York: Simon & Schuster.

Pinkney, G. J. (1992). *Back Home*. Ill. Jerry Pinkney. New York: Dial.

Pochocki E. (1993). *Wildflower Tea*. Ill. by Roger Essley. New York: Simon & Schuster.

Provensen, A. & Provensen, M. (1988). *The Year at the Maple Hill Farm*. New York: Macmillan.

Rylant, C. (1991). *Night in the Country*. Ill. by Mary Szilagyi. New York: Macmillan.

Schweiger, A. (1993). *Autumn Days*. New York: Puffin.

Siebert, D. (1989). *Heartland*. Ill. by Wendell Minor. New York: Crowell.

Waddell, M. (1992). *Farmer Duck*. Ill. by Helen Oxenbury. Cambridge, MA: Candlewick.

Whelan, G. (1992). *Bringing the Farmhouse Home*. Ill. by Jada Rowland. New York: Simon & Schuster.

Wild, M. (1990). *The Very Best of Friends*. Ill. by Julie Vivas. San Diego: Harcourt Brace Jovanovich.

▪ Poetry:

"At the Farm" by John Ciardi in: Bennett, J. (1991). *A Cup of Starshine*. Ill. by Graham Percy. San Diego: Harcourt Brace Jovanovich. (page 32)

"I Love My Darling Tractor" in: Causley, C. (1986). Early in the Morning. Ill. by Michael Foreman. New York: Viking Kestrel. (pages 48–49)

"Harvest Home" by Arthur Guiterman in: Prelutsky, J. (1983). The Random House Book of Poetry for Children. Ill. by Arnold Lobel. New York: Random House. (page 45)

Activities for Extension:

1. Using *City Sounds* (Emberely, 1989) as a model, ask children to create "country sounds."

2. Using *Fighting Words* (Merriam, 1992) as a model, ask children to contrast city and country living.

3. Brainstorm crops that are harvested in the fall. Write harvest poems or vignettes.

4. Ask students to bring in crops that are harvested in the fall. Create a display.

5. Taste recipes using crops that are harvested in the fall.

N·O·V·E·M·B·E·R 3

■ Date: November 3

■ This date is special because:

It is Sandwich Day.

It is the birthday of the John Montague, Fourth Earl of Sandwich, the creator of the first sandwich (1718).

Books that relate to this date

■ Picture Books:

Lester, H. (1992). *Me First.* Ill. by Lynn Munsinger. Boston: Houghton Mifflin.

McLean, B. (1990). *The Best Peanut Butter Sandwich in the Whole World.* Ill. by Katherine Helmer. New York: Firefly.

Pelham, D. (1991). *Sam's Sandwich.* New York: Dutton.

Riley, M. (1992). *Bogart's Sandwich.* New York: Parkwest.

Wolcott, P. (1991). *Tunafish Sandwiches.* Ill. by Hand Zander. New York: Random House.

Ziefert, H. (1987). *So Hungry!* New York: Random House.

■ Poetry:

"If I Were a. . ." by Karla Kuskin in: de Regniers, B. S., and others. (1988) *Sing a Song of Popcorn.* Ill. by nine Caldecott Medal artists. New York: Scholastic. (page 105)

"An Alarming Sandwich" in: Kennedy, X. J. (1975). *One Winter Night in August.* Ill. by David McPhail. (page 48)

Activities for Extension:

1. Ask students to design their fantasy sandwich.

2. Allow students to make posters advertising their sandwich.

3. Brainstorm sandwich ingredients. Itemize according to categories, such as meat, cheese, condiments, etc.

4. Using *Me First* (Lester, 1992) as a starting point, brainstorm other homophones.

5. Students can write a story or poem using these brainstormed lists.

N·O·V·E·M·B·E·R 11

■ Date: November 11

■ This date is special because:
It is Veteran's Day.

Books that relate to this date

■ Picture Books:

Black, W. B. (1991). *Blitzkrieg*. New York: Crestwood House.

Bunting, E. (1990). *The Wall*. Ill. by Ronald Himler. New York: Clarion.

Durell, A. and Sachs, M. (1990). *The Big Book for Peace*. Ill. by Jon Agee & others. New York: Dutton.

Gallaz, C. and Innocenti, R. (1985). *Rose Blanche*. Mankato, MN: Creative Education.

Gauch, P. L. (1988). *Thunder at Gettysburg*. New York: Bantam Doubleday Dell.

Hall, D. (1994). *The Farm, Summer 1942*. Ill. by Barry Moser. New York: Dial.

"Veterans' Day" by Jean Craighead George in:
Low, A. (1991) *The Family Read-Aloud Holiday Treasury*. Ill. by Marc Brown. Boston: Little, Brown & Co. (pages 118–121)

Ray, D. (1990). *My Daddy Was a Soldier: A World War Two Story*. New York: Holiday.

Stevenson, J. (1992). *Don't You Know There's a War On?* New York: Greenwillow.

Yolen, J. (1991). *All Those Secrets of the World*. Boston: Little, Brown.

■ Novelette:

Kudlinski, K. V. (1993). *Pearl Harbor Is Burning! A Story of WW II*. Ill. by Ronald Himler. New York: Puffin.

■ Novels:

Giff, P. R. (1991). *The War Began at Supper: Letters to Miss Loria*. Ill. by B. Lewin. New York: Delacorte.

Hest, A. (1991). *Love You, Soldier*. New York: Macmillan.

Westall, R. (1989). *Blitzcat*. New York: Scholastic.

■ Poetry:

"Armistice Day, World War I" in:
Lewis, C. (1987) *Long Ago in Oregon*. Ill. by Joel Fontaine. New York: Harper & Row. (pages 50–51)

"At the Graveyard on Decoration Day" in:
Lewis, C. (1987). *Long Ago in Oregon*. Ill. by Joel Fontaine. New York: Harper & Row. (pages 26–27)

"Wars" in:
Little, J. (1989). *Hey World, Here I Am!* Ill. by Sue Truesdell. New York: Harper & Row. (page 10)

1. Call a local veteran's association and invite a speaker to come and talk to the class.

2. Ask students to read *The Wall* (Bunting, 1990) and write about how the young boy felt at the end of the story.

3. Students can send letters to servicemen and women overseas.

4. Invite students to interview older relatives about their memories of war and veterans in their families.

5. Encourage students to write thank-you notes to a local veteran's association.

N·O·V·E·M·B·E·R 13

■ **Date:** November 13

■ **This date is special because:**
It is Peanut Butter Day.

Books that relate to this date

■ Picture Books:

Donna, N. (1976). *The Peanut Cookbook.* Ill. by Robert Quackenbush. New York: Lothrop, Lee & Shepard.

Palacios, A. (1990). *Peanut Butter, Apple Butter, Cinnamon Toast: Food Riddles for You to Guess.* Ill. by Ben Mahan. Milwaukee: Raintree.

Robbins, K. (1991). *Make Me A Peanut Butter Sandwich and a Glass of Milk.* New York: Scholastic.

Russell, S. P. (1970). *Peanuts, Popcorn, Ice Cream, Candy, and Soda Pop, and How They Began.* Ill. by Ralph J. McDonald. New York: Abingdon Press.

Westcott, N. B. (1987). *Peanut Butter and Jelly: A Play Rhyme.* New York: Dutton.

■ Novel:

Mitchell, B. (1986). *A Pocketful of Goobers: A Story about George Washington Carver.* Ill. by Peter E. Hanson. Minneapolis: Carolrhoda.

■ Poetry:

"Peanut-Butter Sandwich" in: Silverstein, S. (1974). *Where the Sidewalk Ends.* New York: Harper & Row. (page 84)

Westcott, N. B. (1987). *Peanut Butter and Jelly.* New York: Dutton.

  ## Activities for Extension:

1. Ask students to write the directions for making a peanut butter sandwich.

2. List possible sandwich combinations with peanut butter. For example: peanut butter and dill pickles, peanut butter and jelly.

3. Brainstorm other food items that can be made with peanut butter.

4. Using the *Peanut Cookbook* (Donna, 1976), make homemade peanut butter.

5. Add motions to the book, *Peanut Butter and Jelly: A Play Rhyme* (Wesctcott, 1987), and encourage students to perform.

N·O·V·E·M·B·E·R 16

■ **Date:** November 16

■ **This date is special because:**
It is William C. Handy's birthday (1873).

William C. Handy was a composer, bandleader, and known as the "Father of the Blues."

Books that relate to this date

■ **Picture Books:**

Birchman, D. F. (1992). *Brother Billy Bronto's Bygone Band*. Ill. by John O'Brien. New York: Lothrop, Lee & Shepard.

Catalano, D. (1992). *Wolf Plays Alone*. New York: Philomel.

Drews, H. (1993). *My First Music Book*. New York: Dorling Kindersley.

Fleischman, P. (1988). *Rondo in C*. Ill. by Janet Wentworth. New York: Harper & Row.

Fowler, S. G. (1992). *Fog*. Ill. by Jim Fowler. New York: Greenwillow.

Hausherr, R. (1992). *What Instrument Is This?*. New York: Scholastic.

Hurd, T. (1984). *Mama Don't Allow*. New York: Harper & Row.

Maxner, J. (1989). *Nicholas Cricket*. Ill. by William Joyce. New York: Harper & Row.

Pitts, M. (1980). *Ty's One-Man Band*. Ill. by Margot Tomes. New York: Four Winds.

Raschka, C. (1992). *Charlie Parker Played Be Bop*. New York: Orchard.

Schroeder, A. (1991). *Josephine Baker*. New York: Chelsea House.

Schroeder, A. (1989). *Ragtime Tumpie*. Ill. by Bernie Fuchs. Boston: Little, Brown.

Williams, V. B. (1984). *Music, Music for Everyone*. New York: Greenwillow.

■ **Novel:**

Mitchell, B. (1987). *Raggin': A Story about Scott Joplin*. Ill. by Hetty Mitchell. Minneapolis: Carolrhoda.

■ **Poetry:**

Causley, C. (1986). *Early in the Morning*. Illus. by Michael Foreman. Music by Anthony Castro. New York: Viking Kestrel.

1. Find some blues music in the library. Play for the class. Ask students to illustrate how the music makes them feel.

2. Students can design an album cover for their favorite blues music.

3. Ask students to write their own original songs.

4. Take a survey of favorite kinds of music. Chart the results in a picture graph.

5. Ask students to bring in and share their favorite music.

6. Read the lyrics to music aloud as poetry.

■ **Date:** November 17

■ **This date is special because:**
It is Clock Day.

It is the day that Eli Terry patented his design for the first American-made clock.

Books that relate to this date

■ Picture Books:

Christelow, E. (1983). *Mr. Murphy's Marvelous Invention.* New York: Clarion.

Gibbons, G. (1979). *Clocks and How They Go.* New York: Crowell.

Grossman, B. (1990). *The Guy Who Was 5 Minutes Late.* Ill. by Judy Glasser. New York: Harper.

Havill, J. (1988). *Leroy and the Clock.* Ill. by Janet Wentworth. Boston: Houghton Mifflin.

Konigsburg, E. L. (1991). *Samuel Todd's Book of Great Inventions.* New York: Atheneum.

Krensky, S. (1989). *Big Time Bears.* Ill. by Maryann Cocca-Leffler. Boston: Little, Brown.

Lloyd, D. (1986). *The Stopwatch.* Ill. by Penny Dale. New York: Lippincott.

McMillan, B. (1989). *Time To...* New York: Lothrop, Lee & Shepard.

Siegfried, A. (1991). *Clocks! How Time Flies.* Ill. by Hans Poppel. New York: Lerner.

Taber, A. (1993). *The Boy Who Stopped Time.* New York: McElderry.

Turner, G. (1990). *Once Upon a Time.* New York: Viking.

Yorinks, A. (1988). *Bravo, Minski.* Ill. by Richard Egielski. New York: Farrar, Straus & Giroux.

Ziner, F. (1982). *Time.* New York: Childrens Press.

Zubrowski, B. (1988). *Clocks.* Ill. by Roy Doty. New York: Morrow.

■ Poetry:

"Lengths of Time" by Phyllis McGinley in:
de Regniers, B. S., and others. (1988). *Sing a Song of Popcorn.* Ill. by nine Caldecott Medal artists. New York: Scholastic. (page 88)

"Time" in:
Esbensen, B. (1992). *Who Shrank My Grandmother's House?* Ill. by Eric Beddows. (page 15)

Hopkins, L. B. (1993). *It's about Time!* Ill. by Matt Novak. New York: Simon and Schuster.

"Calendars and Clocks" poems by various authors in:
Kennedy, X. J. & Kennedy, D. M. (1992). *Talking Like the Rain.* Ill. by Jane Dyer. Boston: Little, Brown. (pages 77–80)

"Grandfather Clock" in:
Livingston, M. C. (1985). *Worlds I Know and Other Poems*. Ill. by Tim Arnold. New York: Antheneum. (page 21)

""The Clock Ticks" in:
Merriam, E. (1973). *Out Loud*. Ill. by Harriet Sherman. New York: Antheneum. (pages 44–45)

Activities for Extension:

1. Ask students to design different kinds of clocks.

2. Using *Time to...* (McMillan, 1989), students can make their own books that describe their schedules.

3. Practice telling time.

4. Label the classroom clock with the "five after, ten after," etc., ways of describing time.

5. Ask students to take a survey of the different times people go to bed and wake up.

N·O·V·E·M·B·E·R 26

■ Date: November 26

■ This date is special because:
It is the date the first national Thanksgiving Day was observed (1789).

Books that relate to this date
■ Picture Books:

Anderson, J. (1984). *The First Thanksgiving Feast.* Photos by George Ancona. Boston: Clarion/Houghton Mifflin.

Barkin, C. (1987). *Happy Thanksgiving!* Ill. by Giori Carmi. New York: Lothrop, Lee & Shepard.

Bunting, E. (1988). *How Many Days to America?* Ill. by Beth Peck. New York: Clarion.

Bunting, E. (1991). *A Turkey for Thanksgiving.* Ill. by Diane de Groat. New York: Clarion.

Celsi, Teresa. (1989). *Squanto and the First Thanksgiving.* Ill. by Pam Ford Johnson. Milwaukee: Raintree.

Cohen, M. (1987). *Don't Eat Too Much Turkey!* Ill. by Lillian Hoban. New York: Greenwillow.

Cohen, B. (1983). *Molly's Pilgrim.* Ill. by Michael J. Deraney. New York: Lothrop.

Cuyler, M. (1990). *Daisy's Crazy Thanksgiving.* Ill. by Robin Kramer. New York: Holt.

Dragonwagon, C. (1987). *Alligator Arrived with Apples: A Potluck Alphabet Feast.* Ill. by Jose Aruego & Ariane Dewey. New York: Macmillan.

Gibbons, Gail. (1983). *Thanksgiving Day.* New York: Holiday.

Harness, C. (1992). *Three Young Pilgrims.* New York: Bradbury.

Kroll, S. (1988). *Oh, What a Thanksgiving!* Ill. by S. D. Schindler. New York: Scholastic.

Nikola-Lisa, W. (1991). *1, 2, 3 Thanksgiving!* Ill. by Robin Kramer. Morton Grove, IL: Whitman.

Raphael, E. & Bolognese, D. (1991). *The Story of The First Thanksgiving.* New York: Scholastic.

Schachtman, T. (1985). *Parade!* Photos by Chuch Saaf. New York: Macmillan.

Waters, K. (1993). *Samuel Eaton's Day.* Photos by Russ Kendall. New York: Scholastic.

Weisgard, L. (1988). *The Plymouth Thanksgiving.* New York: Bantam Doubleday Dell.

Wickstrom, S. (1990). *Turkey on the Loose!* New York: Dial.

■ Novel:

Smith, J. L. (1990). *The Turkey's Side of It: Adam Joshua's Thanksgiving.* Ill. by Dick Gackenbach. New York: Harper & Row.

■ Poetry:

"Thanksgiving" in:
Livingston, M. C. (1985). *Celebrations.*
Ill. by Leonard Everett Fisher. New
York: Holiday House. (page 29)

"Giving Thanks Giving Thanks" in:
Merriam, E. (1986). *Fresh Paint.* Ill. by
David Frampton. New York: Macmillan.

Pilkey, D. (1990). *'Twas the Night
Before Thanksgiving.* New York:
Orchard.

Activities for Extension:

1. Ask students to make a list of things to be thankful for this year.

2. Plan a Thanksgiving dinner using the grocery ads. Calculate the cost.

3. Allow students to describe their Thanksgiving traditions. Collect stories in a class book.

4. Read *Molly's Pilgrim* (Cohen, 1983) and watch the video. Compare and contrast. Which did students prefer?

5. Read *How Many Days to America?* (Bunting, 1991). Discuss immigration today.

N·O·V·E·M·B·E·R 28

■ **Date:** November 28

■ **This date is special because:**
It is Ed Young's birthday (1931).

Books that relate to this date

■ **Picture Books:**

Calhoun, M. (1992). *While I Sleep*. Ill. by Ed Young. New York: Morrow.

Carlstrom, N. W. (1991). *Goodbye Geese*. Ill. by Ed Young. New York: Philomel.

Coleridge, S. T. (1992). *The Rime of the Ancient Mariner*. Ill. by Ed Young. New York: Atheneum.

Hearn, L. (1989). *The Voice of the Great Bell*. Ill. by Ed Young. Boston: Little, Brown.

Howe, J. (1987). *I Wish I Were a Butterfly*. Ill. by Ed Young. San Diego: Harcourt Brace Jovanovich.

Lewis, R. (1988). *In the Night, Still Dark*. Ill. by Ed Young. New York: Atheneum.

Louie, Ai-Ling. (1982). *Yeh Shen: A Cinderella Story from China*. Ill. by Ed Young. New York: Philomel.

Martin, R. (1985). *Foolish Rabbit's Big Mistake*. Ill. by Ed Young. New York: Putnam.

Melmed, L. K. (1993). *The First Song Ever Sung*. Ill. by Ed Young. New York: Lothrop.

Oppenheim, S.L. (1994). *Iblis*. Ill. by Ed Young. San Diego: Harcourt.

Osofsky, A. (1992). *Dreamcatcher*. Ill. by Ed Young. New York: Orchard.

Root, P. (1985). *Moon Tiger*. Ill. by Ed Young. New York: Holt, Rinehart & Winston.

Wilde, O. (1989). *The Happy Prince*. Ill. by Ed Young. New York: Simon & Schuster.

Young, E. (1980). *High on a Hill*. New York: Collins.

Young, E. (1989). *Lon Po Po*. New York: Philomel.

Young, E. (1984). *The Other Bone*. New York: Harper & Row.

Young, E. (1992). *Seven Blind Mice*. New York: Philomel.

Young, E. (1983). *Up a Tree*. New York: Harper & Row.

■ **Resource Book:**

Kovacs, D. & Preller, J. (1991). *Meet the Authors and Illustrators: 60 Creators of Favorite Children's Books Talk About Their Work*. New York: Scholastic. (pages 70–71)

1. Read *Lon Po Po* (Young, 1989). Compare and contrast with other versions of Red Riding Hood.

2. Create watercolor illustrations of another folktale or fairy tale.

3. Compare Ed Young's *Cinderella* with *The Egyptian Cinderella* by Shirley Climo, illustrated by Ruth Heller.

4. Students can do a creative drama presentation of their favorite Ed Young fairy tale.

5. Ask students to write their own fairy tale complete with a moral.

DECEMBER

- **This month is special because:** It is Human Rights Month.

Books that relate to this month
- **Picture Books:**

Anderson, D. (1986). *Friends*. Elgin, IL: Chariot Books.

Baden. (1985). *The Greatest Gift Is Love*. St. Louis, MO: Concordia.

Berry, J. (1986). *Teach Me about Friends*. Danbury, CT: Grolier Inc.

Brown, M. (1988). *Oh, Kojo! How Could You!* New York: Dial.

Brown, M. (1989). *What's So Funny, Ketu?* New York: Dial.

Cavan, S. (1993). *Thurgood Marshall and Equal Rights*. Brookfield, CT: Millbrook Press.

Daniel, B. (1991). *Count on Your Friends*. Good Apple.

Dellinger, A. (1985). *Hugging*. Ill. by Jenny Williams. St. Paul, MN: Childs World.

Dupre, R. (1993). *Agassu: Legend of the Leopard King*. Minneapolis, MN: Carolrhoda.

Hallinan, P. K. (1985). *That's What a Friend Is*. Hambleton-Hill.

Hays, M. (1990). *The Tin Heart*. New York: Macmillan.

Herbert, J. (1985). *Love Is Kind*. Elgin, IL: Chariot Books.

Kalman, B. (1985). *Fun with My Friends*. New York: Crabtree Pub Co.

Levine, E. (1990). *If You Lived At the Time of Martin Luther King*. New York: Scholastic.

Marzollo, J. (1993). *Happy Birthday, Martin Luther King*. New York: Scholastic.

Morris, B. (1987). *Friends Help Me*. Nashville, TN: Broadman.

Preschool Color and Learn: Making Friends and Sharing. (1992). New York: Scholastic.

Roberts, S. *Friendship*. Ill. by Linda Hohag. St. Paul, MN: Childs World.

Aardema, V. (1988). *Bimwili and the Zimwi.* Ill. by Susan Meddaugh. New York: Dial.

Aliki. (1982). *We Are Best Friends.* New York: Greenwillow.

Activities for Extension:

1. Encourage students to make friendship bracelets and to swap them with friends.

2. Human Right's leaders look for ways to make the world a better place for everyone to live in. Invite students to brainstorm how the classroom can be made a better place.

3. Divide the class in pairs. Ask each child to think of three nice things about his or her partner. Ask children to share their words of kindness with the class.

4. Encourage students to make a collage of people that have helped the Human Rights cause. Some children might choose to illustrate a poster, instead.

5. Brainstorm with students why it's good to be kind to everyone.

6. Have a "Be Kind to Every Person" Day.

H·A·N·U·K·K·A·H

Date: Varies in December

This date is special because:
It is Hanukkah.

Books that relate to this date

Picture Books:

Adler, D. A. (1989). *Happy Hanukkah Rebus*. Ill. by Jan Palmer. New York: Viking.

Adler, D. A. (1982). *A Picture Book of Hanukkah*. Holiday House.

Burns, M. (1981). *The Hanukkah Book*. Ill. by Martha Weston. New York: Macmillan.

Chaikin, M. (1990). *Hanukkah*. Ill. by Ellen Weiss. New York: Holiday House.

Chaikin, M. (1981). *Light Another Candle: The Story and Meaning of Hanukkah*. Ill. by Demi. New York: Clarion.

Cooper, D. (1989). *Hanukkah Songs and Games*. New York: Random House.

de Paola, T. (1989). *My First Chanukah*. New York: Putnam.

Ehrlich, A. (1989). *The Story of Hanukkah*. Ill. by Ori Sherman. New York: Dial.

Gellman, E. (1992). *Jeremy's Dreidel*. Ill. by Judith Friedman. New York: Kar-Ben Copies.

Goldin, B. D. (1988). *Just Enough Is Plenty: A Hanukkah Tale*. Ill. by Seymour Chwast. New York: Viking.

Jaffe, N. (1992). *In the Month of Kislve: A Story for Hanukkah*. Ill. by Louise August. New York: Viking.

Katz, B. (1992). *A Family Hanukkah*. Ill. by Caryl Herzfeld. New York: Random House.

Kimmel, E. A. (1993). *Asher and the Capmakers: A Hanukkah Story*. Ill. by Will Hillenbrand. New York: Holiday House.

Kimmel, E. a. (1990). *The Chanukkah Guest*. Ill. by Giora Carmi. New York: Holiday House.

Kimmel, E. A. (1989). *Hershel and the Hanukkah Goblins*. Ill. by Trina Schart Hyman. New York: Holiday House.

Kimmelman, L. & Kimmelman, J. (1992). *Hanukkah Lights and Hanukkah Nights*. New York: HarperCollins.

Koralek, J. (1990). *Hanukkah: The Festival of Lights*. Ill. by Juan Wijngaard. New York: Lothrop.

Manushkin, F. (1990). *Latkes and Applesauce: A Hanukkah Story*. New York: Scholastic.

Rosen, M. (1992). *Elijah's Angel*. Ill. by Aminah Brenda Lynn Robinson. San Diego: Harcourt Brace Jovanovich.

Schotter, R. (1991). *Hanukkah!* Ill. by Marylin Hafner. Boston: Little, Brown.

Silverman, M. (1987). *Festival of Lights: The Story of Hanukkah*. Ill. by C. S. Ewing. New York: Simon & Schuster.

Novels:

Cohen, B. (1993). *The Christmas Revolution*. New York: Dell.

Singer, I. B. (1980). *The Power of Light: 8 Stories about Hanukkah.* Ill. by Irene Lieblich. New York: Farrar, Straus & Giroux.

■ Poetry:

"Dreidel" by J. Patrick Lewis and "First Night of Hanukkah" by Ruth Roston in: Livingston, M. C. (1986). *Poems for Jewish Holidays.* Ill. by Lloyd Bloom. New York: Holiday House. (page 12, 13)

"Light the Festive Candles (for Hanukkah)" in: Prelutsky, J. (1983). *The Random House Book of Poetry For Children.* Ill. by Arnold Lobel. New York: Random House. (page 48)

"Dreidel Song" by Efraim Rosenzweig in: Prelutsky, J. (1986). *Read-Aloud Rhymes for the Very Young.* Ill. by Marc Brown. New York: Knopf. (page 52)

■ Resource Book:

Browkaw, M. & Gilban, A. (1991). *The Penny Whistle Christmas Party Book: Including Hanukkah, New Year's & Twelfth Night Family Parties.* Ill. by Jill Weber. New York: Simon & Schuster.

Activities for Extension:

1. Make potato latkes. Grate the following:

    6 medium potatoes   1 onion
    1 large carrot

Add: 2 eggs, 1/4 cup matzo meal, and 1/4 cup oil. Fry large spoonfuls in hot oil until golden brown. Serve with applesauce.

2. Make a dreidel and play. First, all players get 10–15 objects (pennies, candy pieces, etc.). All players put one object in the pot or middle. Then, each player takes turns spinning the dreidel. Each letter on the dreidel has a meaning:

    N (nisht)—nothing. If it lands on this letter, the player does nothing.
    G (ganz)—all. Player takes everything in the pot.
    H (halb)—half. Player takes half of what's in the pot.
    S (shtel)—put in. Player puts two objects in the pot.

(Source: *Latkes and Applesauce: A Hanukkah Story,* Manushkin, 1993.)

3. Match the following Hanukkah words with their definitions in a pocket chart.

    dreidel—spinning top   latkes—potato pancakes
    menorah—candle holder   shamash—helper candle

4. Light Hanukkah candles and explain what each day represents.

5. Eat Jewish foods, such as matzo balls, bagels, and lox.

D·E·CEM·B·E·R 3

■ Date: December 3

■ This date is special because:

It is Gilbert Stuart's birthday (1755).

Gilbert Stuart was an American portrait painter.

Books that relate to this date

■ Picture Books:

Alcorn, J. (1991). *Rembrandt's Beret or the Painter's Crown.* Ill. by Stephen Alcorn. New York: Tambourine.

Baker, A. (1986). *Benjamin's Portrait.* New York: Lothrop.

Bang, M. (1981). *Tye May and the Magic Brush.* New York: Greenwillow.

Demi. (1980). *Liang and the Magic Paintbrush.* New York: Holt.

Harley, R. (1990). *Mary's Tiger.* Ill. by Sue Porter. San Diego: Harcourt Brace Jovanovich.

Kesselman, W. A. (1980). *Emma.* Ill. by Barbara Cooney. Garden City, NY: Doubleday.

Rylant, C. (1988). *All I See.* Ill. by Peter Catalanotto. New York: Orchard.

Schwartz, A. (1983). *Begin at the Beginning.* New York: Macmillan.

Zadrzynska, E. (1990) *The Girl with a Watering Can.* Ill. by Arnold Skanick. New York: Chameleon.

■ Novel:

Conrad, P. (1991). *Prairie Visions: The Life and Times of Solomon Butcher.* New York: Harper.

■ Poetry:

"Frame for a Picture" in:
Merriam, E. (1986). *Fresh Paint.* Ill. by David Frampton. New York: Macmillan.

"Me" by Walter de la Mare and "Me" by Karla Kuskin in:
Prelutsky, J. (1983). *The Random House Book of Poetry for Children.* Ill. by Arnold Lobel. New York: Random House. (pages 118–119)

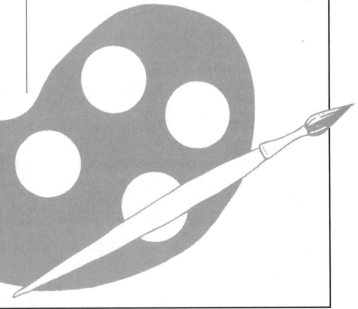

1. Students can do self-portraits.

2. Ask students to make a frame for their self-portraits to give to parents or caregivers.

3. Allow students to do a word portrait of themselves using words found in the newspaper.

4. Read *Prairie Visions: The Life and Times of Solomon Butcher* (Conrad, 1991). Discuss the lives of these people. How were they different from and similar to students' lives? Encourage students to write about it.

5. Brainstorm famous portraits. Ask groups of children to find a print of each of the famous ones. Share with class.

6. Students can send for a magnet button with their picture on it. Each student should include a photo of himself or herself, a long self-addressed envelope, and $1.00 and mail to:

> Professor Bob
> 135 Echo Drive
> Chambersburg, PA 17201

(From *Free Stuff for Kids*, Meadowbrook Press, 1993, page 35)

D·E·C·E·M·B·E·R 14

■ **Date:** December 14

■ **This date is special because:**
It is Insect Day.

It is the annual meeting of the Entomological Society of America.

Books that relate to this date

■ **Picture Books:**

Bailey, Jill. (1989). *The Life Cycle of a Grasshopper*. New York: Bookwright.

Batten, M. (1992). *Nature's Tricksters*. Boston: Little, Brown.

Bernhard, E. (1993). *Dragonfly*. Ill. by Durga Bernhard. New York: Holiday House.

Bernhard, E. (1992). *Ladybug*. Ill. by Durga Bernhard. New York: Holiday House.

Brenner, B. & Chardiet, B. (1993). *Where's That Insect?* Ill. by Carol Schwartz. New York: Cartwheel Books.

Brinckloe, J. (1985). *Fireflies!* New York:Macmillan.

Brown, R. (1988). *Ladybug, Ladybug*. New York: Dutton.

Carle, E. (1989). *Animals, Animals*. New York: Putnam.

Carle, E. (1990). *The Very Quiet Cricket*. New York: Putnam.

Carle, E. (1984). *The Very Busy Spider*. New York: Putnam.

Carle, E. (1969). *The Very Hungry Caterpillar*. New York: Philomel.

Cole, Joanna. (1984). *An Insect's Body*. New York: Morrow.

Danks, Hugh. (1987). *The Bug Book*. New York: Workman.

Dorros, A. (1987). *Ant Cities*. New York: Crowell.

Florian, D. (1986). *Discovering Butterflies*. New York: Scribners.

Florian, D. (1989). *Nature Walk*. New York: Greenwillow.

Gibbons, G. (1989). *Monarch Butterfly*. New York: Holiday House.

Gibbons, G. (1993). *Spiders*. New York: Holiday House.

Goor, R. and Goor, N. (1990). *Insect Metamorphosis: From Egg to Adult*. New York: Atheneum.

Graham, A. (1983). *Busy Bugs*. New York: Dodd.

Hall, K. and Eisenberg, L. (1986). *Buggy Riddles*. New York: Dial.

Henwood, C. (1988). *Spiders*. New York: Watts.

Howe, J. (1987). *I Wish I Were A Butterfly*. Ill. by Ed Young. San Diego: Harcourt Brace Jovanovich.

Jukes, M. (1984). *Like Jake and Me*. Ill. by Lloyd Bloom. New York: Knopf.

Kimmel, E. (1988). *Anasi and the Moss-Covered Rock*. Ill. by Janet Stevens. New York: Holiday House.

Lavies, B. (1990). *Backyard Hunter: The Praying Mantis*. New York: Dutton.

Maxner, Joyce. (1991). *Lady Bugatti*. New York: Lothrop.

Maxner, Joyce. (1989). *Nicholas Cricket*. Ill. by William Joyce. New York: Harper & Row.

Merrill, J. (1992). *The Girl Who Loved Caterpillars*. Ill. by Floyd Cooper. New York: Philomel. (Japanese folktale)

Mound, Laurence. (1990). *Eyewitness Books: Insect*. New York: Knopf.

Parker, N. W. and Wright, J. R. (1987). *Bugs*. New York: Greenwillow.

Parsons, A. (1990). *Amazing Spiders*. Photos by Jerry Young. New York: Knopf.

Patent, D. (1986). *Mosquitoes*. New York: Holiday House.

Pelham, D. (1990). *Sam's Sandwich*. New York: Dutton.

Pallotta, J. (1986). *The Icky Bug Alphabet Book*. Ill. by Ralph Masiello. Watertown, MA: Charlesbridge.

Pallotta, J. (1992). *The Icky Bug Counting Book*. New York: Trumpet Club.

Roop, P. and Roop, C. (1986). *Going Buggy! Jokes about Insects*. Minneapolis: Lerner.

Van Allsburg, C. (1988). *Two Bad Ants*. Boston: Houghton Mifflin.

Watts, B. (1985). *Butterfly and Caterpillar*. Morristown, NJ: Silver Burdett.

Watts, B. (1988). *Dragonfly*. Morristown, NJ: Silver Burdett.

Whalley, P. (1988). *Eyewitness Books: Butterfly & Moth*. New York: Knopf.

Yoshi. (1990). *The Butterfly Hunt*. New York: Picture Book Studio.

■ Poetry:

Fisher, A. (1986). *When It Comes to Bugs: Poems*. Ill. by Chris and Bruce Degen. New York: Harper & Row.

Fleischman, P. (1988). *Joyful Noise*. Ill. by Eric Beddows. New York: Harper & Row.

Hoberman, M. (1976). *Bugs: Poems*. New York: Viking.

"Who Pulled the Plug in My Ant Farm?" and "Mosquitoes, Mosquitoes" in: Prelutsky, J. (1990). *Something BIG Has Been Here*. Ill. by James Stevenson. New York: Greenwillow. (pages 70-71, 136-137)

Rounds, G. (1990). *I Know an Old Lady Who Swallowed a Fly*. New York: Holiday House.

Westcott, N. B. (1980). *I Know an Old Lady Who Swallowed a Fly*. Boston: Little, Brown.

Activities for Extension:

1. Keep a classroom insect journal noting bugs seen during the day, week and month.

2. Invite an entomologist or a beekeeper to come to class and talk about different types of insects.

3. Read *Joyful Noise* (Fleischman, 1988) and ask students to perform it in pairs.

4. Take a nature walk with the class. Keep a count of all the insects you see.

DECEMBER 22

■ **Date:** December 22

■ **This date is special because:**
It is Jerry Pinkney's birthday (1939).

Books that relate to this date
■ Picture Books illustrated by Pinkney:

Aardema, V. (1989). *Rabbit Makes a Monkey of Lion: A Swahili Tale*. New York: Dial.

Adoff, A. (1991). *In for Winter, Out for Spring*. San Diego: Harcourt Brace Jovanovich.

Carlstrom, N. W. (1987). *Wild, Wild Sunflower Child Anna*. New York: Macmillan.

Coyle, R. (1988). *My First Baking Book*. New York: Workman.

Dragonwagon, C. (1986). *Half a Moon and One Whole Star*. New York: Macmillan.

Dragonwagon, C. (1990). *Home Place*. New York: Macmillan.

Flournoy, V. (1985). *The Patchwork Quilt*. New York: Dial.

Forest, H. (1990). *The Woman Who Flummoxed the Fairies: An Old Tale From Scotland*. Ill. by Susan Gaber. San Diego: Harcourt Brace Jovanovich.

Hamilton, V. (1992). *Drylongso*. San Diego: Harcourt Brace Jovanovich.

Harris, J. C. (1988). *More Tales of Uncle Remus*. New York: Dial.

Levitin, S. (1991). *The Man Who Kept His Heart in a Bucket*. New York: Dial.

MacDonald, E. (1989). *Miss Poppy and the Honey Cake*. Ill. by Claire Smith. New York: Dial.

MacDonald, M. (1990). *Hedgehog Bakes a Cake*. Ill. by Lynn Munsinger. New York: Bantam.

Marzollo, J. (1990). *Pretend You're a Cat*. New York: Dial.

McKissack, P. (1988). *Mirandy and Brother Wind*. New York: Knopf.

Parker, N. W. (1983). *Love from Aunt Betty*. New York: Dodd, Mead.

Pinkney, G. J. (1992). *Back Home*. New York: Dial.

Polacco, P. (1990). *Thundercake*. New York: Philomel.

San Souci, R. (1989). *The Talking Eggs: A Folktale from the American South*. New York: Dial.

Singer, M. (1989). *Turtle in July*. New York: Macmillan.

Spurr, E. (1991). *The Biggest Birthday Cake in the World*. San Diego: Harcourt Brace Jovanovich.

Taylor, J. (1988). *Dudley Bakes a Cake*. Ill. by Peter Cross. New York: Putnam.

Watson, C. (1989). *Valentine Foxes*. New York: Orchard.

Willard, N. (1990). *The High Rise Glorious Skittle Skat Roarious Sky Pie Angel Food Cake*. Ill. by Richard Jesse Watson. San Diego: Harcourt Brace Jovanovich.

■ Resource Books:

Cumings, P. (1992). *Talking With Artists*. New York: Bradbury. (pages 60-65) (additional information about Jerry Pinkney)

Kovacs, D. & Preller, J. (1991). *Meet the Authors and Illustrators: 60 Creators of Favorite Children's Books Talk about Their Work*. New York: Scholastic. (pages 50–51)

Activities for Extension:

1. Add actions to *Pretend You Are a Cat* (Marzollo, 1990) and ask students to act it out.

2. Perform a puppet show of *The Talking Eggs* (San Souci, 1989).

3. Read *Home Place* (Dragonwagon, 1990). Ask students to imagine and write about what might be left from their houses after 100 years.

4. After reading *Mirandy and Brother Wind* (McKissack, 1988), have a cake walk with little snack cakes. Discuss different interpretations of cake walks. Brainstorm different types of cakes. Students can collect cake recipes and make a booklet or write about their favorite cakes after reading some of the following books and poems about cake.

Hennessy, B. G. (1990). *Jake Baked the Cake*. New York: Viking.

Nobisso, J. & Kranjnc, A. C. (1993). *For the Sake of a Cake*. New York: Rizzoli.

"Chocolate Cake" by Nina Payne in: Prelutsky, J. (1983). *The Random House Book of Poetry*. Ill. by Arnold Lobel. New York: Random House. (page 148).

Robart, R. (1986). *The Cake the Mack Ate*. Boston: Little, Brown.

Wayman, J. (1988). *Don't Burn Down the Birthday Cake*. Houston: Heartstone.

D·E·C·E·M·B·E·R 25

■ **Date:** December 25

■ **This date is special because:**
It is Christmas.

Books that relate to this date

■ **Picture Books:**

Ames, M. (1990). *Grandpa Jake and the Grand Christmas*. New York: Scribner.

Aoki, H. G. (1991). *Santa's Favorite Story*. Ill. by Ivan Gantscher. New York: Scholastic.

Brett, J. (1990). *The Wild Christmas Reindeer*. New York: Putnam.

Bunting, E. (1992). *The Day before Christmas*. Ill. by Beth Peck. New York: Clarion.

Bunting, E. (1991). *Night Tree*. Ill. by Ted Rand. San Diego: Harcourt Brace Jovanovich.

Carrier, L. (1989). *The Snowy Path*. Saxonville, MA: Picture Book Studio.

Civardi, A. (1991). *The Secrets of Santa*. Ill. by Clive Scruton. New York: Simon & Schuster.

Clifton, L. (1991). *Everett Anderson's Christmas Coming*. Ill. by Jan Spivey Gilchrist. New York: Holt.

Climo, S. (1982). *The Cobweb Christmas*. Ill. by Joe Lasker. New York: Crowell.

Cuyler, M. (1987). *Fat Santa*. Ill. by Marsha Winborn. New York: Holt.

Day, A. (1990). *Carl's Christmas*. New York: Farrar, Straus & Giroux.

de Paola, T. (1987). *An Early American Christmas*. New York: Holiday House.

Dubanevich, A. (1986). *Pigs at Christmas*. New York: Bradbury.

Dugan, M. (1988). *Wombats Don't Have Christmas?* Ill. by Jane Burrell.

Fox, M. (1988). *With Love, at Christmas*. Ill. by Gary Lippincott. Nashville: Abingdon.

George, W. T. (1992). *Christmas at Long Pond*. Ill. by Lindsay Barrett George. New York: Greenwillow.

Godden, R. (1992). *The Story of Holly and Ivy*. Ill. by Barbara Cooney. New York: Scholastic.

Goode, D. (1990). *Diane Goode's American Christmas*. New York: Dutton.

Greenburg, D. (1993). *Young Santa*. Ill. by Warren Miller. New York: Puffin.

Harvey, B. (1990). *My Prairie Christmas*. Ill. by Deborah Kogan Ray. New York: Holiday House.

Haywood, C. (1986). *How the Reindeer Saved Santa*. Ill. by Victor Ambrus. New York: Morrow.

Heath, A. (1992). *Sofie's Role*. Ill. by Sheila Hamanaka. New York: Four Winds. (recipes for Marzipan and Cinnamon Stars on endpapers)

Holabird, K. (1985). *Angelina's Christmas.* Ill. by Helen Craig. New York: Potter.

Houston, G. (1988). *The Year of the Perfect Christmas* Tree. Ill. by Barbara Cooney. New York: Dial.

"January" by John Updike in: Prelutsky, J. (Ed.) (1983). *The Random House Book of Poetry for Children*. Ill. by Arnold Lobel. New York: Random House. (page 50)

Howard, E. F. (1989). *Chita's Christmas Tree*. Ill. by Floyd Cooper. New York: Bradbury. (African American)

Howe, J. (1988). *The Fright Before Christmas*. Ill. by Leslie Morrill. New York: Morrow.

Hyman, T. S. (1991). *How Six Found Christmas*. New York: Holiday House.

Impey, R. (1988). *A Letter to Santa Claus*. Ill. by Sue Porter. New York: Delacorte.

Jukes, M. (1987). *Lights around the Palm*. Ill. by Stacey Shuett. New York: Random House.

Kellogg, S. (1992). *The Christmas Witch*. New York: Dial.

Koralek, J. (1989). *The Cobweb Curtain*. Ill. by Pauline Baynes. New York: Henry Holt.

Leighton, M. R. (1992). *An Ellis Island Christmas*. Ill. by Dennis Nolan. New York: Viking.

Lindgren, A. (1991). *A Calf for Christmas*. Ill. by Marit Tornqvist. New York: R & S Books.

Neville, M. (1992). *The Christmas Tree Ride*. Ill. by Megan Lloyd. New York: Holiday House.

Nixon, J. L. (1992). *That's the Spirit, Claude*. Ill. by Tracey Campbell Pearson. New York: Viking.

Pilkington, B. (1990). *Grandpa Claus*. Minneapolis: Carolrhoda.

Proysen, A. & Ahlbom, J. (1992). *Christmas Eve at Santa's*. New York: R & S Books.

Pryor, B. (1990). *Merry Christmas Amanda and April*. Ill. by Diane de Groat. New York: Morrow.

Rollins, C. H. (1993). *Christmas Gif': An Anthology of Christmas Poems, Songs, and Stories Written by and about African Americans*. Ill. by Ashley Bryan. New York: Morrow. (African American)

Rylant, C. (1988). *Henry and Mudge in the Sparkle Days*. Ill. by Sucie Stevenson. New York: Bradbury.

Sharmat, M. W. (1990). *I'm Santa Claus and I'm Famous*. Ill. by Marylin Hafner. New York: Holiday House.

Spier, P. (1983). *Christmas*. Garden City, NY: Doubleday.

Stevenson, J. (1981). *The Night after Christmas*. New York: Greenwillow.

Trivas, I. (1988). *Emma's Christmas*. New York: Orchard.

Tyler, L. W. (1990). *The After-Christmas Tree*. Ill. by Susan Davis. New York: Viking.

Wells, R. (1975). *Morris's Disappearing Bag*. New York: Dutton.

Wild, M. (1991). *Thank You, Santa*. Ill. by Kerry Argent. New York: Scholastic.

Wilhelm, H. (1989). *Schnitzel's First Christmas*. New York: Simon & Schuster.

Wood, A. (1988). *The Horrible Holidays*. Ill. by Rosekrans Hoffman.

Yolen, J. (1991). *Hark! A Christmas Sampler*. Ill. by Tomie de Paola. New York: Putnam.

■ Novels:

Davies, V. (1991). *Miracle on 34th Street*. Ill. by Tomie de Paola. New York: Scholastic.

Greenberg, M. H. (1991). *A Newbery Christmas: 14 Stories of Christmas by Newbery Award Winning Authors*. New York: Delacorte.

Hamilton, V. (1989). *The Bells of Christmas*. Ill. by Lambert Davis. San Diego: Harcourt Brace Jovanovich. (African Americans)

Hautzig, D. (1992). *The Nutcracker Ballet*. Ill. by Carolyn Ewing. New York: Random House.

Robinson, B. (1972). *The Best Christmas Pageant Ever*. Ill. by Judith Gwyn Brown. New York: Harper & Row.

Rylant, C. (1987). *Children of Christmas: Stories for the Season*. Ill. by S. D. Schindler. New York: Orchard.

■ Poetry:

"Day Before Christmas" by Marchette Chute in:
de Regniers, B. S., and others. (1988). *Sing a Song of Popcorn*. New York: Scholastic. (page 89)

Duntze, D. (1992). *The Twelve Days of Christmas*. New York: North-South.

Edens, C. (1991). *Santa Cows*. Ill. by Daniel Lane. New York: Green Tiger Press.

Frost, R. (1990). *Christmas Trees*. Ill. by Ted Rand. New York: Holt.

Hague, M. (1991). *Deck the Halls*. New York: Holt.

Hague, M. (1991). *O Christmas Tree*. New York: Holt.

Kennedy, X. J. (1992). *The Beasts of Bethlehem*. Ill. by Michael McCurday. New York: McElderry.

"Christmas Eve" in:
Livingston, M. C. (1985). *Celebrations*. Ill. by Leonard Everett Fisher. New York: Holiday House. (page 31)

Moore, C. (1985). *The Night Before Christmas*. Ill. by James Marshall. New York: Scholastic.

Prelutsky, J. (1981). *It's Christmas*. Ill. by Marylin Hafner. New York: Greenwillow.

■ Resource Book:

Browkaw, M. & Gilban, A. (1991). *The Penny Whistle Christmas Party Book: Including Hanukkah, New Year's & Twelfth Night Family Parties*. Ill. by Jill Weber. New York: Simon & Schuster.

Activities for Extension:

1. Share family Christmas traditions.

2. Ask students to make an advent calendar with special treats for every day of December.

3. Discuss Christmas customs around the world.

4. Ask students to write about their favorite Christmas.

5. Students can match the following countries with their "Merry Christmas" greetings in a pocket chart.

China—Sheng Dan Kuai Le
Denmark—Glaedelig Jul
France—Joyeux Noel
Italy—Buon Natale

Poland—Wesolych Swiat
Spain/Mexico—Feliz Navidad
Sweden—God Ju

D·E·C·E·M·B·E·R 26

■ **Date:** December 26

■ **This date is special because:**
It is Kwanzaa.

Books that relate to this date

■ **Picture Books:**

Chocolate, D. M. N. (1990). *Kwanzaa*. Ill. by Melodye Rosales. Chicago: Childrens Press.

Chocolate, D. M. N. (1992). *My First Kwanzaa Book*. Ill. by Cal Massey. New York: Scholastic.

Freeman, D. R. (1992). *Kwanzaa*. Ill. by Dorothy Rhodes Freeman & Diane M. Macmillan. Hillside, NJ: Enslow.

Hoyt-Goldsmith, D. (1993). *Celebrating Kwanzaa*. Photos by Lawrence Migdale. New York: Holiday House.

Porter, A. P. (1991). *Kwanzaa*. Ill. by Janice Lee Porter. Minneapolis: Carolrhoda.

Pinkney, A. D. (1993). *Seven Candles for Kwanzaa*. Ill. by Brian Pinkney. New York: Dial.

■ **Poetry:**

"Candlelight and Moth Wings" in: Zolotow, C. (1987). *Everything Glistens and Everything Sings*. Ill. by Margot Tomes. San Diego: Harcourt Brace Jovanovich.(page 30)

Activities for Extension:

1. Match the Swahili words with the English terms in a pocket chart. These are the seven principles of Kwanzaa:

       umojo (oo-MO-jah)—unity

       kujichagulia (koo-jee-cha-goo-LEE-ah)—self-determination

       ujima (oo-JEE-mah)—collective work and responsibility

       ujamma (oo-jah-MAH)—cooperative economics

       nia (NEE-ah)—purpose

       kuumba (koo-OOM-bah)—creativity

       imani (ee-MAH-nee)—faith

2. Encourage students to do research on Kwanzaa.

3. Using black, red, and green construction paper, students can make strips and weave into placemats.

4. Using *Moja Means One* (Feelings, 1971) and *Jambo Means Hello* (Feelings, 1974), make a pocket chart activity of Swahili and English words.

moja (mo-jah)—1

mbili (m-bee-lee)—2

tatu (ta-too)—3

nne (n-nay)—4

tano (tah-no)—5

sita (see-tah)—6

saba (sah-bah)—7

nane (nah-nay)—8

tisa (tee-sah)—9

kumi (koo-mee)—10

baba (bah-bah)—father

chakula (cha-koo-lah)—food

jambo (jahm-bow)—hello

mama (mah-mah)—mother

rafiki (rah-fee-key)—friend

shule (shoe-lay)—school

tembo (tem-bow)—elephant

wahtoto (wah-toe-toe)—children

5. Using the illustrations in *Kwanzaa* (Chocolate, 1990), ask students to create kofias (hats) out of construction paper.

D·E·C·E·M·B·E·R 29

■ Date: December 29

■ This date is special because:
It is Molly Bang's birthday (1943).

Books that relate to this date

■ Picture Books:

Cassedy, S. & Suetake, K. (1992). *Red Dragonfly on My Shoulder: Haiku*. New York: HarperCollins.

Bang, B. (1975). *The Old Woman and the Red Pumpkin: A Bengali Folktale*. New York: Macmillan.

Bang, B. (1978). *The Old Woman and the Rice Thief*. New York: Greenwillow.

Bang, B. (1978). *Tuntuni, the Tailor Bird*. New York: Greenwillow.

Bang, M. (1977). *The Buried Moon and Other Stories*. New York: Scribner.

Bang, M. (1983). *Dawn*. New York: Morrow.

Bang, M. (1988). *Delphine*. New York: Morrow.

Bang, M. (1973). *The Goblin's Giggle and Other Stories*. New York: Macmillan.

Bang, M. (1980). *The Grey Lady and the Strawberry Snatcher*. New York: Four Winds.

Bang, M. (1973). *The Man from the Village Deep in the Mountains and Other Japanese Folk Tales*. New York: Macmillan.

Bang, M. (1985). *Paper Crane*. New York: Greenwillow.

Bang, M. (1983). *10, 9, 8*. New York: Greenwillow.

Bang, M. (1981). *Tye May and the Magic Brush*. New York: Greenwillow.

Bang, M. (1976). *Wiley and the Hairy Man*. New York: Macmillan.

Bang, M. (1991). *Yellow Ball*. New York: Morrow.

■ Resource Book:

Kovacs, D. & Preller, J. (1991). Meet the Authors and Illustrators: 60 Creators of Favorite Children's Books Talk about Their Work. New York: Scholastic. (pages 14–15)

1. Invite students to make a nonconventional alphabet book modeled after *10, 9, 8* (Bang, 1983)

2. Using *10, 9, 8* (Bang, 1983), students can practice counting backwards.

3. Molly Bang wrote *10, 9, 8* (Bang, 1983) for her daughter when Molly was away from her daughter. Encourage students to discuss how writing can help when a person misses someone.

4. Read some of Molly Bang's books and vote on a class favorite.

5. Read *Red Dragonfly on My Shoulder: Haiku* (Cassedy & Suetake, 1992) and the following book:

Higginson, W. J. (1991). *Wind in the Long Grass: A Collection of Haiku.* Ill. by Sandra Speidel. New York: Simon & Schuster.

Ask students to write and illustrate their own haiku.

SPECIAL DAYS

S·N·O·W D·A·Y·S

■ **Date:** Any day that it snows

■ **This date is special because:**
It is a day to celebrate cold weather.

Books that relate to this date

■ **Picture Books:**

Agee, J. (1982). *If Snow Falls: A Story for December*. New York: Pantheon.

Aragon, J. C. (1988). *Winter Harvest*. Ill. by Leslie Baker. Boston: Little, Brown.

Arnold, T. (1988). *The Winter Mittens*. New York: McElderry.

Barasch, L. (1993). *A Winter Walk*. New York: Ticknor & Fields.

Bauer, C. F. (1987). *Midnight Snowman*. Ill. by Catherine Stock. New York: Atheneum.

Bauer, C. F. (1986). *Snowy Day: Stories and Poems*. Ill. by Margaret Tomes. New York: Lippincott.

Branley, F. M. (1986). *Snow Is Falling*. Ill. by Holly Keller. New York: Crowell.

Brett, J. (1989). *The Mitten*. New York: Putnam.

Briggs, R. (1978). *The Snowman*. New York: Random House.

Butterworth, N. (1989). *One Snowy Night*. Boston: Little, Brown.

Carlstrom, N. W. (1992). *The Snow Speaks*. Ill. by Jane Dyer. Boston: Little, Brown.

Cosgrove, M. (1980). *It's Snowing!* New York: Dodd, Mead.

Downing, J. (1989). *White Snow, Blue Feather*. New York: Bradbury.

Ewart, C. (1992). *One Cold Night*. New York: Putnam.

Fradin, D. (1983). *Blizzards and Winter Weather*. Chicago: Childrens Press.

Goffstein, M. B. (1986). *Our Snowman*. New York: Harper & Row.

Harshman, M. (1990). *Snow Company*. Ill. by Leslie W. Bowman. New York: Cobblehill.

Hartley, D. (1993). *Up North in Winter*. Ill. by Lydia Dabcovich. New York: Puffin.

Hoban, J. (1989). *Amy Loves the Snow*. Ill. by Lillian Hoban. New York: Harper & Row.

Johnston, T. (1993). *The Last Snow of Winter*. Ill. by Friso Henstra. New York: Tambourine.

Kahl, J. D. (1992). *Wet Weather: Rain Showers and Snowfall*. Minneapolis: Lerner.

Keller, H. (1988). *Geraldine's Big Snow*. New York: Greenwillow.

Khalsa, D. K. (1992). *The Snow Cat*. New York: Potter.

Levine, C. A. (1981). *Snow Fun.* Ill. by Tom Huffman. New York: Watts.

Lobe, M. (1984). *The Snowman Who Went for a Walk.* Ill. by Winifried Opgennoorth. New York: Morrow.

Maestro, B. (1989). *Snow Day.* Ill. by Giulio Maestro. New York: Scholastic.

McCully, E. A. (1985). *First Snow.* New York: Harper & Row.

Miller, N. (1990). *Emmett's Snowball.* Ill. by Suan Guevara. New York: Holt.

Morgan, A. (1985). *Sadie and the Snowman.* Ill. by Brenda Clark. New York: Scholastic.

Neitzel, S. (1989). *The Jacket I Wear in the Snow.* Ill. by Nancy Winslow Parker. New York: Greenwillow.

Rockwell, A. (1987). *The First Snowfall.* New York: Macmillan.

Schweniger, A. (1993). *Wintertime.* New York: Puffin.

Silverman, E. (1991). *Warm in Winter.* Ill. by Michael J. Deraney. New York: Macmillan.

Stevenson, J. (1991). *Brrr!* New York: Greenwillow.

Sugarman, J. G. (1985). *Snowflakes.* Ill. by Jennifer Dewey. Boston: Little, Brown.

Vigna, J. (1989). *Boot Weather.* Niles, IL: Whitman.

Webster, H. (1988). *Winter Book.* Ill. by Irene Trivas. New York: Scribner.

Williams, T. T. (1984). *The Secret Language of Snow.* Ill. by Jennifer Dewey. San Francisco: Sierra Club.

 Ziefert, H. (1988). *Snow Magic.* Ill. by Claire Schumacher. New York: Viking.

Zolotow, C. (1988). *Something Is Going to Happen.* Ill. by Catherine Stock. New York: Harper.

■ Novels:

Kehret, P. (1989). *Nightmare Mountain.* New York: Dutton.

Lawson, L. (1989). *Addie's Dakota Winter.* New York: Whitman.

■ Poetry:

Florian, D. (1987). *A Winter's Day.* New York: Greenwillow.

"On the First Snowfall" in: Merriam, E. (1986). *Fresh Paint.* Ill. by David Frampton. New York: Macmillan.

Prelutsky, J. (1984). *It's Snowing! It's Snowing!* Ill. by Jeanne Titherington. New York: Greenwillow.

"First Snow" by Marie Louise Allen, "Icy" by Rhoda W. Bacmeister, "January" by Maurice Sendak, "Snowman" by David McCord, and "Snow" by Karla Kuskin in: Prelutsky, J. (1986). Read-Aloud Rhymes for the Very Young. Ill. by Marc Brown. New York: Knopf. (pages 76–77)

Winthrop, E. (1989). Sledding. Ill. by Sarah Wilson. New York: Harper & Row.

"The First Snow" in: Zolotow, C. (1987). Everything Glistens and Everything Sings. Ill. by Margot Tomes. San Diego: Harcourt Brace Jovanovich. (page 72)

1. Encourage students to tell the story of the biggest snowfall they remember or have read about.

2. Students can make snow ice cream. Brainstorm possible ingredients and experiment (snow, sugar, flavorings to taste). If there is no snow, used crushed ice.

3. Students can make snow globes using jars. Collect baby food jars, fill with water and decorate. Use small plastic animals and crushed eggshells for the snow.

4. Challenge students to write a song about snow. Brainstorm other songs about snow.

5. Ask students to make snow pictures using shaving cream or a whipped topping to create a winter scene.

6. Allow students to make sentence strips of the separate sentences in *The Jacket I Wear in the Snow* (Neitzel, 1989). After reading the book, students can put the sentences in the correct order in a pocket chart. Rewrite the story with another season, such as "The Swimsuit I Wear in the Summer" or "The Sweater I Wear in the Fall."

RAIN DAYS

- **Date:** Any day that it rains

- **This date is special because:**
It is a day to celebrate rainy weather.

Books that relate to this date
- **Picture Books:**

Aardema, V. (1981). *Bringing the Rain to Kapiti Plain*. Ill. by Beatriz Vida. New York: Dial. (Africa)

Albert, B. (1993). *Windsongs and Rainbows*. Ill. by Susan Stillman. New York: Simon & Schuster.

Anderson, L. (1989). *Stina*. New York: Greenwillow.

Barber, A. (1990). *The Mousehole Cat*. Ill. by Nicola Bayley. New York: Macmillan.

Bauer, C. F. (1986). *Rainy Day: Stories and Poems*. Ill. by Michele Chessare. New York: Lippincott.

Bennett, D. (1988). *Rain*. Ill. by Rosalinda Kightley. New York: Bantam.

Blegvad, L. (1987). *Rainy Day Kate*. Ill. by Erik Blegvad. New York: McElderry.

Branley, F. M. (1985). *Flash, Crash, Rumble, & Roll*. Ill. by Barbara & Ed Emberley. New York: Crowell.

Branley, F. M. (1987). *It's Raining Cats and Dogs*. Ill. by True Kelley. Boston: Houghton Mifflin.

Carlstrom, N. W. (1993). *What Does the Rain Play?* Ill. by Henry Sorensen. New York: Macmillan.

Fradin, D. (1983). *Droughts*. Chicago: Childrens Press.

Hamilton, V. (1992). *Drylongso*. Ill. by Jerry Pinkney. San Diego: Harcourt Brace Jovanovich.

Hines, A. G. (1992). *Rumble Thumble Boom!* New York: Greenwillow.

Kahl, J. D. (1992). *Weatherwise: Learning about the Weather*. Minneapolis: Lerner.

Kahl, J. D. (1992). *Wet Weather: Rain Showers and Snowfall*. Minneapolis: Lerner.

Kalan, R. (1978). *Rain*. Ill. by Donald Crews. New York: Greenwillow.

Knutson, K. (1992). Muddigush. New York: Macmillan.

Kramer, S. (1993). *Lightning*. Photos by Warren Faidley. Minneapolis: Carolrhoda.

Kramer, S. (1993). *Tornado*. Minneapolis: Carolrhoda.

Lyon, G. E. (1990). *Come a Tide*. Ill. by Stephen Gammell. New York: Orchard.

Newton, J. (1983). *Rain Shadow*. Ill. by Susan Bonners. New York: Crowell.

Nikola-Lisa, W. (1993). *Storm*. Ill. by Michael Hays. New York: Atheneum.

Nobisso, J. (1992). *Shh! The Whale Is Smiling*. Ill. by Maureen Hyde. New York: Simon & Schuster.

Novak, M. (1986). *Rolling*. New York: Bradbury.

Otto, C. (1990). *That Sky, That Rain*. Ill. by Megan Lloyd. New York: Crowell.

Peters, L. W. (1991). *Water's Way*. Ill. by Ted Rand. New York: Arcade.

Polacco, P. (1990). *Thunder Cake*. New York: Philomel.

Pooley, S. (1993). *It's Raining, It's Pouring*. New York: Greenwillow.

Serfozo, M. (1990). *Rain Talk*. Ill. by Keiko Narahashi. New York: McElderry.

Simon, S. (1989). *Storms*. New York: Morrow.

Spier, P. (1982). *Rain*. Garden City, NY: Doubleday.

Stanley, S. (1993). *The Rains Are Coming*. New York: Greenwillow. (Zaire)

Stewart, D. (1993). *The Dove*. Ill. by Jude Daly. New York: Greenwillow. (Africa)

Stolz, M. (1988). *Storm in the Night*. Ill. by Pat Cummings. New York: Harper. (African American)

Sussman, S. (1982). *Hippo Thunder*. Ill. by John C. Wallner. Niles, IL: Whitman.

Szilagy, M. (1985). *Thunderstorm*. New York: Bradbury.

Wiesner, D. (1990). *Hurricane*. New York: Clarion.

Wyler, R. (1989). *Raindrops and Rainbows*. Ill. by James Steven Petruccio. New York: Messner.

■ Novel:

Ruckman, I. (1984). *Night of the Twisters*. New York: Crowell.

■ Poetry:

Bauer, C. F. (1986). *Rainy Day: Stories and Poems*. Ill. by Michele Chessare.

"Country Rain" by Aileen Fisher & "Rain" by Romesh Gunesekera in: Bennett, J. (1991). A *Cup of Starshine*. Ill. by Graham Percy. San Diego: Harcourt Brace Jovanovich. (pages 41, 50)

"Hurricane" by Dionne Brand in: Booth, D. (1990). *'Til All the Stars Have Fallen*. Ill. by Kady MacDonald Denton. New York: Viking. (page 72)

Carlstrom, N. W. (1990). *It's about Time, Jesse Bear*. Ill. by Burce Degen. New York: Macmillan.

"Four Poems for Roy G Biv" and "Rainbow Making" in: Esbensen, B. (1992). *Who Shrank My Granmother's House? Poems of Discovery*. Ill. by Eric Beddows. New York: HarperCollins. (pages 24–25, 29–30)

"Sudden Storm" by Elizabeth Coatsworth, "Never Mind the Rain" by N.M. Bodecker, "Sun After Rain" by Norma Farber, and "Downpour" by Myra Cohn Livingston in: Hopkins, L. B. (1973). *Surprises* Ill. by Megan Lloyd. New York: Harper. (pages 44–46, 51–52)

Martin, B. & Archambault, J. (1988). *Listen to the Rain*. Ill. by James Endicott. New York: Holt.

"I Like to Look in Puddles" in: Moore, L. (1992). *Sunflakes: Poems for Children*. Ill. by Jan Ormerod. New York: Clarion. (pages 15–21

1. Read some of the books on pages 199-200 and make a sensory chart about rain:

smells like:	
sounds like:	
tastes like:	
looks like:	
feels like:	

2. Use the words from the chart above to make rain poems.

3. Read *Rain Talk* (Serfozo, 1990) and brainstorm other sound words for the chart.

4. Ask students to write the words for the wordless book *Rain* (Spier, 1982).

5. Brainstorm different types of cakes and cake ingredients. Then ask students to taste cupcakes made from the recipe at the back of *Thunder Cake* (Pollaco, 1990). Challenge them to predict the 9 ingredients and the one secret ingredient. Then read the book and see how many they got correct. Discuss other unusual ingredients in cakes (such as mayonnaise and zucchini).

6. Rainy Day Games: Encourage students to make a board game from their favorite children's book and play it on rainy days.

H·O·T D·A·Y·S

■ **Date:** Any day that it is hot

■ **This date is special because:**
It is a day to celebrate hot weather.

Books that relate to this date

■ Picture Books:

Baker, L. (1990). *Morning Beach*. Boston: Little, Brown.

Barrett, J. (1978). *Cloudy with a Chance of Meatballs*. Ill. by Ron Barrett. New York: Macmillan.

Borden, L. (1993). *Albie the Lifeguard*. Ill. by Elizabeth Sayles. New York: Scholastic.

Brown, K. (1989). *Willy's Summer Dream*. San Diego: Harcourt Brace Jovanovich.

Calmenson, S. (1994). *Hotter Than a Hot Dog!* Ill. by Elivia. Boston: Little, Brown.

Caple, K. (1990). *The Coolest Place in Town*. Boston: Houghton Mifflin.

Cosgrove, B. (1991). *Weather*. New York: Knopf.

Davies, K. (1992). *Weather*. New York: Steck-Vaughn.

Factor, J. (1987). *Summer*. New York: Viking Kestrel.

Hedderwick, M. (1989). *P. D. Peebles' Summer or Winter Book*. Boston: Little, Brown.

Michels, T. (1992). *What a Beautiful Day!* Ill. by Thomas Muller. Minneapolis: Carolrhoda.

Rodowsky, C. (1990). *Dog Days*. Ill. by Kathleen Collins Howell. New York: Farrar, Straus & Giroux.

Weiss, N. (1992). *On A Hot, Hot Day*. New York: Putnam.

Zolotow, C. (1993). *Summer Is. . . .* Ill. by Ruth Lercher Bornstein. New York: Crowell.

■ Poetry:

"Under the Hottest Summer Sun" in:
Adoff, A. (1988). *Greens*. Ill. by Betsy Lewin. New York: Lothrop, Lee & Shepard. (page 16)

"Too Hot to Sleep" by Sid Marty in:
Booth, D. (1989). *'Til All the Stars Have Fallen*. Ill. by Kady MacDonald Denton. New York: Viking. (pages 84–85)

"Sun and I" in:
Chandra, D. (1988). *Balloons and Other Poems*. Ill. by Leslie Bowman. New York: Farrar, Straus & Giroux. (page 29)

"In August" by Marchette Chute in:
Hopkins, L. B. (1984). *Surprises*. Ill. by Megan Lloyed. New York: Harper & Row. (pages 48–49)

"The Sun Is Stuck" in:
Livingston, M. C. (1984). *A Song I Sang to You*. Ill. by Margot Tomes. San Diego: Harcourt Brace Jovanovich. (page 40)

"August Heat" in:
Prelutsky, J. (1986). Read-Aloud Rhymes for the Very Young. Ill. by Marc Brown. New York: Knopf. (page 32)

"It's Hot" in:
Silverstein, S. (1981). A Light in the Attic. New York: Harper & Row.

1. Ask students to write about a time when they were really hot. Describe how they felt.

2. Brainstorm ways to cool off on a hot day.

3. Invite students to illustrate their favorite way to cool off.

4. Students can record the daily temperature as it climbs.

5. Ask students to bring in recipes for cool fruit drinks. Create a class book of cool, refreshing class drinks.

M·O·V·I·N·G DAY

■ **Date:** Any day that someone is moving or has moved

■ **This date is special because:**

It is a day to wish someone well or to welcome someone.

Books that relate to this date
■ Picture Books:

Aliki. (1982). *We Are Best Friends*. New York: Greenwillow.

Carlstrom, N. W. (1990). *I'm Not Moving, Mama!* Ill. by Thor Wickstrom. New York: Macmillan.

Dorros, A. (1992). *This Is My House*. New York: Scholastic.

Fiday, B. (1990). *Time to Go*. Ill. by Thomas Allen. San Diego: Harcourt Brace Jovanovich.

Hendry, D. (1989). *The Not-Anywhere House*. Ill. by Thor Wickstrom. New York: Lothrop.

Johnson, A. (1992). *The Leaving Morning*. Ill. by David Soman. New York: Orchard.

Jukes, M. (1993). *I'll See You in My Dreams*. Ill. by Stacey Schuett. New York: Knopf.

Komaiko, L. (1987). *Annie Bananie*. Ill. by Laura Cornell. New York: Harper & Row.

Levine, E. (1991). *Not the Piano, Mrs. Medley!* Ill. by S. D. Schindler. New York: Orchard.

McLerran, A. (1992). *I Want to Go Home*. Ill. by Jill Kastner. New York: Tambourine.

O'Donnell, E. L. (1987). *Maggie Doesn't Want to Move*. Ill. by Amy Schwartz. New York: Four Winds.

Petty, K. (1987). *Moving House*. New York: Watts.

Sharmat, M. W. (1978). *Mitchell Is Moving*. Ill. by Jose Aruego & Ariane Dewey. New York: Macmillan.

Waber, B. (1988). *Ira Says Goodbye*. Boston: Houghton Mifflin.

Woodruff, E. (1991). *The Wing Shop*. Ill. by Stephen Gammell. New York: Holiday House.

■ Novels:

Billington, E. T. (1984). *The Move*. New York: Warne.

Caseley, J. (1991). *Hurricane Harry*. New York: Greenwillow.

Caseley, J. (1992). *Starring Dorothy Kane*. New York: Greenwillow.

Paterson, K. (1991). *The Smallest Cow in the World*. Ill. by Jane Clark Brown. New York: HarperCollins.

■ Poetry:

"Poem" by Langston Hughes in: de Regniers, B. S. (1988) *Sing A Song of Popcorn*. Ill. by nine Caldecott Medal artists. New York: Scholastic. (page 116)

"Girl Who's Moved Around" in: Kennedy, X. J. (1985). *The Forgetful Wishing Well*. Ill. by Monica Incisa. New York: Atheneum. (page 4)

"So Long, See You Later" in: Merriam, E. (1992). *The Singing Green*. Ill. by Kathleen Collins Howell. New York: Morrow. (page 18)

"The New Kid on the Block" in: Prelutsky, J. (1984). *The New Kid on the Block*. Ill. by James Stevenson. New York: Greenwillow. (page 7)

"We Moved about a Week Ago" in: Prelutsky, J. (1990). *Something Big Has Been Here*. Ill. by James Stevenson. New York: Greenwillow. (page 94)

"How Do You Say Goodbye?" in: Simmie, L. (1984). *Auntie's Knitting a Baby*. Ill. by Anne Simmie. New York: Orchard. (page 66)

"Since Hanna Moved Away" in: Viorst, J. (1981). *If I Were in Charge of the World and Other Worries*. Ill. by Lynne Cherry. New York: Atheneum. (page 54)

"Absent Friend" in: Zolotow, C. (1987). *Everything Glistens and Everything Sings*. Ill. by Margot Tomes. San Diego: Harcourt Brace Jovanovich. (page 21)

Activities for Extension:

1. Ask students to make a handbook of information that would be helpful for a new kid in their school.

2. Students can make a going-away card packet for the child who is moving. Include addresses, phone numbers, stationery, and best wishes from the class.

3. Ask children to discuss what five things they would pack first if they were moving.

4. Create a welcome banner complete with signatures and encouraging messages for a new student.

5. Make a list of interesting places to go in your community for the new student. Take the class to one site.

B·I·R·T·H·D·A·Y·S

■ **Date:** Any birthday

■ **This date is special because:**
It is a day to celebrate someone's birthday.

Books that relate to this date
■ **Picture Books:**

Anderson, L. (1991). *Stina's Visit*. New York: Greenwillow.

Anholt, L. & Anholt, C. (1993). *Can You Guess?* New York: Puffin.

Argent, K. (1991). *Happy Birthday, Wombat!* Boston: Little, Brown.

Arnold, C. (1987). *Everybody Has a Birthday*. Ill. by Anthony Accardo. New York: Watts.

Asch, F. (1982). *Happy Birthday, Moon*. Englewood Cliffs, NJ: Prentice-Hall.

Barrett, J. (1992). *Benjamin's 365 Birthdays*. Ill. by Ron Barrett. New York: Aladdin.

Base, G. (1989). *The 11th Hour: A Curious Mystery*. New York: Abrams.

Brandenberg, F. (1983). *Aunt Nina and Her Nephews and Nieces*. Ill. by Aliki. New York: Greenwillow.

Brown, M. (1989). *Arthur's Birthday*. Boston: Little, Brown.

Calmenson, S. (1983). *The Birthday Hat*. Ill. by Susan Ganter. New York: Grosset & Dunlap.

Carle, E. (1972). *The Secret Birthday Message*. New York: Crowell.

Caseley, J. (1989) *Three Happy Birthdays*. New York: Greenwillow.

Charlip, R. (1987). *Handtalk Birthday: A Number and Story Book in Sign Language*. Photos by Remy Charlip, Mary Beth, & George Ancona. New York: Four Winds.

Cole, J. (1993). *Pin the Tail on the Donkey and Other Party Games*. Ill. by Alan Tiegreen. New York: Morrow.

Dragonwagon, C. (1993). *Annie Flies the Birthday Bike*. Ill. by Emily Arnold McCully. New York: Macmillan.

Fox, M. (1989). *Night Noises*. Ill. by Terry Denton. San Diego: Harcourt Brace Jovanovich.

Frasier, D. (1991). *On the Day You Were Born*. San Diego: Harcourt Brace Jovanovich.

Gantos, J. (1990). *Happy Birthday, Rotten Ralph*. Ill. by Nicola Rubel. Boston: Houghton Mifflin.

Gibbons, G. (1986). *Happy Birthday*. New York: Holiday House.

Giff, P. R. (1986). *Happy Birthday, Ronald Morgan*. Ill. by Susanna Natti. New York: Viking.

Goennel, H. (1992). *It's My Birthday*. New York: Tambourine.

Hest, A. (1993). *Nana's Birthday Pary*. Ill. by Amy Schwartz. New York: Morrow.

Hill, E. (1982). *Spot's Birthday Party*. New York: Putnam.

Ichikawa, S. & Laird, E. (1988). *Happy Birthday! A Book of Celebrations* New York: Philomel.

Jonas, A. (1992). *The 13th Clue*. New York: Greenwillow.

Keller, H. (1990). *Henry's Happy Birthday*. New York: Greenwillow.

Kiser, S. A. (1989). *The Birthday Thing*.

Kleven, E. (1993). *Ernst*. New York: Puffin.

Lankfrod, M. D. (1992). *Hopscotch Around the World*. Ill. by K. Milone. New York: Morrow.

Merriam, E. (1986). *The Birthday Door*. Ill. by Peter Thornton. New York: Morrow.

Modell, F. (1988). *Ice Cream Soup*. New York: Greenwillow.

Motomara, M. (1989). *Happy Birthday*. Ill. by Mary Young Duarte. Milwaukee: Raintree.

Noble, T. H. (1989). *Jimmy's Boa and the Big Splash Birthday Bash*. Ill. by Steven Kellogg. New York: Dial.

Pearson, S. (1987). *Happy Birthday, Grampie*. Ill. by Ronald Himler.

Pepper, D. (1986). *The Happy Birthday Book*. Ill. by Dennis Pepper & David Jackson. Oxford: Oxford University Press.

Perl, L. (1984). *Candles, Cakes, and Donkey Tails: Birthday Symbols and Celebrations*. Ill. by Victoria de Carrea. New York: Clarion.

Polacco, P. (1991). *Some Birthday*. New York: Simon & Schuster.

Poltarness, W. (1993). *A Most Memorable Birthday*. Ill. by Paul Cline and Judy the Sieck. New York: Green Tiger Press.

Pryor, B. (1993). *Birthday Blizzard*. Ill. by Molly Delaney. New York: Morrow.

Rylant, C. (1987). *Birthday Presents*. Ill. by Sucie Stevenson. New York: Orchard.

Shannon, G. (1983). *The Surprise*. Ill. by Jose Aruego & Arianne Dewey. New York: Greenwillow.

Steptoe, J. (1991). *Birthday*. New York: Holt.

Walter, M. P. (1989). *Have a Happy...* Ill. by Carole Byard. New York: Lothrop.

Wild, M. (1993). *The Slumber Party*. Ill. by David Cox. New York: Ticknor & Fields.

■ Novels:

Conrad, P. (1988). *Staying Nine*. Ill. by Mike Wimmer. New York: Harper.

Danzinger, P. (1989). *Everyone Else's Parents Said Yes*. New York: Delacorte.

Mahy, M. (1993). *The Birthday Burglar and a Very Wicked Headmistress*. Ill. by Margaret Chamberlain. New York: Beech Tree.

■ Poetry:

Goldstein, B. S. (1993). *Happy Birthday!* Ill. by Jose Aruego & Ariane Dewey. New York: Doubleday.

Hopkins, L. B. (1991). *Happy Birthday*. Ill. by Hilary Knight. New York: Simon & Schuster.

Livingston, M. C. (1989). *Birthday Poems*. Ill. by Margot Tomes. New York: Holiday House.

"Birthday" in:
Livingston, M. C. (1985). *Celebrations*. Ill. by Leonard Everett Fisher. New York: Holiday House. (page 32)

"The Wish" by Ann Friday, "Birthdays" by Mary Ann Hoberman, and "Five Years Old" by Marie Louise Allen in:
Prelutsky, J. (1986). *Read-Aloud Rhymes for the Very Young*. Ill. by Marc Brown. New York: Knopf. (page 29)

■ Resource Book:

Bresnahan, M. & Macfarlane, J. G. (1988). *The Happiest Birthdays: Great Theme Parties for Young Children*. New York: Viking.

1. Make a class birthday calendar showing the date of every person's birthday.

2. Decorate a T-shirt for a birthday. Let the birthday child wear it on his or her birthday.

3. Students can create a birthday hat for the birthday child.

4. Students can make a birthday card for the birthday child. Remind everyone to only include positive comments in the card.

5. Celebrate 1/2 year birthdays for students with summer birthdays.

6. Play various games using *Hopscotch Around the World* (Lankford, 1992). Invent other games to play at a birthday party.